NOT QUITE AUSTRALIAN

Peter Mares is a contributing editor for *Inside Story*, an adjunct fellow at the Swinburne Institute for Social Research and a senior moderator with the Cranlana Programme. A former ABC broadcaster, he is the author of the award-winning book *Borderline: Australia's Response to Refugees and Asylum Seekers in the Wake of the Tampa*, and has written for the *Age*, *Australian Financial Review* and *Griffith Review*. He lives in Melbourne with his wife and son.

NOT QUITE AUSTRALIAN

How Temporary Migration Is Changing the Nation

Peter Mares

TEXT PUBLISHING MELBOURNE AUSTRALIA

textpublishing.com.au
The Text Publishing Company
Swann House
22 William Street
Melbourne Victoria 3000
Australia

Copyright © Peter Mares 2016

The moral right of Peter Mares to be identified as the author of this work has been asserted.

All rights reserved. Without limiting the rights under copyright above, no part of this publication shall be reproduced, stored in or introduced into a retrieval system, or transmitted in any form or by any means (electronic, mechanical, photocopying, recording or otherwise), without the prior permission of both the copyright owner and the publisher of this book.

First published in 2016 by The Text Publishing Company

Book design by Imogen Stubbs
Typeset by J & M Typesetting
Index by Karen Gillen

Printed in Australia by Griffin Press, an accredited ISO/NZS 14001:2004 Environmental Management System printer

National Library of Australia Cataloguing-in-Publication entry :
Creator: Mares, Peter, author.
Title: Not quite Australian : how temporary migration is changing the nation.
ISBN: 9781925355116 (paperback)
ISBN: 9781922253705 (ebook)
Notes: Includes index.
Subjects: Emigration and immigration.
          Australia—Emigration and immigration.
          Australia—Social conditions.
Dewey Number: 304.894

This book is printed on paper certified against the Forest Stewardship Council® Standards. Griffin Press holds FSC chain-of-custody certification SGS-COC-005088. FSC promotes environmentally responsible, socially beneficial and economically viable management of the world's forests.

For Julie—your love and wisdom keep me on course

Contents

Introduction		1
Chapter 1:	The New Metics	11
Chapter 2:	The Rise and Rise of Temporary Migration	30
Chapter 3:	Mind the Gap!	65
Chapter 4:	Indefinitely Temporary	96
Chapter 5:	New Zealanders	128
Chapter 6:	Fear in the Family	154
Chapter 7:	Asylum Seekers and Refugees	180
Chapter 8:	The Pros and Cons of Temporary Migrant Labour	207
Chapter 9:	De Facto Labour Migration	233
Chapter 10:	An Unsettled World	258
Chapter 11:	Flexibility and Indifference	270
Conclusion		293
Postscript		305
Acknowledgments		306
Endnotes		308
Index		349

It is a great discouragement to an individual, and a still greater one to a class, to be left out of the constitution; to be reduced to plead from outside the door to the arbiters of their destiny, not taken into consultation within. The maximum of the invigorating effect of freedom upon the character is only obtained when the person acted on either is, or is looking forward to becoming, a citizen as fully privileged as any other.

JOHN STUART MILL,
Considerations on Representative Government, 1861

Introduction

Not Quite Australian

It's a blustery Australia Day in Taylor Park, a scrubby reserve in the centre of Torquay, the nation's self-proclaimed surfing capital at the start of Victoria's Great Ocean Road. The crowd is flecked with blue, white and red: one particularly enthusiastic woman has wrapped herself in an Australian-flag beach towel and plonked an Australian-flag baseball cap on her head; another has draped a large Australian flag over the back of her aluminium deckchair; many more people are clutching the small plastic flags on white sticks that are being handed out by senior citizens from the Lions Club.

Later the Lions Club will put on a free barbeque brunch of sausages and soft drinks, but for now, attention is focused on 13 people standing in a straggly line with their backs to the ocean. They are making a commitment to Australia:

2   Not Quite Australian

> From this time forward, under God [these two words are optional],
> I pledge my loyalty to Australia and its people,
> whose democratic beliefs I share,
> whose rights and liberties I respect, and
> whose laws I will uphold and obey.

Afterwards, each new citizen receives a certificate, a native seedling and hearty congratulations from their political representatives—the Mayor of the Surf Coast Shire and their local state and federal MPs—who can now be said to truly represent them, since, from this time forward, as citizens, they also vote.

On Australian Day 2016, the 13 people buffeted by Torquay's onshore breeze were among more than 16,000 immigrants from 154 different countries taking the pledge at close to 400 similar ceremonies around the nation. In a statement to mark the occasion, Immigration Minister Peter Dutton said, 'Australia Day provides the opportunity for all of us to openly reflect on what it means to be Australian.'[1]

What *does* it mean to be Australian? In the second decade of the twenty-first century, this apparently simple question is increasingly difficult to answer.

In his comments, Peter Dutton described citizenship as 'the common bond uniting all Australians'. We might perhaps accept this if we define 'Australian' in a narrow legal sense as someone who can hold an Australian passport and has the right (and obligation) to vote, two things not generally available to other people who nevertheless call Australia home. To say that citizenship is the common bond that unites *all* Australians is, however, to exclude hundreds of thousands of people—perhaps millions—with strong connections to the nation.

The census, the register of births and deaths, and the close monitoring of border movements enable us to count Australia's population with some degree of confidence—24 million and rising. Yet there is less certainty about how many *citizens* Australia has. The best data comes from the census, which asks whether or not you are an Australian citizen. In 2011, more than 18 million people (85 per cent of respondents) marked the box for 'yes'; almost two million (nine per cent) answered 'no' and one and a quarter million (six per cent) failed to respond to the question.

Since short-term visitors to Australia are excluded from these figures, this suggests that there are two million people living in Australia who are not citizens and a significant number who may be confused about their status. Who are these people and what is their experience?

Those who did not respond to the question on the census form may be unsure of the correct answer—migrants who arrive as children, for example, can come of age in Australia assuming that they are citizens until they get a rude shock when they apply for a job with the federal public service, try to join the defence force, register to vote or run into serious trouble with the law.

Of those declaring that they are not citizens, many will be migrants who have settled in Australia on a permanent visa but who have not taken the pledge of citizenship. Why not? Perhaps they have not yet got around to it. Perhaps they have decided not to take out Australian citizenship because they do not wish to renounce a legal connection to their previous homeland: some countries—such as Japan—make dual citizenship impossible; others—such as Germany—make it difficult. Perhaps they see no benefit in pledging loyalty to Australia since they migrated from the United Kingdom before 1984 and gained all the advantages of citizenship—including voting rights—without ever becoming citizens.[2] Perhaps they want to avoid the obligations of citizenship—such as having to sit on a jury or cast a ballot. Perhaps, despite living here, they do not identify as Australian, and so do not wish to become citizens.

Or perhaps they belong to the growing cohort of long-term but temporary migrants who are the focus of my attention. Today there are more than one million people who fit this category—they include international students, working holidaymakers, skilled workers on 457 visas, asylum seekers, refugees and New Zealanders who arrived after 2001. Ten years ago this group was much smaller than it is now—perhaps a quarter of its current size—but temporary migration has increased rapidly; and, as it increases, it changes the nation.

Most temporary migrants are of working age, and, by my calculation, they now make up between eight and nine per cent of the labour force. Some will sojourn here for a few months or a few years and then return, more or less happily, to the country they came from, or move on to somewhere else. As they depart, other temporary migrants arrive to replenish their ranks, seeking experience, income, education, adventure or a future life as an Australian. A significant proportion of these temporary migrants will make the successful transition to permanent residence. Once they have achieved 'PR' (and clocked up at least four years' residence), they will be eligible to stand and swear loyalty as a citizen of Australia at a ceremony like the one I witnessed in Torquay.

Other temporary migrants will be unable to take this step. They will have lived in Australia for just as long or longer, they will feel that they belong here, they will have invested their money, sweat and hope in an Australian future and they will strongly desire to become full members of the political community and contribute more to the life of the nation. They will be unable to take the pledge of citizenship, however, because they cannot find a pathway to permanent residence. They are the settlers who remain unsettled.

There may be as many as 200,000 New Zealanders who fall into this category, because they do not have the right skills or earn enough money to get a permanent visa as the necessary precursor to citizenship, even though they can expect to live in Australia for the rest of their lives. Some 30,000 people who arrived by boat may also fit this picture—asylum seekers on bridging visas and refugees on temporary protection visas, who are barred by law from ever settling permanently in Australia, regardless of the fact that it is impossible for them to return home or travel anywhere else. Then there is an unknown number of international-student graduates, skilled workers on 457 visas and other temporary migrants who have lived lawfully in Australia for many years, but who have so far been unable to secure permanent status. There is no way of knowing how many people sit in this last group because they fall outside the statistical net. What can be said with some certainty is that in 2013 there were an estimated 65,000 people living in Australia on temporary visas who first arrived in the country on a temporary visa between six and 10 years earlier.

The logic of the immigration minister's Australia Day comments is that people who live in Australia on temporary visas cannot be called Australian because they do not share the common bond of citizenship that unites 'us' all. Who constitutes this 'us'? If 'us' is restricted to citizens, then it is a very narrow definition indeed. Even if we expand the circle of 'us' to include permanent residents, how are we to describe these other long-term but temporary residents of the nation? Are they 'non-Australian'? Are they perhaps 'un-Australian'?

I describe them as 'not quite Australian': they live here, contribute to the economic and cultural life of the nation, pay its taxes and obey its laws, but lack access to a range of government services and benefits, and are denied the right to vote. Despite all the rules and pronouncements that supposedly guarantee equal treatment in the workplace, temporary migrants do not stand on the same firm legal ground as citizens and permanent residents, and are consequently at greater risk of exploitation and abuse. Their visa status often makes them vulnerable to unreasonable employer demands—for example, a migrant worker might need their employer's support for an application for permanent residence or a second working-holiday visa. In times of trouble and challenge—if they are employed by a firm that goes bust, suffer a workplace accident, fall chronically ill, are subjected to domestic violence, have a child, end a relationship, become homeless—then they may find themselves falling between stools, because they do not fit any of the three standard categories into which people are generally classified by Australia's administrative and legal systems: citizen, permanent resident or short-term visitor.

At the end of the twentieth century the number of temporary migrants in Australia was small and this was less of an issue. As recently as a decade ago, politicians could declare, with little fear of contradiction, that Australia did not have guest workers. At the time, prime minister John Howard maintained that Australia has always preferred permanent settlement over temporary migration. 'I think you either invite somebody to your country to stay as a permanent resident or a citizen or you don't,' he declared. This is the same man who, about 10 years earlier, in 1996, had overseen the introduction of the 457 temporary skilled-worker visa.

As the 457 visa celebrates its twentieth anniversary, temporary migration has become a significant, permanent and expanding feature of the Australian way of life. It may be a temporary migrant who picks the fruit and vegetables we eat, cuts and packs our raw meat, digs up our minerals, cleans our offices, makes our coffees, drives our taxis, prescribes our medicine, cares for our aged parents or serves our takeaway meals. The fees paid by international students help to keep our universities solvent and hold down tertiary education costs for domestic students.

Granted, we still have large-scale permanent migration, but it is increasingly a two-step program; these days most 'new' settlers are actually 'old' temporary migrants—people who have already been living in Australia for at least two years. One of my concerns is with the fate of those temporary migrants who are unable to take that second step—who are indefinitely or permanently temporary, trapped in the status of being 'not quite Australian'.

I use the term 'not quite Australian' in another sense, too—to indicate that the rise of temporary migration sits uncomfortably with the stories we tell ourselves as a nation.

The permanent exhibition in Melbourne's Immigration Museum in the old Customs House on the banks of the Yarra begins with a room called 'Leaving Home'. It offers five core narratives of emigration—of people seeking freedom, escaping war and conflict, fleeing disaster, searching for a better life, and reuniting with family. The second room—'Immigrant Stories and a Timeline'—tracks the changing pattern of migration to Australia, from early colonisation, through growing anti-Chinese sentiment in the second half of the nineteenth century and the first immigration restriction laws after Federation, to the mass resettlement of the postwar era and the multiculturalism of the late twentieth century. The centrepiece of the third and largest room, 'Journeys of a Lifetime', is the re-creation of a ship. Entering at the stern you move between cabins from different historical eras, from the cramped accommodation below decks during the age of sail to the bunk beds of a passenger liner in the postwar period. Emerging from the bow, the exhibition continues with interactive displays showing the development of air routes to Australia. In the final room, 'Getting In', visitors can take a dictation test or sit an interview with a simulated immigration official to see whether or not they will be admitted as a migrant.

The displays are engaging and informative, but they are also out of date: they frame the migration experience entirely in terms of permanent and intentional settlement, both on the part of the migrant and on the part of the nation. This is consistent with the deeply engrained (if problematic) idea of Australia as a settler society, in which the migrant stepping onto Australian soil for the first time is also walking forward into a new Australian life.

The many personal stories used to illustrate the migration experience all conform to this narrative, as does the museum's breakdown of immigration policy into four main periods: the end of convict transportation (1840–1900), White Australia (1901–45), European migration (1946–72) and multiculturalism (1973–today). But the museum's 'today' is now a 'yesterday'—immigration to Australia in the second decade of the twenty-first century is a very different experience to what has gone before; it is more contingent and contractual. Most migrants arrive on temporary visas to do a job or buy an education; they may have set their sights on making a home here, or they may not, and in either case, the experience of actually living in Australia may prompt a change of heart over time. Increasingly,

Australia's future citizens are selected from among these temporary arrivals, though whether or not any particular person will be permitted to settle is a different question.

This new era of migration poses challenges and problems. What does it mean, for example, for our version of multiculturalism? In a landmark speech in 1981, prime minister Malcolm Fraser said that multiculturalism 'is about equality of opportunity for the members of all groups to participate in and benefit from Australia's social, economic and political life'. Thirty years later, Labor immigration minister Chris Bowen echoed Fraser's sentiments when he declared that the genius of Australian multiculturalism lies in the fact that it is 'citizenship based' and that 'people who share respect for our democratic beliefs, laws and rights are welcome to join us as full partners with equal rights'.

What if these statements are no longer true? What if we have created a society in which, to use Fraser's words, not everyone is a 'full and equal' participant? If, instead, a significant proportion of our population and our workforce are 'partial and unequal' participants and not welcome to join as 'full partners'?

Immigration Minister Peter Dutton's remarks on Australia Day 2016 suggest that citizenship gives rise to the franchise; once you make the pledge, then you get to cast a ballot. This renders the right to vote in a democracy as something bestowed by government on those who successfully jump through the hoops of language tests, health checks and skills assessments. But surely causation in democracy runs the other way—it is by dint of living and participating in the life of the nation that you gain the right to political representation and political voice. Anyone who is present within the boundaries of the state for a significant period acquires rights. We may admit migrants to live, work or study here temporarily, but over time, they start becoming Australian, in the sense of having an increasing stake in the life of the nation. The longer they stay, the more Australian, in this sense, they become. Though it may be hard to say after what period of time the threshold is crossed, at some point the core principles of democracy require that migrants must be included as full and equal partners with an equal opportunity 'to participate in and benefit from Australia's social, economic and political life'—and this includes the opportunity to recite the pledge of citizenship at a barbeque brunch and receive a native plant as a symbol of their belonging.

1 | The New *Metics*

When I was a child, my parents would delight in telling the story of their landfall in Australia on Boxing Day, 1954. The way my late father recalled it, or the way I recall him telling it to me, a future work colleague greeted them on Fremantle dock 'with a crate of crayfish tucked under one arm and a crate of beer tucked under the other'. My mother does not remember it exactly the same way, but she does remember crayfish, sunshine, peaches and wine at lunch on their first day in Perth, along with her surprise at being offered immediate part-time work as a tutor, based on a cursory question about her qualifications and experience. 'After the grim, grey days of postwar England,' she says, 'I thought we had landed in heaven.'

At the time, my parents had no intention of settling permanently in Australia. When they said their farewells to family on the docks at Tilbury six weeks earlier, they thought they were embarking on a three-year adventure. My father was a recent university graduate and his immediate job prospects in Britain were limited. Mum, a teacher, had supported him through his studies, but now she had a new baby, my eldest sister, to care for. So when the University of Western Australia offered Dad a temporary contract, my parents decided that he should take it. The intention was to stay for a few years at most, just long enough for my father to get sufficient experience to land a 'proper' job back in England.

'We didn't see ourselves as migrants,' says Mum.

There were many adjustments to be made. Summers so hot 'you could fry an egg on the doorstep'. Wide open spaces that gave my mum vertigo—the first time they drove east through the hills from Perth and got a vista of wheat fields stretching as far the eye could see, she found the vastness so overwhelming that she was afraid to let go of the door of the car.

Overall, though, my parents loved Perth and enjoyed their new life in Australia. After a couple of years, they moved to Adelaide, where my father was offered an ongoing position. Initially my mother was devastated, having relinquished the joys of a house in Nedlands on the edge of Perth's vast Kings Park to take up residence in Blair Athol in Adelaide's comparatively desolate northern suburbs. But she settled in, built her career there and still lives in Adelaide today.

Although my parents were English, they were part of the great wave of migration that saw Australia extend a welcome to people beyond Great Britain and Ireland. The massive postwar resettlement of displaced persons, or DPs, marked the first of what historian Eric Richards calls 'two seismic changes, which worked as social revolutions in the otherwise relative calm of modern Australian history'.[1]

Recruiting migrants from Continental Europe rather than just the United Kingdom marked a significant and sharp break with past policy. Today, the policy is often held up as a shining example of Australian humanitarianism and generosity towards refugees. It was nothing of the sort. As Klaus Neumann reminds us in his book *Across the Seas*, Australia selected displaced Europeans as migrants 'not because they had been displaced, but because they were freely available'.[2] The supply of British migrants had fallen off, and for Arthur Calwell, Australia's first immigration minister, DPs appealed as a convenient, alternative source of acceptable migrants to help the nation populate rather than perish. (DPs were convenient because the International Refugee Organisation organised the shipping and contributed to the cost of bringing them to Australia.[3])

In keeping with the White Australia policy, preference was initially given to northern Europeans with 'Aryan' and Anglo-Saxon features, but, before long, southern Europeans were also deemed acceptable.[4] As Gwenda Tavan records in her history of the long, slow death of the White Australia policy, by the late 1960s, Australia immigration officials keen to attract more migrants were redefining the boundaries of Europe to include Turkey, so that Turks could be classified as 'European' and pass the test of whiteness.[5]

Not all of these postwar migrants ended up making lives for themselves in Australia. There were high rates of 'settler loss' as many people returned to their homelands during the late 1950s and 1960s, as my parents had intended to do. It was Mum and Dad's first visit 'home', six years after arriving in Perth, that eventually turned them into migrants; the trip alerted them to the fact that life for a young family remained much tougher in England than it was in Australia.

From the outset it was clear, however, that my parents, like other

European migrants, could choose to stay in Australia permanently if they wanted to. Indeed, it was more or less expected that they *would* stay. Australia's migration program was designed to increase the population and build the nation.

Growing up, one of my favourite novels was John O'Grady's *They're a Weird Mob,* written, supposedly, by Italian journalist Nino Culotta. Nino is sent to Sydney on assignment, but soon abandons his attempts to write articles about Australia and instead devotes himself with gusto to his new life as a brickie's labourer. As a child in the 1960s, I found Nino's decision plausible. The rough-and-ready but generous treatment that Nino receives from his Australian workmates gelled with my father's story of being greeted on the docks with crates of crayfish and beer. I enjoyed the slapstick humour and the language games in the novel, and I think, as much as anything, it appealed to me because of its cheerful tone and happy ending. This was an optimistic account of the great postwar migration and its possibilities—the social reality that I was growing up in—and it was a story that ended well both for the migrants and for Australia. (In my last year of primary school I had a crush on the daughter of Italian market gardeners so perhaps that gave me extra cause to be romantically invested in the book's happy ending.)

Re-reading *They're a Weird Mob* as an adult, I was struck by how contingent the happy ending is on Nino's capacity to adapt to Australian ways—to abandon established patterns of behaviour and conform to the conservative, masculine, alcohol-assisted culture of his mates. The prevailing belief, reflected in policy, was that migrants should assimilate; there was no sense that 'New Australians' might shape a new, or different, Australia. In the concluding passages, Nino sounds a stern warning to his fellow migrants:

> There are far too many New Australians in this country who are still mentally living in their homelands, who mix with people of their own nationality, and try to retain their own language and customs. Who even try to persuade Australians to adopt his customs and manners. Cut it out. There is no better way of life in the world than that of the Australian…Learn his way. Learn his language. Get yourself accepted as one of him; and you will enter a world that you never dreamed existed. And once you have entered it, you will never leave it.[6]

Promoted by Calwell as an alternative to derogatory terms like 'reffos', 'DPs' and 'Balts',[7] the term 'New Australian' was, and is, clumsy and patronising. It was always applied selectively—I doubt my English parents were ever called 'New Australians'. It smacks of a 'sons of the soil' nativism, points to a hierarchy of belonging and promotes expectation of complete assimilation, in which non Anglo-Celtic migrants, like the fictional Nino Culotta, completely divorce themselves from their cultural origins. As Malcolm Fraser put it in his landmark speech on multiculturalism, they were expected to 'shed their identities like snakes their skins'.[8] Yet, despite all these limitations, historian John Hirst makes an important point when he argues that the label 'New Australian' was at one level welcoming: 'They were not guest workers but future citizens,' he writes.[9] *They're a Weird Mob* may offer a narrow, tightly defined path to inclusion and acceptance, but it does assume that inclusion and acceptance are the ultimate goal and that before long 'migrants' become 'Australians'.

In the 1950s and 1960s, British subjects like my parents qualified for citizenship after just one year of residence in Australia; migrants from other parts of Europe could gain citizenship after five years. From the moment they stepped off the gangway or walked down the aeroplane steps, migrants with the correct racial characteristics were on a short, straight path to becoming full members of the Australian political community, should they choose to do so.

This is not to discount or diminish the social and cultural exclusion of 'wogs' and 'dagos': the discrimination and insults, the humiliations over such trivial matters as accents or strange food, the bullying and beatings in school grounds and workplaces. John O'Grady/Nino Culotta did not tell anywhere near the full story. The hierarchy of belonging—some would call it the privileging of whiteness—was reinforced and entrenched in everyday behaviours and attitudes. The benign term 'settler society' glosses over the racially structured violence—organised and spontaneous—that was required to dispossess Australia's Indigenous peoples and that continues to be used to police the boundaries of Australian-ness today, whether it be in the turning around of asylum-seeker boats or events like the Cronulla riots.

Nevertheless, in an essential legal sense, European 'New Australians' were granted equal status with the Australian-born—after five years they could vote, run for office, sit on juries and work for the federal government. They were, or could choose to become, citizens.

The situation was different for non-Europeans. The presence of a small number of Asians or Pacific Islanders was tolerated under certain circumstances—as traders, for example, or as fee-paying students, or as spouses (a prominent example being Japanese war brides)—but their stay was generally deemed to be temporary, and required a 'certificate of exemption' that had to be periodically renewed. Even after the *Migration Act 1958* abolished exemption certificates (along with the notorious dictation test used as a tool to enforce the White Australia policy), people deemed to have less than 75 per cent 'European blood' were still required to obtain a temporary entry permit issued at the discretion of the immigration minister.[10] Non-European migrants had to be resident in Australia for at least 15 years before they could seek citizenship. In 1964, the former champion cyclist turned cautiously reformist immigration minister Hubert Opperman brought this discrimination to the attention of prime minister Robert Menzies. Menzies responded: 'Good thing, too—right sort of discrimination.'[11] The policy eventually changed in 1966, after Harold Holt took over as prime minister.[12]

The end of the White Australia policy was the second of Eric Richards' two seismic changes. If Holt prepared the grave, then Whitlam buried the policy. Reforms enacted under his leadership in 1973 extended citizenship to all lawful migrants after three years' residence, regardless of how they looked, where they came from or what they believed in.

Today, most Australians would find it absurd and offensive that certain migrants should be denied membership of the national political community due to their ethnic origins or skin tone. I hope that most would also agree that 15 years is far too long a time for a migrant to have to spend proving his or her credentials as a citizen—to be present in Australia without being accepted as Australian. We might feel particularly strongly about this when migrants arrive as children and spend formative years growing to adulthood in Australia.

Yet in the twenty-first century we are again creating circumstances in which it is possible, as it was under the White Australia policy, for migrants to live in Australia for very long periods of time without being included in the political community of the nation. Our immigration policies are no longer racially based or racially motivated, but for an increasing number of migrants, they hold the potential to replicate the type of civic exclusion experienced by non-European residents prior to 1973. It is a fundamental tenet of a liberal democracy that those who live by the laws of a nation, who contribute to the nation through their labour and their taxes, should also have an equal say in the running of the nation. This principle is in danger of being undermined as the result of what I see as a third seismic change in the formation of the nation.

The shift has been less obvious and dramatic than the mass migration of DPs from Europe, or the large-scale resettlement of Indochinese refugees under Fraser—the first major practical manifestation of the end of the White Australia policy. Yet over the two decades since the mid-1990s, Australia has been fundamentally recasting the way it 'does' migration. Key developments have been the introduction of 457 temporary work visas, the internationalisation of Australia's education system, the expansion of the working-holiday-maker scheme and changes to the status of New Zealanders living in Australia. Each of these policies has had its own rationale and has developed a separate trajectory and momentum. When they come to public attention, each is generally dealt with as a discrete issue. It is only when we consider these policies together that a fuller picture of Australia's new migration system begins to emerge.

The Nino Culotta story, the story of my parents and countless other postwar European migrants, of a short, straight pathway from fresh-off-the-boat 'New Australian' to full legal citizen, is no longer the norm. Most migrants to Australia now arrive on temporary visas. As with past waves of migrants, not all of them want to continue down the pathway to permanent residency and citizenship. Many temporary migrants are happy to sojourn in Australia and then move on. A considerable number, however, do wish to stay and build lives here. They may come with that plan, or their intentions may change, as my parents' did. In many cases, the prospect of permanent residency and citizenship will have been a carrot dangled before their eyes prior to arrival, as an added incentive for a student to pay fees at an Australian university rather than a British one, for example, or to encourage a nurse to take up a medical job in an isolated clinic or remote hospital that is struggling to find local staff.

But the route from temporariness to permanence can have many twists and turns. As Shanthi Robertson has observed in relation to international students, the rise of temporary migration is radically different from the permanent settler migration that characterised Australian policy in the second half of the twentieth century. In the twenty-first century, she writes, Australia has created '"staggered" migration processes, characterised by multiple "gates" of membership that migrants must past through to enter the nation state'.[13] As a result, 'paradigms of settlement, permanent residency and full citizenship... are being destabilised'.[14]

Discrimination against non-Europeans under the White Australia policy is a reminder that the postwar migrant pathway from arrival to citizenship was never fully inclusive or comprehensive. The mythologising of Australia's immigration success story omits mention of the mostly Asian migrants who were forced to be temporary by law, whose desire to settle was denied because of their racial background. We also tend to forget that more than one in five postwar settlers did not stay and returned home or moved on elsewhere.[15]

In this sense, the 'permanent settler' model was never completely accurate: neither objectively, since many migrants chose not to stay, or were not allowed to stay because of their skin colour, nor subjectively, in the minds of arriving migrants, since some never intended to settle, even if they eventually did. Nevertheless, the settler-society model has become the dominant paradigm and continues to have a profound influence on shaping our collective sense of the kind of Australia we live in. It may be partly mythical, but widely accepted myths have their own generative power in shaping a shared reality and a common understanding of who we are or seek to be as a nation.

The act of migration—so often depicted at the symbolic moment of disembarking onto Australian soil from an ocean liner or aeroplane—is celebrated as the first step towards establishing a new life in a new land, a journey that will lead in due course to the granting of citizenship. The idea of Australia as a settler society is deeply embedded and widely propagated. Politicians from both sides of parliament continue to present it as a given that Australia is a place of permanent, not temporary, migration, even when they are in positions to know how much the ground has shifted over the past 20 years.

At the Pacific Islands forum in 2005, Liberal prime minister John Howard rejected calls for Australia to set up a seasonal labour scheme for Pacific Island workers in the following terms. 'We have always had a preference for permanent settlement or permanent migration,' he said. 'I think you either invite somebody to your country to stay as a permanent resident or a citizen or you don't.'[16] Howard was doing more than whiting out the nineteenth-century history of blackbirding from Melanesia—he was creating a clear distinction between the type of postwar migration that Australia engaged in, and that practised by countries in Western Europe. He was shoring up the notion of

Australia as a settler society. A year later, treasurer Peter Costello buttressed the argument, telling Pacific finance ministers, 'Australia has never been a guest worker country.'[17]

In 2011, Labor immigration minister Chris Bowen put further props in support of the settler society, echoing Costello by confidently declaring in a speech on multiculturalism that 'we are not a guest worker society'. According to Bowen, the 'genius' of Australian multiculturalism lies in the fact that it is 'citizenship centred', unlike in other countries, where people arrive as 'guest workers' and are given 'little encouragement to take out citizenship' and 'little incentive to become full, contributing members of that society'.[18]

Despite such pronouncements, the settler-society model has been increasingly unsettled by successive changes to migration policy. Flawed and incomplete as the process was under the White Australia policy, for half a century after World War II there was a clear route from migration to membership—an understanding that to make the journey to Australia as a migrant was also to go through an open gate on a path that led to citizenship. As 'New Australians', migrants could choose to belong, at least in a legal sense. While citizenship might not guarantee immediate cultural acceptance and equality in everyday practice, it provides a solid foundation from which to claim a place, express identity, assert rights and make your voice heard.

Today, Australia's migration system looks very different. Increasingly we have a two-step or 'try before you buy' migration program: migrants arrive on temporary visas and have the potential, but not the certainty, of converting that status into permanent residency. The second step is mostly made by two groups of temporary migrants—international students who have graduated from Australian universities, and skilled workers who have initially come to Australia on temporary 457 visas. In some cases categories merge, creating two or more steps. A temporary migrant might first arrive, for example, as a student, then move on to a two-year 485 post-study work visa after graduation, before moving on to a 457 temporary skilled-worker visa with the aim of getting employer sponsorship for permanent residency.

Regardless of how long a temporary migrant stays, however, there is no guarantee that he or she will be able to take the second (or third or fourth) step to permanency. In place of a supposedly straightforward two-step migration process, they may find themselves moving around in circles, jumping repeatedly from one temporary visa to another. If they cannot leap to a safe landing before their temporary visa options are exhausted, then they are out.

New Zealanders are in a different category. They can remain in Australia as long as they choose—barring serious criminal conviction—but while New Zealanders can attempt to settle and build their lives here with no fear that their visas will expire, that does not qualify them for residency, and the rights and entitlements and sense of belonging that flow from the status of being permanent. A significant number of New Zealanders will never qualify for permanent residency no matter how long they live here, which means that they can never become citizens and full members of the Australian body politic. Again, this contradicts the fundamental principles of liberal democracy.

Two-step migration has many advantages for government, employers and tertiary institutions, but it also throws up potential problems, particularly given that Australia's permanent migration program has an annual cap on numbers while the temporary migration program is open-ended. If the number of temporary migrants wanting to convert to permanent residency exceeds the number of places available in the annual program, then we could have a build-up of frustrated 'not-quite-Australians' jumping across (or falling between) a succession of temporary-visa stepping stones.

Already, the number of long-term but temporary migrants with work rights exceeds one million people and makes up a significant proportion of our labour force. While the phenomenon of temporary migration gets some public attention, discussion tends to be narrowly focused on whether temporary migrant workers are taking 'Aussie' jobs or being exploited in the workplace. These are important issues, but to focus on them solely is to lose sight of the larger trends.

In this book, I am particularly concerned about two potential outcomes of the paradigm shift away from the settler-society model, both of which flow from the fact that the annual intake of permanent migrants to Australia is subject to a cap, while the number of temporary migrants is not.

The first potential outcome is for a growing number of temporary migrants to be active and engaged members of Australian society for extended periods of time—by which I mean five years or more—without necessarily being able to access permanent residency or citizenship. The second potential outcome is that an increasingly large and increasingly significant share of Australia's population and labour force will be made up of temporary migrants.

My contention is that the logic of Australia's temporary migration system as it currently operates will inevitably generate both these outcomes.

This prompts the following question, posed in a different context by North American political philosopher Joseph Carens: what is the place of long-term temporary migrants on the 'normative map' of Australian liberal democracy?[19] Carens asks whether liberal democracies should be able to admit people to their societies for an extended period of time 'without putting them on a path to citizenship and without granting them most of the rights that citizens enjoy'.[20] His answer (framed as question of justice, rather than political pragmatism) inclines towards a no. His reasoning is more detailed and complex than I can do justice to here, but a couple of key points, condensed from some of his extensive writing on this issue, may help to show why I find Carens' argument compelling.

Firstly, as 'embodied creatures' our lives unfold within physical space. In the contemporary world, the spaces in which we live 'are organised politically primarily as territories governed by states'.[21] Time spent actually living in a state creates ties that lay down the foundation for a claim to membership: 'Home is where one lives, and where one lives is the crucial variable for interests and for identity, both empirically and normatively.'[22] The longer a person lives in a given state, the stronger becomes their claim 'to full membership in society and to the enjoyment of the same rights as citizens, including, eventually, citizenship itself'.[23] In other words, the passage of time carries a moral force that cannot be ignored.[24] States are 'obliged to respect the claims of belonging that arise from living in a political community on an ongoing basis'.[25]

Carens' second fundamental concern is with the ethical responsibilities that arise towards migrants in states that are committed to 'democratic principles'. These principles flow from the liberal assumption that all human beings have equal moral worth and that no one should suffer discrimination on the grounds of race, gender or religious belief. On this basis, political systems should be representative, fair, and based on majority rule and the consent of the governed, while respecting the rights and freedoms of individuals and the rule of law. I use the term 'liberal democracy' as shorthand for an equivalent understanding. If we are truly committed to such principles, as Australians avowedly are, then, Carens argues, this will significantly constrain the range of policy responses that a liberal democracy can offer to the ethical dilemmas thrown up by migration in general, and by long-term temporary migration in particular.[26]

To date, the important questions raised by Carens have not engaged the attention of many Australian policymakers, journalists or analysts. In fact, we even lack the appropriate language to discuss these issues. The term 'guest worker' (or *Gastarbeiter*) with its specific historical connotations and geographical references is inadequate to encompass a range of temporary migrants that includes highly skilled professionals, university students and jobbing backpackers. 'Guest worker' also implies a blanket official understanding that these temporary migrants will leave after a limited stay, whereas many long-term temporary migrants to Australia hope to become permanent residents, and formal mechanisms exist for a considerable number of temporary migrants to make that transition.

So the term 'guest worker' will not do. A more accurate but rather clumsy formulation would be 'long-term temporary migrants with work rights', but this also falls short. It does tolerably well in capturing three of the main groups that I am interested in—skilled workers on 457 visas, international students and working holiday-makers—but does not cover New Zealanders, whose special category visa (subclass 444) renders their presence in Australia neither temporary nor permanent, but rather indefinite. Nor does it capture well the situation of refugees on temporary protection visas, who are in the first place refugees, not migrants, and who may also be in Australia indefinitely, without achieving either permanent residence or citizenship.

Alternative terms that are sometimes offered for long-term temporary migrants with work rights include 'denizens' and 'sojourners', but the one that seems to me to best hit the mark comes from American political philosopher Michael Walzer. In his landmark book *Spheres of Justice*, Walzer compares long-term temporary migrants to the *metics* of ancient Athens. The *metics* were foreigners resident in the city. (Aristotle was a notable *metic*.) They enjoyed greater freedoms than slaves, including the right to conduct business, but were excluded from membership of the polis and its decision-making:

> 'We throw open our city to the world,' said Pericles in his Funeral Oration, 'and never exclude foreigners from any opportunity.' So the *metics* came willingly to Athens, drawn by economic opportunity, perhaps also by the city's 'air of freedom'. Most of them never rose above the rank of laborer or 'mechanic', but some prospered: in fourth-century Athens, *metics* were represented among the wealthiest merchants. Athenian freedom, however, they shared only in its negative forms. Though they were required to join in the defense of the city, they had no political rights at all; nor did their descendants. Nor did they share in the most basic of welfare rights: 'Foreigners were excluded from the distribution of corn.'[27]

The main categories of temporary migrants that I discuss in this book are very different from one another. Those who hold 457 visas are primarily here to work at a particular job—though this may not be true of their spouses or children. Most international students are primarily here to study, even if some have their sights set on permanent residency in the long term. Working holidaymakers are young and mobile, and they must leave Australia after a maximum stay of two years or else shift to a different visa category. New Zealanders can live and work in Australia for as long as they choose, and come and go across the Tasman at will. Refugees on temporary protection visas have landed in Australia in a desperate search for a safe place to live.

While these temporary migrants have different characteristics, they all have certain important things in common: they have the right to work, and are expected to pay taxes and abide by the laws of the state, yet like the *metics* of ancient Athens they have no say in choosing the representatives who make those laws; they cannot vote or run for office and have, at best, only restricted access to government services and welfare systems.

The response may be—so what? This is a contract freely entered into. Temporary migrants come here to study or work with no promise that permanent residency will ever be part of the deal. In other words, temporary migrants have accepted the terms of the bargain that got them a visa; they have made their beds and should lie in them without complaint. But migration—even temporary migration—is always more than a transaction. The longer a migrant stays in a country, the more the contractual nature of the original arrangement recedes into the background and the more the sense of attachment and engagement with the host nation tends to grow. We are social beings. We live together in communities. Society and culture are shaped by our interactions. We establish bonds of connection, interdependence and mutuality. Out of those bonds grows an ethic of reciprocity and obligation. That ethic will eventually make its presence felt, no matter how hard we seek to ignore it.

There is a tendency to treat permanent settlement and temporary migration as if they were 'two quite separate and unrelated processes'.[28] While it would be overstating the case to deploy the oft-repeated phrase that there is nothing more permanent than a temporary migrant, the very concept of two-step migration shows that the two are interconnected and that any attempt to draw a neat distinction between the two categories will produce a false dichotomy. So Australian policymakers are fooling themselves if they think that the expansion of various forms of temporary migration in ever greater numbers can be neatly packaged up and kept in a separate box from questions of settlement, residency, citizenship, rights and obligation.

In an Australian context, Joseph Carens' question about where long-term temporary migrants fit on the 'normative map' of liberal democracy seems to me to break down into two more specific sub-questions. These two core questions animate this book.

Firstly, how long is it reasonable for a migrant to live in Australia without being accepted as an Australian? Long-term temporary migrants are neither visitors nor permanent residents; they work and study, pay taxes and university fees, abide by local laws and contribute to the economic and cultural life of the nation in myriad ways. Yet, like the *metics* of ancient Greece, they remain on the outer.

Secondly, what sort of country we want Australia to be? Do we hold to the positive conception—however historically simplistic—of Australia as a settler society where migrants become full members of the political community and make this country their home? Or are we content for the proportion of *metics*—of provisional, not-quite-Australians—to continue to grow? In other words, is there a threshold we should not cross—a point at which the number of long-term temporary migrants tips the balance and changes the nature of Australian society and the assumptions underpinning Australian multiculturalism?

Clearly these questions have both ethical and practical dimensions. I will return to them and attempt to offer some responses to them in the final chapter. Readers may not agree with my conclusions and suggestions, but I hope they will engage with the questions themselves. As the number of Australia's twenty-first-century *metics* grows, we need to start talking more seriously about the way temporary-visa schemes are changing the nation.

2 | The Rise and Rise of Temporary Migration

As a child growing up in the Adelaide Hills, I saw in a trip to the city the promise of a treat. If we went out in the evening to see a play or a movie, my parents might indulge me afterwards with *tartufo* or *cassata* from the Flash Gelati Bar in Hindley Street. Later, as a teenager, I would sometimes meet my father for lunch at the university. After the meal he would invariably take me to a small Italian cafe in the ornate Adelaide Arcade for a short black or a cappuccino. In the mid-1970s this was one of the few places equipped with an espresso machine. Gelato and espresso were novelties—gifts to the tastebuds of Adelaide courtesy of the postwar wave of Italian migrants.

Between 1947 and 1954, Australia's Italian-born population more than tripled in size. It doubled again between 1954 and 1961, and continued to grow for several more years, peaking at around 290,000 people in the 1971 census.¹ For at least 30 years, the Italian-born were second to the British as the largest overseas-born group in Australia.

In Melbourne, postwar migrants gave the suburb of Carlton its genuine Italian flavour. As Italian migration fell away and the existing Italian-born community aged, Carlton's Lygon Street coffee strip risked becoming a caricature of its former self, its Italian reputation hanging by a slender thread. Thanks to a new wave of Italian migrants, Lygon Street has got its zip back. In late 2015, when I ate lunch at a self-proclaimed *Gastronomia Italiana*, the waiter told me that all the stylish young staff in the establishment were recent Italian migrants. He said some of them (I suspect most) were here on temporary visas; others had made the transition to permanent residence.

The same phenomenon is evident in Sydney. Over dinner in a chic new pizzeria in Walsh Bay, Michele (Mike) Grigoletti and his colleague Silvia Pianelli have fun guessing which regions of Italy the waiters hail from by their accents. Both Grigoletti and Pianelli settled in Australia relatively recently, and they devote much of their time to gathering data and stories from the new wave of Italian migration of which they are a part.

Grigoletti and Pianelli felt that the authorities in Italy and Australia were not paying due attention to the dynamics and challenges of the new migration. To try to make the issue more visible they formed an independent study group called *Australia Solo Andata* (Australia One Way) and secured modest funding from the *Migrantes Foundation*, an offshoot of the Italian Bishops Conference. As well as producing written reports, they have made a film called *88 Giorni* (*88 Days*), documenting the experiences of young Italians seeking to secure a second working-holiday visa by labouring for at least three months on Australian farms.

Many of the young Italians they interview would never have conceived of working in agriculture in their homeland. 'I would never have imagined in my whole life that I would be working as a watermelon picker,' says one young man. Harvest work is hot, dirty, difficult and poorly paid. In Italy, just as in Australia, it is work largely reserved for migrants. 'I now understand how foreign workers feel,' says another backpacker in the film. 'Here, I am the immigrant.'

Like backpackers from other countries, some young Italians have been abused, exploited and underpaid. 'Mildura's farms are the worst thing that has ever happened in my life,' says one. A young woman remarks that if you work hard, then at least you should be treated with respect.

Yet if the interviews are anything to go by, many young Italians find their work picking pumpkins or driving tractors surprisingly enjoyable, in some cases even liberating. Some decide they want to stay. 'Australia opens your horizons and makes you feel incredibly young,' says one. 'Perhaps it was necessary to go to the other side of the world. Italy doesn't offer us this opportunity.'

When Mike Grigoletti tells me that the scale of *temporary* Italian migration to Australia today rivals the *permanent* migration that changed the flavours of my Adelaide childhood, I am surprised. When I do my own calculations, I find the numbers bear him out (albeit over a much shorter time frame).

Over the two-and-a-half decades from 1947, Australia's Italian-born population increased by an average of about 11,000 people per year; during the peak period between 1954 and 1961, that number was 15,000. By comparison, around 13,000 young Italians have come to Australia as first-time working holidaymakers annually since 2012. A few thousand more have been granted visas as international students, temporary skilled workers or permanent migrants.

Perhaps this new wave of Italian migration will be a short-lived phenomenon that abates as Italy recovers from the long-term effects of the Global Financial Crisis—particularly its high rates of youth unemployment. Or perhaps, as the Migration Policy Institute suggests, southern European nations like Italy have 'in some ways returned to their earlier, more traditional roles, as significant countries of emigration', with the difference that 'migrants today are younger, better educated and more skilled than past waves, with a high proportion of professionals among those leaving'.[2] Whatever the causes of emigration from Italy, it is clear that the nature of temporary Italian immigration to Australia today is qualitatively different from the permanent Italian migration of the 1950s and 1960s.

Yet there is a widespread tendency to conceive of migration through the lens of past experience. Michael Pezzullo, Secretary of the Department of Immigration and Border Protection (and the Australian-born son of Italian migrants) summed this up well in a speech at the Australian National University:

> For many of us, the paradigmatic case for thinking about immigration is still probably best captured in the black-and-white photographs of European migrants arriving on ships and gazing expectantly on the new land that would be their future home. This is often the collective memory, imagery and organising frame for thinking about immigration. Even today, as one walks the halls of my Department, the visual images and cues of this paradigm are everywhere. And yet, as with all revolutions in paradigms of thought and practice, a new reality has

been steadily emerging, in the shadows of that which we used to do, and which is fixed in collective memory.³

It is not that we are unfamiliar with the changes that have been made to policy since the postwar era of mass migration. In the early 1970s, Whitlam and his effervescent immigration minister, Al Grassby, finished the job of burying the White Australia policy, while sharply cutting migrant numbers at the same time. A few years before Whitlam was elected, migrant numbers peaked at 185,000 (in 1969–70). By the time he was dismissed the annual intake had been cut by more than two-thirds: with fewer than 53,000 arrivals, 1975–76 holds the record for the lowest migrant intake of any year since World War II.⁴

Malcolm Fraser, who took over from Whitlam, is remembered for opening Australia's doors to refugees from Indochina. As well as responding intelligently to the first wave of 'boat people', in 1977 Fraser added a planned humanitarian component to Australia's migration program and introduced a refugee determination policy for assessing claims lodged by asylum seekers onshore. In 1978, in response to the Galbally Report on Post-Arrival Programs and Services to Migrants, Fraser formalised the policy of multiculturalism. His starting point was 'recognition and appreciation of the fact that the Australian population is derived from a wide variety of ethnic and cultural backgrounds'. He conceived multiculturalism as an attempt to give substance to the 'principles of equal opportunity and equality of access' for all Australians, and to respond to specific migrant needs (for such things as adult English classes, translating and interpreting services, and multilingual broadcasting).⁵

It was Fraser, too, who in 1979 first introduced the 'points test'. Borrowed from Canada and known technically as the 'Numerical

Multifactor Assessment System', the test was a migrant-selection tool that could be used to weight different characteristics of migrants, such as family ties to Australia, occupational skills and language proficiency.[6]

Family and humanitarian migration dominated in the Fraser years, but during the Hawke–Keating era from 1983 onwards the points test was tweaked to give greater weight to skills, qualifications and work experience. This shift accelerated over the life of the Howard government as the migration program was re-conceptualised as an economic lever that could be used to lift growth and productivity. In the first full year of the Hawke government (1983–84), family reunion accounted for around 80 per cent of Australia's migration intake and skilled migration 20 per cent; by the end of the Howard years (2006–2007) those proportions had been almost reversed: skilled migration accounted for about 70 per cent of the program and family migration 30 per cent.[7] (The humanitarian intake, which had risen above 20,000 people per year under Fraser, was pretty static, hovering around 12,000 places under the Hawke, Keating and Howard governments.[8])

By the end of the century, Australia's immigration program had been radically overhauled: the postwar policy of mass migration to boost numbers in the population and the labour force had been replaced by one focused on selecting people with specific skills that were deemed to be in high demand in the Australian economy. The boundaries of the family stream had been drawn so tightly that it might almost have been called the partner stream, since more than 80 per cent of all 'family' visas were issued to spouses or fiancés. Almost all the rest went to dependent children and parents.[9] The era in which family migration might have extended to brothers, sisters, uncles, aunties or cousins was long gone. If you were not the partner of an

Australian, and aspired to migrate to Australia, then the qualities you needed to possess were youth, English-language fluency, good health, professional qualifications and work experience. Skin tone and style of dress no longer mattered. As a result, rather than drawing migrants almost exclusively from Europe, by the end of the century Australia's intake had become global, with more migrants coming from countries in Asia than from any other region.[10]

There was, nevertheless, a strong thread of continuity. In 2000, it would have still been possible, without fear of contradiction, to describe Australia as a settler society in which temporary migration played a small but insignificant role. A decade and a half later, we can no longer say this. We can now see that Australia has made a permanent shift to temporary migration. Of course, permanent settlement continues, but it is now part of a hybrid system, intricately and intimately entwined with a much larger program of temporary entry, which serves as the primary gateway to establishing a life in Australia.

What is more, we have moved from a permanent migration intake that was centrally planned and tightly controlled by government, to a temporary-migration regime that is flexible and responsive. Rather than setting targets, government manages flows: migration numbers are largely driven by employers' demand for skilled workers, by the desires of backpackers to travel and work here, and by the capacity of Australian tertiary institutions to attract international enrolments.

In some respects, Australia's new hybrid migration model may be more efficient than the twentieth-century model of permanent settlement that preceded it—in delivering improved labour-market outcomes among recent migrants, for example. In other ways, its performance is yet to be evaluated. It is unclear, for example, what, if any, impact the rise of temporary migration may have on social cohesion, multiculturalism and national identity. The new reality of a two-step, employer-driven migration scheme also throws up practical and ethical challenges that we are only just beginning to acknowledge.

The radical makeover of the migration program was incremental. For a long time the cumulative impact was hard to identify, because it flowed from disparate and disconnected initiatives that were not necessarily considered to fall under the heading of migration. As a result there was little public debate about the transformation as it was unfolding.

The speed and scale of change only started to become apparent towards the end of the first decade of the twenty-first century, when it was already in full bloom, although most of the seeds were sown earlier. In the 1980s, Australia began opening up its higher-education system to international students. In 1996, the 457 or temporary skilled-worker program was established—so small a scheme that at first it appeared insignificant. In 1999, temporary protection visas were introduced for refugees who had arrived without a valid visa, and in 2001 changes were made to the way New Zealanders could access welfare—a measure that was not a migration reform per se. In 2005, in response to pressure from the agricultural lobby, there was some ostensibly minor tinkering to the working-holidaymaker scheme to enable backpackers to get a second 12-month visa if they did seasonal jobs in rural areas.

Each seemingly self-contained and apparently inconsequential change had its own logic, and each gained its own momentum. Initially the changes did not appear to be connected or to cohere to any overarching design. So while there was debate about specific issues, like the effect of the internationalisation of education on teaching in Australian universities, or the impact of the 457 visa scheme on labour rights, such issues were rarely considered to be part of a larger discussion about migration. Yet their combined impact has altered Australia's migration program in profound ways. It is only when we see these changes in this broader context that the contours of Australia's new hybrid system become visible.

So when we think about migration today, many of us may still have in our minds the twentieth-century permanent-settler model that is so familiar to us. Politicians rarely do much to dissuade us from this perspective. Occasionally, however, a senior government figure like Michael Pezzullo acknowledges that we are in a different era.

Pezzullo's frankness was evident in a candid speech to staff to mark Australia Day 2015. At the time he was a new man in a new role: formerly the head of Customs, he was now secretary of an amalgamated Department of Immigration and Border Protection with its own armed Border Protection Force. (Some insiders saw the amalgamation as more of a takeover of Immigration by Customs that shifted the department's focus from migration to national security. Several senior bureaucrats left to work in other areas of government.[11]) Pezzullo contended that settlement was the story of Australia's past since 1788, but not the story of its future. While settlement would surely continue, '"engagement" with the world', driven by globalisation, was now at the heart of the Australian story. As a result, it was time to 'reframe our national self-understanding' and to declare that 'the mission of mass migration that was set for us in 1945 is long accomplished'. Pezzullo told immigration staff that their primary task was no longer settlement but gate-keeping, and 'the overwhelming and predominant role of the department will be to act as the open conduits of Australia's engagement with the world around us, whether for the purposes of trade, travel or migration—for time-limited purposes or for tomorrow's settlers'.[12]

The thrust of Pezzullo's speech is neatly symbolised in a change to his department's website; the established URL—www.immi.gov.au—was replaced with www.border.gov.au. Pezzullo's speech also serves to underline my overall point: temporary migration is no longer a marginal phenomenon at the edges of our immigration program. Nor is it an interim setting. Temporary migration is a central plank of policy. It is integral to boosting the responsiveness of the labour market to changing economic conditions, enabling employers to access a supply of workers at all skill levels who can be more easily hired or let go as the situation demands. Much of Australia's fruit and vegetable crop is harvested by foreign backpackers on working-holiday visas and almost one in four students enrolled in an Australian university now comes from overseas.[13] In some major institutions, such as RMIT in Melbourne, the proportion is closer to one in two students.[14] In an era of declining government funding, the fees international students pay help keep our higher-education sector afloat and maintain the viability of tertiary study for domestic students. Temporary migration has also become a primary mechanism by which we select and filter future citizens.

This permanent shift to temporary migration was not part of a platform promised and implemented by a newly elected reformist government. It did not flow from the recommendations of a landmark departmental review, a parliamentary inquiry or an expert panel. Rather, the increasing emphasis on temporary migration has gradually but steadily emerged over a period of about 20 years, without much public discussion or critical analysis. The rise and rise of temporary migration is not so much the result of deliberate policy settings as the cumulative outcome of four distinct programs, each with its own momentum and rationale, which now cohere, to a greater and lesser degree, around a demand-driven, employer-led hybrid system of two-step migration.

457 visas

The best known and most contentious of these four distinct programs is the temporary skilled-worker scheme (usually referred to by its visa subclass as a 457 visa).

In 1961, a young graduate of Bombay University arrived in Sydney to take up a temporary position as the New India Assurance Company's representative in Australia. The White Australia policy was in force, so Neville Roach had no expectation of staying for long, let alone settling for life. When he decided he wanted to change careers and work in information technology, the Australian government gave Roach a permit to remain for another seven years, on the understanding that this would be the one and only extension to his stay. By this time he was living in Adelaide, where the Indian community numbered just 27 people.

More than half a century later, Neville Roach AO can look back on a successful career as chief executive and chair of Fujitsu Australia and an impressive record of public service and civic engagement. The list of his appointments includes periods as chair of the National Multicultural Advisory Council, as deputy chair of SBS and as a member of the federal government's Cooperative Research Centres committee.[15]

By the time of Roach's arrival in Australia the cracks in the White

Australia policy were already apparent. In 1960, the Immigration Reform Group at the University of Melbourne had published *Control or Colour Bar? A Proposal for Change in Australia's Immigration Policy*. Priced at 3 shillings, the slim paperbound booklet sparked a national debate that eventually spelled the end of the White Australia policy, opening the way for Neville Roach to become an Australian citizen and to play a direct role in shaping future immigration policy through the creation of the 457 visa. The visa was introduced soon after John Howard came to office in 1996, but had its origins in an inquiry commissioned when Paul Keating was prime minister. Neville Roach chaired the inquiry committee—the Committee of Inquiry into the Temporary Entry of Business People and Highly Skilled Specialists, to give its full title—and its 1995 report became known as the Roach Report.[16]

Reading the report today highlights the extent to which the 457 program has outgrown its origins. Roach's committee was primarily concerned with smoothing the process of 'intra-company transfers'—making it quicker and easier for international corporations to bring senior executives and technical specialists into the country—at a time when the Australian economy was opening up and two-way flows of skilled labour were growing. The Roach Report warned that other countries could retaliate against Australia's 'overly restrictive' temporary-entry rules, and that could prevent Australians from working overseas.

Australia was in a period of major economic change, with manufacturing declining and services growing. In a world where 'trade in services is based on different countries developing specialised skills in different areas', Roach argued that it was 'not realistic for Australia to attempt to develop specialised skills in all areas'. Keating and his predecessor, Bob Hawke, had been working to link Australia more closely with its near neighbours, and Roach hoped a revamped visa system would foster 'greater integration into the international business environment—in particular the Asia Pacific region'.

From today's perspective, though, what is most striking about the Roach Report is its attempt to strictly define the boundaries of temporary entry. According to Roach, the new arrangements were 'not meant to apply to the traditional skilled trades or to professions like nursing and teaching'. Yet today, about one in every five 457-visa holders has a trade qualification and nurses are one of the biggest professional groups recruited under the scheme. (Teachers on 457 visas are less common, but university lecturers are high on the list.)

Roach warned that temporary entry must not be seen 'as an instrument for overcoming long-term labour-market deficiencies'. Immigration ministers have echoed that view. In mid-2013, for example, Labor's Brendan O'Connor asserted that the 457-visa program was only intended 'to fill temporary skills shortages in some sectors and regions'[17] and should be used 'as a last resort'.[18] But O'Connor was either misinformed or being disingenuous, for by then the 457 scheme had become something much bigger and more complex than Roach envisaged.

In the first full year of the scheme (1996–97), the number of 457 visas issued was 25,000; over the next 15 years this grew fivefold to more than 125,000 (in 2011–12).[19] In mid-2015, there were 188,000 people living in Australia on 457 visas, counting both primary and secondary visa holders.[20] (A secondary visa holder is a spouse or dependent child.) A little more than half of the primary visa holders were categorised as 'Skill Level 1', meaning that their qualifications or experience were commensurate with a bachelor or higher level degree. About a fifth were at Skill Level 2, meaning they held a diploma, and just under a quarter were at Skill Level 3, which equates to a vocational Certificate III or IV. (The remainder were either unclassified or at lower skill levels.) In 2015 the major countries of origin for 457-visa holders were India and the United Kingdom (each accounting for about one-fifth of the primary 457-visa holders in Australia), followed by Ireland, the Philippines and China (each making up about eight per cent of the program).[21]

In comparison to the total size of the Australian labour force, the 457-visa scheme is very small, but it has become an important component of workforce planning that is popular with employers, not least because its flexibility enables them to respond rapidly to changing needs.

International students

In the two decades since Neville Roach wrote his report, the increasing internationalisation of the Australian economy has gone hand in hand with the internationalisation of the Australian education system. This process began a decade earlier, when the Hawke government allowed Australian universities to accept full-fee-paying international students. By 1996, Australia was already granting more than 100,000 international student visas each year. Over the next decade, the numbers almost tripled.

The surge in international enrolments through the early 2000s was not driven solely by the quality of Australia's educational offering or by Australia's price advantage over Britain and the United States. A major reason the program expanded so rapidly was that the Howard government established a more direct link between study in Australia and permanent residency. After 1999, applicants who had obtained their diploma, trade or degree in Australia gained five extra marks in the migration points test.[22] Another 10 bonus points were offered to applicants with a qualification on a new schedule of occupations deemed to be in short supply in Australia (called the Migration Occupations in Demand List, or MODL). International students and education marketers quickly latched onto the fact that certain courses of study now offered a smoother and clearer path to permanent residency. In 2001, the government made the path easier by allowing international students to apply for a permanent visa onshore after they completed their studies—previously graduates had to leave Australia before applying—and by exempting them from having to demonstrate work experience in their field. Then, in 2005, the government expanded the number of trades on the MODL, adding in qualifications in cooking, hospitality and hairdressing that could be gained with a one-year course of study. The vocational-training sector exploded with courses directly targeting this migration pathway, both responding to and prompting a greater surge in international student numbers.

It is hard to be sure exactly why the Howard government made these changes. In part, no doubt, ministers and bureaucrats were responding to intense lobbying by interested parties—particularly the universities, TAFEs and private training colleges. The leaders of those institutions were in turn desperate to find new sources of revenue under a government that preferred to hand out tax cuts than to increase funding for post-school education. This was also the era of the minerals boom, when unemployment was low and it appeared Australia might be headed for chronic skills shortages, so creating an education and training pathway to permanent residence might have seemed like a good idea at the time. In retrospect, the Howard-era changes look like knee-jerk responses to specific issues and pressures, rather than coherent and considered policy.

In 2009, the Rudd government wound back many of these measures, breaking the nexus between study and residency that had generated a massive backlog in valid applications for permanent skilled migration. Combined with the deterring effects of a high Australian dollar and racist attacks on Indian students, this produced a dramatic 16 per cent fall in new applications from one year to the next. Universities, TAFEs and private education providers reacted with alarm; they had increasingly come to rely on international-student fees to meet budget targets. The sector lobbied for action to prop up the industry and government responded by dangling a new carrot to attract international students, revamping an existing post-study work visa—the 485 subclass—to make it easier for overseas students to stay on in Australia and work for up to four years after graduation. In response to the visa change—and to the fall in the value of the Australian dollar—international student numbers began to rise again, and to approach previous record highs. By mid-2015, the number of international students and student graduates living in Australia had climbed above 400,000. The five biggest source countries were all in Asia: China (22 per cent of the total), India (13 per cent), Vietnam, South Korea and Nepal (around five per cent each).[23]

In order to be granted a visa to study in Australia, prospective students must satisfy the 'genuine temporary entrant requirement'. This 'integrity measure' is designed to ensure that international students do not use the visa program 'as a way of maintaining de facto permanent residency in Australia'.[24] Factors that decision-makers must consider in applying the test include whether wage rates in an applicant's homeland are much lower than in Australia, whether the prospective student may be required to do compulsory military service and whether the home country is subject to political and civil unrest.[25] The immigration department's website notes that the genuine temporary-entry test 'is not designed to exclude those students who, after studying in Australia, go on to develop the skills required by the Australian labour market and apply to obtain permanent residency'.[26] Or, as the ministerial guidelines put it, a prospective student must have 'a genuine intention to enter and remain in Australia temporarily, notwithstanding the potential for this intention to change over time to an intention to utilise lawful means to remain in Australia for an extended period or permanently'.[27]

International students must also demonstrate or declare that they have 'genuine access to sufficient funds' from 'an acceptable source' to meet the costs of living and studying in Australia for the first year or two of their stay.[28] Whether or not students are required to prove or only attest that they have enough money depends on which country they come from and which course they are studying; a student from Germany will be granted streamlined processing, whereas a student from Bangladesh will be assessed to pose a much greater 'immigration risk' and will be expected to furnish evidence of their financial resources.[29] In 2015, students had to have access to a minimum of $18,610 per year for living costs, on top of paying for course fees and a return airfare.[30] This is independent of any income they might hope to get by working in Australia. Overseas students are permitted to work up to 40 hours per fortnight during term time and without limit during course breaks.

There is an obvious tension between the genuine temporary-entry requirement and the sufficient-funds test, and other aspects of Australia's international student program—between the desire to tightly control Australia's borders and the desire to maximise enrolments at Australian universities and vocational colleges; between using the prospect of permanent residency and the enticement of work rights during and after study as bait to lure students to Australia and the fear of debasing the education system; between international education as a high turnover export industry and international education as a selection gateway for permanent skilled residents.

Working holidaymakers

We can see similar tensions at work in the expansion of the working-holidaymaker program that grants travellers aged 18 to 30 a visa (the 417 subclass) to live and work in Australia for a year.

The working-holidaymaker scheme has existed since 1975. It is a reciprocal arrangement that was initially limited to Canada, the United Kingdom and Ireland, with Japan joining in the 1980s.[31] Since then, agreements have been established with a further 15 countries or territories—Belgium, the Republic of Cyprus, Denmark, Estonia, Finland, France, Germany, Hong Kong, Italy, South Korea, Malta, the Netherlands, Norway, Sweden and Taiwan.[32] The expansion of the scheme to these other countries began in the mid-1990s—around the same time as the 457 visa was introduced—and has been part of the rapid growth of temporary migration to Australia over the past 20 years.

The increase in numbers has also been accompanied by an increase in scope. In 1997, a Senate inquiry into the scheme recommended that 'the original intention of the working-holiday program be reinforced so that it remains a program which provides an opportunity for an extended holiday with incidental work and is not used either to resolve labour-market problems in Australia or as a mechanism by which people can circumvent normal migration processes in order to remain in Australia, particularly in employment-related categories'.[33]

The recommendation was ignored and the Senate report's concerns about the working-holiday visa being used primarily for work rather than travel or to plug gaps in the labour market accurately anticipated the future shape of the program.

In April 2005, in response to persistent lobbying from rural employers complaining about labour shortages, the federal government changed the rules of the visa to encourage backpackers to take up seasonal agricultural jobs. It did this by offering a second 12-month visa to travellers who engaged in at least three months (88 days) of 'harvest work'.[34] A year later, the range of jobs that merited a second visa was expanded and now includes plant and animal cultivation, tree farming and felling, fishing and pearling, and mining and construction.[35] The only requirement for a second visa is that the work is undertaken in a regional area, which includes anywhere in Australia except the ACT and eight major urban centres (Sydney, Wollongong, Newcastle, the NSW Central Coast, Melbourne, Brisbane, the Gold Coast and Perth). Originally, too, a working holidaymaker could remain with any one employer for a maximum period of three months; this threshold was subsequently doubled to six months.[36] Over the course of the decade from 2001, the number of 417 visas issued each year grew 250 per cent, from fewer than 80,000 to almost 200,000.[37]

In the mid-2000s, the Howard government also established a more restrictive reciprocal 'work and holiday' arrangement (a 462 subclass visa), which is limited to travellers aged 18 to 30 who have a post-school qualification and speak 'functional English'. The first agreement under the work and holiday scheme was struck with Thailand in August 2005 and the program has now been extended to another 14 countries—Argentina, Bangladesh, Chile, China,

Indonesia, Malaysia, Poland, Portugal, Slovak Republic, Slovenia, Spain, Turkey, the United States and Uruguay, with Israel, Greece, Papua New Guinea and Vietnam expected to join the list soon.[38] With the exception of the United States, there is an annual cap on the number of visas that can be issued to any particular country. (Thailand, for example, is limited to 500 visas, Indonesia to 1,000, Bangladesh and Papua New Guinea to just 100). The 462 visa cannot be extended for an additional 12 months. In comparison to the working-holidaymaker program the number of visas issued under the work and holiday program remains small, though it, too, has grown rapidly in recent years, from fewer than 2,000 visas in 2006–2007 to almost 12,000 in 2014–15.[39]

As of June 2015, there were around 144,000 working holiday-makers present in Australia: about 20 per cent of them came from the United Kingdom, around 35 per cent were from other European countries (primarily France, Germany, Italy and Ireland), almost 39 per cent were from Asia (mostly Taiwan, South Korea, Japan and Hong Kong) and the rest were from the Americas (largely Canada and the United States).[40]

Several aims merge in the working-holiday arrangements, including encouraging tourism to Australia, improving diplomatic ties and the desire to open up reciprocal opportunities for young Australians to gain experience travelling and working overseas. But changes to the scheme also reveal how government has increasingly used it to meet employer demand for a mobile, flexible, often low-skilled workforce that can be deployed or laid off in accord with changing labour-market needs. The immigration department fact sheet says that working-holiday visas 'encourage cultural exchange and closer ties between countries, by allowing young people to have an extended holiday and supplement their funds with short-term employment'.[41] To be eligible for the visa, applicants must be 'genuine visitors'.[42] It is obvious, however, that the 417 and 462 visas are no longer the preserve of individual travellers seeking to eke out their holiday savings by doing a few odd jobs. While there are certainly still many backpackers who fit this stereotype, evidence is mounting that working-holiday visas are increasingly the province of highly organised migration brokers and labour-hire firms. Researcher Shanthi Robertson has found that agents in source countries recruit and organise temporary migrants specifically for the 417 visa, often with exaggerated promises of the pay and conditions that they can expect in Australia.[43] Her finding is supported by Sherry Huang, a former working holidaymaker from Taiwan, who is now an organiser with the National Union of Workers. She told a Senate inquiry that shopfront recruitment agencies in Taiwan charge migrant workers thousands of dollars to organise jobs in Australia. 'It is like a whole set of programs—a whole package,' she told the committee. 'They are offering the flight ticket. They even arrange the same car, accommodation. They then tell you, "I will find you a job", which you have to pay a certain amount of money for. But it is really a lot.'[44]

New Zealanders

In many ways New Zealanders do not fit neatly into the category of temporary migration. They can live and work in Australia for as long as they choose, under a visa that is issued on arrival. This special category visa (subclass 444) is, however, defined in the Migration Act as a 'temporary' visa, even though it allows for an indefinite stay. In 2001, the Howard government sought to discourage long-term movement to Australia by certain categories of New Zealanders, by changing the definition of a 'resident' in social-security laws so as to deliberately exclude Kiwis. The effect was not to deter new arrivals as intended, but to make the lives of New Zealanders who choose to settle in Australia more precarious. It also added a significant and growing new cohort to the body of temporary migrants present in Australia at any one time.

The exact number of New Zealanders resident in Australia on temporary visas is difficult to quantify, since Kiwis can come and go at will and are always issued a new special category visa on arrival, regardless of how long they intend to stay. According to official statistics there were 653,830 New Zealand visa holders present in Australia on 30 June 2015. This snapshot, however, includes anyone in Australia on a short-term holiday or business trip (which may account for around 100,000 people out of the total). It also includes a significant number of New Zealanders who moved to Australia prior to 2001, and who retained the rights granted to them at that time, making them more akin to permanent residents than temporary migrants. In 2013, two researchers at Victoria University in Wellington calculated that the number of 'unprotected' New Zealanders living in Australia was 'around 185,000 (but steadily growing)'.[45]

Other temporary migrants

There are three other smaller but significant groups of temporary migrants who are relevant to this discussion: refugees and asylum seekers, seasonal workers and overstayers.

Asylum seekers are issued with bridging visas as they await the outcome of the government's refugee determination procedure—a process that can take many years. At the end of 2015, there were around 30,000 people in this position, most of whom arrived in Australia by boat from Indonesia in 2012 and 2013.[46] Under current policy it will be almost impossible for any of these asylum seekers to ever become permanent residents. If they are recognised as refugees, they will be moved onto temporary protection visas (reintroduced by the Abbott government in late 2014). When their visas expire, they will either have to prove they face a continuing threat of persecution in their homeland or leave Australia.

The second group, seasonal workers, are Pacific Islanders and East Timorese who come to Australia to take up jobs in agriculture and tourism. They are perhaps better described as 'circular migrants' than 'temporary migrants', since they can only stay in Australia for part of the year—in most cases for a maximum of six months—before returning to their homeland, although they may return again and again in subsequent years. They come to Australia under the Seasonal Worker Programme, which is run by the Department of Employment rather than by the immigration department (though immigration issues the 416 special program visa). At the same time as seeking to meet labour-market needs in agriculture, the program is designed to contribute to international development by boosting employment, incomes and skills in nations that are major recipients of Australian foreign aid. First introduced as a pilot in 2009 and then established as an ongoing program in 2012, the scheme has been subject to a tight annual cap on numbers. In 2014–15 there were only 3,250 places in the scheme.[47] Numbers are likely to expand in coming years, however, since the cap has been removed and the scheme has been expanded to more sectors of the economy.[48]

The third group of temporary migrants who should be mentioned are overstayers—popularly called illegal immigrants and technically termed 'unlawful non-citizens' by the immigration bureaucracy. These are people who arrived on a legitimate visa, usually a tourist visa, and failed to depart when that visa expired. In June 2011 the immigration department estimated that there were 58,000 overstayers in Australia.[49] Their nationality broadly reflects the mix of people who visit Australia, with the largest groups coming from China, the United States, Malaysia, the United Kingdom and India. As undocumented migrants, overstayers are potentially vulnerable to exploitation and abuse, particularly in the workplace; however, many stay for a relatively short time after their visas expire before leaving of their own accord. About 30 per cent of overstayers have been in Australia for less than two years while around 37 per cent have been living below the radar for more than 10 years.[50] Given that Australia has more than seven million visitor arrivals every year, the number of overstayers is very small and has been relatively constant for many years, despite the growth of tourism and international education. Australia's lack of land borders and rigorous universal visa system means that it has very few undocumented migrants relative to comparable developed nations in Europe and North America.

Each of the distinct forms of temporary migration described above aimed to deliver a particular benefit or respond to a particular problem, but they have gained their own dynamics, evolving into something with more extensive and far-reaching implications than was originally conceived.

There are many differences between these classes of temporary migrants. The entitlement to access public services varies according to the type of visa they hold or the country they come from. New Zealanders, for example, can access Medicare, as can citizens of some other countries with which Australia has reciprocal arrangements (like the United Kingdom), but most temporary migrants are required to take out private health insurance and to cover the full costs of any medical treatment.

Some temporary migrants come to Australia primarily to work, under dedicated migrant labour programs like the 457-visa scheme; others come primarily to study or to travel, but may also join the workforce, and often end up concentrated in particular sectors of the economy that are notorious for low payment and poor conditions, such as students working in hospitality and backpackers labouring in agriculture. In this sense, Australia's student-visa program and the working-holidaymaker scheme are categorised by legal scholar Joo-Cheong Tham and his colleagues as de facto migrant labour programs; they not only bring in students and encourage tourism, but also supply workers to meet the employment needs of specific business sectors.[51] Dedicated and de facto temporary labour migration is now a permanent feature of Australia's market economy.

Some temporary migrants intend to stay a long time; others plan to leave after just a few months. Some aspire to permanent residency; others have no intention of making Australia home. In many cases, their aims and hopes are not fixed, but change with time and experience. All these categories of temporary migrants can be distinguished from tourists, however, in that they are authorised to work in Australia and to remain here for an extended period of time. All, too, can be distinguished from Australian residents and citizens, who do not share in the characteristic of temporariness. Temporary migrants, the new *metics*, are non-Australians, at least in a legal sense, no matter how long they have been here. This can make life precarious in all sorts of ways.

The scale of temporary migration

There are various ways of measuring the extent of temporary migration. You can count the number of temporary visas issued in a year, you can compare temporary and permanent migration, or you can measure the number (or stock) of temporary migrants present in the country at any one time. In all cases, it helps to illustrate the data graphically.

Let's begin with the number of visas issued. Chart 1 shows that the number of temporary visas issued annually in the three core categories of 457 workers, international students and working-holidaymakers tripled over a 16-year period, from around 200,000 a year to more than 600,000 a year:

Chart 1: Temporary visas issued by financial year [52]

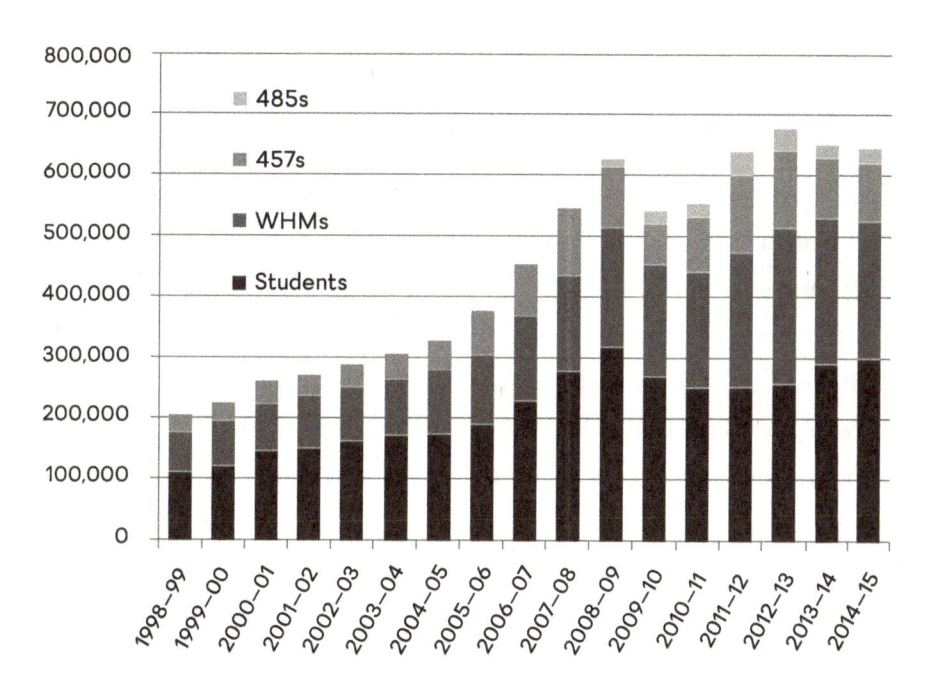

In the opening chapter of this book I posed two questions. Firstly, how long is it reasonable for a migrant to live in Australia without being accepted as an Australian? Secondly, is there a threshold we should not cross if we want to remain a settler nation—a point at which the share of long-term temporary migrants in the population tips the balance and changes the nature of Australian society and Australian multiculturalism?

If the number of long-term temporary migrants with work rights was relatively stable, then these questions might be of less significance. To put it another way, if the number of temporary migrants entering Australia each year was more or less balanced out by the number converting to permanent visas plus the number leaving, then it would be fair to assume that temporary migrants had either become Australians, or had departed, more or less happily, after completing their studies or finishing up in a job. This would make it unlikely that significant numbers of temporary migrants were remaining in Australia for an extended period of time as they moved from one temporary visa to another. It would also mean that the share of the Australian population and workforce living on temporary visas was not increasing. What the data shows, however, is that the stock of temporary migrants present in Australia at any given time has risen steadily. In the seven years from 2006 to 2013 the stock more than doubled, from around 350,000 temporary migrants to close to 800,000. In addition to the main categories of temporary-visa holders (457-visa holders, international students, student graduates and working holidaymakers), Chart 2 includes people on bridging visas. The reason for including these figures is that bridging visas capture two groups relevant to this discussion: international student graduates who are seeking to convert to permanent residency and asylum seekers waiting for their protection claims to be assessed.

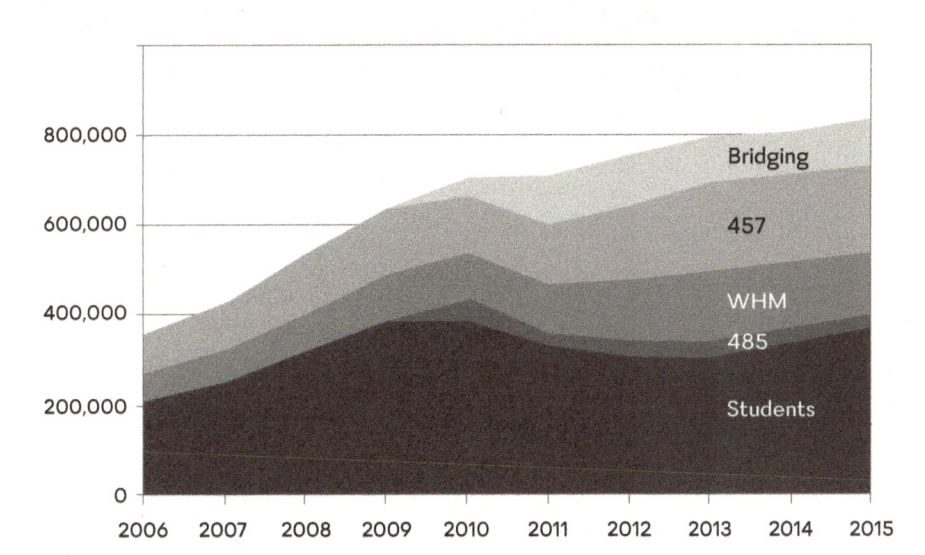

Chart 2: Number (stock) of temporary visa holders present in Australia[53]

[Chart showing stacked areas from 2006 to 2015 with categories: Students, 485, WHM, 457, Bridging; total rising from approximately 350,000 in 2006 to over 800,000 in 2015]

Chart 2 excludes the 200,000 or more New Zealanders who are estimated to have taken up residence in Australia after 2001 and who are officially categorised as temporary-visa holders by the immigration department. If New Zealanders who have settled in Australia since 2001 are included in the count, then the number of temporary migrants present in Australia on 30 June 2015 exceeds one million people. This equates to more than four per cent of the population.

Under the Trans-Tasman Travel Arrangement, New Zealand citizens are free to move to Australia at any time to live and work, and can stay as long as they like. Unlike nationals of all other countries, they do not have to pass any kind of threshold in terms of education, skills or experience. (Australian citizens are equally free to move to New Zealand, but until the last couple of years the movement has been heavily biased in the opposite direction.) As Chart 3 shows, since 2001,

New Zealanders have been steadily adding to Australia's population (although with a significant drop-off after 2012). This is expressed as the contribution of New Zealanders to 'net overseas migration', which is the net increase—or, potentially, net decrease—in population resulting from the difference between long-term immigration and long-term emigration.[54])

Chart 3: Annual contribution of New Zealanders to net overseas migration[55]

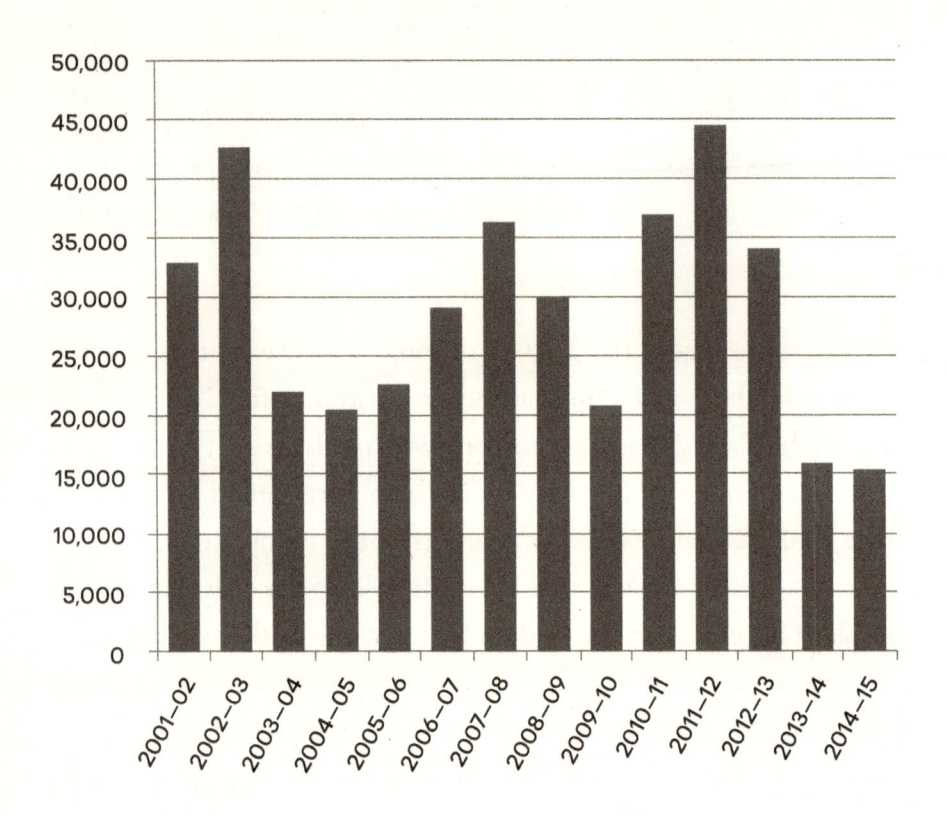

As a proportion of the Australian labour force, temporary migrants are even more significant—if New Zealanders arriving after 2001 are included, then Australia's twenty-first-century *metics*

now constitute up to nine per cent of the workforce. Admittedly, not all of these temporary migrants would be working. A small number are children, some are stay-at-home spouses and some are students fully supported by scholarships or by their families overseas. Some work intermittently, like backpackers supplementing their savings so they can stay on the road longer, and students working part time or in semester breaks. Yet this group are also, on average, much younger than the general population, so their role in the labour market is particularly pronounced in certain age brackets. A calculation prepared by the immigration department in 2010 concluded that working holidaymakers, skilled workers on 457 visas and international students make up around one-fifth of the total labour force aged between 20 and 24.[56] If you included New Zealanders in this calculation then the proportion would be even higher.

While the immigration department does not anticipate that temporary migration will continue to grow as quickly in coming years as it has over the past decade, it nevertheless forecasts that temporary migrants (temporary skilled workers, students, working holidaymakers and New Zealanders) will continue to make a significant contribution to net overseas migration to Australia over the next three years (in the order of between 130,000 and 170,000 people per year, which accounts for 60 to 70 per cent of the anticipated net overseas migration between 2016 and 2018).[57] While a considerable number of temporary migrants will make the transition to permanent residency, the overall stock of temporary migrants present in Australia, and their share of the labour market, is likely to keep growing, not least because the permanent migration program has an annual cap, while the number of temporary migrants admitted to the country is open-ended.

This is particularly important when combined with the fact that a significant proportion of temporary migrants do hope to settle permanently in Australia. The most comprehensive available survey of 457-visa holders (temporary skilled workers), suggests that around 70 per cent intend to apply for permanent residency when their temporary visa expires.[58] In another survey of 457 holders, over one-third of respondents had already applied for permanent residence, close to half intended to apply and fewer than one in six had no intention to seek permanent residence. Almost two-thirds of the surveyed migrants rated seeking permanent residence as an important factor in their decision to come to work in Australia on a temporary visa in the first place. Among those who did not cite permanent residence as a reason for their initial migration, more than half had nevertheless already applied for it or intended to apply for it.[59]

A 2007 survey of international students found 65 per cent intended to seek permanent residency.[60] (One survey of second-year accounting students at a Melbourne University found that 84 per cent intended to seek permanent residency.[61])

Survey results like these underline the potential that over time there will be an increasing mismatch between the aspirations of temporary migrants to become permanent residents and their capacity to realise that goal. This is likely to generate a growing cohort of temporary migrants who continue to live in Australia for extended periods of time on a series of temporary visas, either by repeatedly renewing an existing work visa (such as a 457 visa) or by switching between different visa categories (moving from student visa to 457 visa, for example).

The numbers involved are potentially large and growing. In recent years around half the applications for a 457 visa have been lodged onshore—that is, they were made by people who were already present in Australia as temporary migrants. In the two years between June 2012 and June 2014, this amounted to around 60,000 people moving from one temporary visa to another.[62] Some would have been 457-visa holders extending their stay; others would have been international students who had completed their studies and were moving onto a work visa.

We know that over the same period approximately 93,000 international student graduates extended their stay in Australia by switching to a different temporary-visa category with work rights—around 52,000 moved onto a 485 post-study work visa; close to 34,000 moved onto a 457 temporary skilled-work visa; and 5,700 moved onto a working-holidaymaker visa.[63] This was more than three times the number of student graduates that moved onto a permanent skilled visa.[64] In addition, almost 56,000 international students shifted from one type of study visa to another—from vocational education to university education, for example.[65]

My concern here is that within these statistics there could be a rising number of increasingly frustrated twenty-first-century *metics*—that is, long-term temporary migrants who desire to move along the path to permanent residency, but who fail to make progress towards that goal, and instead move around in circles, jumping precariously from one temporary visa to another.

Data to demonstrate or dismiss this concern is not readily available. The immigration department's publication *Australia's Migration Trends 2012–13* shows that in 2013 there were around 2,000 temporary-visa holders who had been in Australia for 10 or more years since their date of last arrival.[66] This is not a large number, but nor does the statistic actually answer the question that I am trying to ask. Since temporary-visa holders can travel in and out of Australia, a person's date of last arrival does not give a good indication of how long they have been living in Australia on a temporary visa. More relevant would be their length of stay since the date of *first* arrival. The problem is that the department's administrative systems are not set up to collect the data in this way. To calculate the continuous length of stay of migrants moving across different temporary visas would involve the complex and time-consuming matching of arrival and departure data for more than one million individuals.

Another potential source of data is the periodic Australian Bureau of Statistics (ABS) series 'Characteristics of Recent Migrants'. This information is generated from a survey, carried out every three years, that records the progress of migrants who have come to Australia over the past decade in areas such as employment, education and household income. While the survey is not concerned with inquiring about whether or not temporary migrants are progressing to permanent residency and citizenship, some of the data is organised by visa status and year of arrival. This makes it possible to see the number of people who first arrived on a temporary visa and who are still living in Australia on a temporary visa many years later. From the most recent survey, we can glean that in November 2013 there were 18,600 temporary-visa holders in Australia who had first arrived on a temporary visa at least eight years earlier—that is, in 2004 or 2005. Another 46,000 temporary migrants had first arrived in Australia on a temporary visa six or seven years earlier (in 2006 or 2007).[67] This does not mean, however, that they have been living in Australia all that time, since that is not the question that they were being asked. The question posed in the survey was this: 'In which year did you first arrive in Australia to live (for one year or more)?' As a senior ABS analyst explained to me, it cannot be assumed that these temporary entrants have lived continuously in Australia since their first year of arrival; a temporary migrant might have first come to Australia in 2004 as, say, a working holidaymaker, and then returned to their homeland for seven years before coming back to Australia to study or work on another temporary visa in 2012.

So while the immigration department figure of 2,000 visa holders who have been here for more than a decade certainly understates the number of temporary migrants who have lived in Australia on a long-term basis, the ABS figure of 18,600 who have been here at least eight years may overstate it. It should be noted, however, that because the ABS survey is concerned only with 'recent migrants'—that is, those arriving in the previous decade—it does not provide any indication as to whether there are temporary migrants in Australia who first arrived on a temporary visas *more than* 10 years ago. The ABS data also excludes anyone who might have been a child (under 15) at the time of arrival, and who may still be in Australia on a temporary visa. Nor does it include New Zealanders living in Australia for extended periods on the 'temporary' special category visa.

One response might be that, either way, the numbers are relatively small, so there is nothing much to worry about. That is to miss the point. The number of non-Europeans denied citizenship under the White Australia policy's 15-year residency rule was small, too, since not many were admitted in the first place, but that did not make the rule any less abhorrent. Questions of ethics and justice are not decided on head counts, and numbers do not capture the lived experience of those stuck in a precarious state of indefinite temporariness.

Regardless of whether you think the numbers are small or large, the ABS data does suggest that there is an insecure group of migrants whose engagement with Australia via the temporary visa system extends over a long period of time, and the way Australia's visa system is structured makes it possible for increasing numbers of temporary migrants to end up in similar circumstances. This supports Shanthi Robertson's argument that settlement is becoming a staggered, lengthy and uncertain process.

3 | Mind the Gap!
Hidden Traps for Temporary Migrants

Claire Hewitt does not recall very much about the crash. 'I can remember just before the accident realising that the car was going to roll,' she tells me. And that she was afraid rescue workers thought she was dead when they put a sheet over her head—in fact, they were protecting Claire's face from breaking glass as they smashed windows to extricate her from her overturned four-wheel drive. She remembers trying to tell them to just get the vehicle back on its wheels so she could drive on to her appointment in remote Mount Liebig in central Australia. 'I was worried I was going to be late,' she laughs.

Claire is lucky to be alive. Five years on from her accident, her weekly routine still revolves around regular therapy and rehabilitation sessions. Claire and her husband, Terry, remain ensconced in a 'temporary' serviced apartment in the Adelaide beachside suburb of

Glenelg, because it is close to the health services that she regularly attends.

When I visit, Claire is initially tongue-tied. We had spoken at length on the phone for an article that I wrote about Claire's case, but this is the first time we have met face to face. Terry tells me Claire's apparent shyness is a side effect of her accident, which involved massive head injuries as well as 33 chest fractures and severe nerve damage to both arms. We soon get talking, however, partly with the help of Claire's disability dog, an ebullient terrier called Stan, who breaks the ice by constantly jumping onto the couch and inserting himself into the conversation.

Claire tells me that she loved working in central Australia. 'It was my best nursing job ever,' she says. When Claire and Terry migrated to the Northern Territory in 2009, it was no rash decision. The English couple had spent the previous year travelling around Australia in a campervan, deciding where they wanted to live and what they wanted to do. Although Claire could easily have landed a job in a capital city, they fell in love with the outback. 'Working in Sydney or Melbourne would have been just like staying in London,' she says. 'I wanted to do something that I couldn't do anywhere else.'

Claire was 34 years old when she and Terry settled in Alice Springs and she began working on trachoma treatment and prevention in remote Aboriginal communities. Trachoma, an easily treatable and preventable eye disease, is the leading cause of infectious blindness in 59 of the world's poorest countries. With Indigenous communities still afflicted, Australia is the only developed country in the world where trachoma is still active.[1]

Claire was sponsored for a temporary 457 skilled-worker visa by the NT health department, with Terry as the secondary applicant.

He was hoping to build his career as a photographer. Claire says they would have preferred to migrate to Australia on a permanent visa right from the start, but that option wasn't open to them. Authorities in the Northern Territory told her they had had bad experiences sponsoring health professionals for permanent migration: unprepared for local conditions, new arrivals would often quickly decamp to cooler or more urbanised locations. The conditions of a temporary visa make it harder for new migrants to up sticks and leave, because if they want to shift to a different job then they have to find an alternative employer to act as their sponsor in the new location. Claire says health officials led her to believe that if she came on a 457 visa they would sponsor her for permanent residency after 12 months. 'We were in the middle of the paperwork for our application for permanent residency at the time of the accident,' she says.

In May 2010, driving along the notorious Tanami Road that runs north-west through the desert from Alice Springs, Claire lost control of her work vehicle and it rolled six times. She was hospitalised for three months and underwent major surgery, including an operation to transfer a pectoral muscle from her chest to her shoulder to replace a damaged deltoid and restore her ability to raise her left arm—a procedure performed only once before in Australia. Since the accident, Terry has been devoted almost full time to her care.

It's a nightmare story, but Claire's recovery has astounded doctors. More than three years after her accident, Les Koopowitz, a professor of neuro-psychiatry at the University of Adelaide, told me in an email that Claire was attaining 'the type of progress seldom realised following such a serious, devastating and debilitating accident'.

There is no prospect of complete recovery, and Claire knows that she can anticipate 'a lifetime of disability, pain and medical conditions'. She accepts that she can't return to her old job in remote communities, but is nevertheless determined to return to nursing in some capacity. 'Right from the beginning they almost had to hold me down to stop me trying to go back to work,' she says. 'In a way I haven't helped myself. I tried to do too much too soon. My brain has to relearn things and that takes time.'

Throughout the first two years of her rehabilitation, says Claire, the NT health department assured her that it would fully support her eventual return to work, tailoring her duties where necessary. In early 2012 it signed off on her application for permanent residency under the Regional Sponsored Migration Scheme and the relevant documents were submitted to the immigration department. Due to a technicality, however, Claire's application was not processed and had to be resubmitted. For months it seemed nothing was happening. Then, in early 2013, Claire says that the department told her that it was no longer willing or able to sponsor her application for permanent residency because she no longer met the criteria necessary to be considered as a skilled migrant. Claire's injuries and intensive rehabilitation regime had made it impossible, for example, for her to maintain her certificate of registration as a nurse, which requires proof of recent practice and at least 20 hours of continuing professional development per year. With their existing 457 visas due to expire in June 2014, Claire and Terry faced the prospect of being forced to leave Australia.

The implications were profound. Les Koopowitz said that interruptions to Claire's 'continuity of care and environmental stability' could seriously compromise her recovery and render a return to meaningful work 'an unrealistic challenge'. Claire knew that if she could not stay in Australia, then not only would she lose access to the extensive medical and rehabilitation team that had worked with her for the previous three years, but she would also lose any realistic chance of returning to her career as a nurse. Besides, by the time the visa was due to expire, Claire and Terry would have been living in Australia for five years; after all they have been through, Australia was more home to them now than ever.

As the prospect of having to leave Australia loomed large, Claire was distraught. 'Our lives are here,' she told me back then. 'We didn't come here with the intention of having a holiday, we moved ourselves lock, stock and barrel.' Claire pointed out that she was not asking for favours or special treatment, but just 'the same support as would be offered an injured worker who was already lucky enough to be a permanent resident or an Australian citizen'.

At the time of her crash, Claire was at work and driving a government vehicle. In other words, it was a workplace accident and she was covered by workers compensation. The NT's WorkSafe scheme pays Claire's medical bills and she receives 75 per cent of her original salary in compensation for not being able to work. If Claire were a permanent resident or citizen of Australia then this payment would continue until the age of 67. If she were only able to return to work part time, or in a lower-paying job than before, then the workers compensation scheme would top up her salary so that her original income was maintained. Again, this benefit would continue until she turned 67.

But as a temporary migrant Claire's longer-term entitlements were unclear. The NT *Workers Rehabilitation and Compensation Act* makes no reference to a worker's visa status and a case like Claire's had never arisen before. Her legal advice was that if her visa expired and she had to leave Australia and return to the United Kingdom, then any medical bills relating to her accident would continue to be paid. Her entitlements to compensation for her loss of salary would, however, be a different matter. Claire was advised that if she left Australia then her salary payments from WorkSafe would cut out after two, or possibly four, years. After that time, she would have to get by on a disability benefit from the British government.

The NT *Workers Rehabilitation and Compensation Act* says that 'rehabilitation means the process necessary to ensure, as far as is practicable, having regard to community standards from time to time, that an injured worker is restored to the same physical, economic and social condition in which the worker was before suffering the relevant injury'.[2] The Act was clearly set up on the assumption that workers are permanent residents or citizens, and in Claire Hewitt's case, the only way to give proper meaning to the definition of rehabilitation was to enable her to gain that status. Yet in 2013, the NT health department was telling her that she was no longer a good fit with the criteria for a permanent visa.

In theory, Australia's 457-visa system requires potential employers to show that they will provide 'no less favourable terms and conditions of employment' to a 457-visa holder 'than they would to an equivalent Australian in the sponsor's workplace at the same location'.[3] Further, 457-visa holders are entitled to the same 'basic rights and protections in the workplace' as Australian employees.[4] But in Claire's case, the policy appeared to fail. As a temporary migrant who incurred a lifelong disability as the result of an accident at work, she did not, in fact, enjoy the same entitlements and protections provided to a citizen or permanent resident in the same situation.

Things turned out okay for Claire in the end. Members of the NT parliament and the media drew attention to her situation, and her predicament was raised with the federal minister for immigration. In the face of public and political pressure, the NT health department relented and agreed that it would, after all, sponsor her application for a permanent visa. A visa was granted in 2014. When I visited Claire and Terry in May 2015, they were looking forward to becoming Australian citizens in a few months' time.

Even though the eventual outcome for Claire was positive, the deal worked out in her case does not resolve the outstanding contradictions that gave rise to her peculiar circumstances in the first place. While her predicament was highly specific and personal, it is predictable, indeed likely, that similar anomalies will arise in the future.

In fact, two bills that were before the Senate in 2015 would have resulted in manifest discrimination against severely injured workers on temporary visas.[5] The first piece of legislation (the Safety, Rehabilitation and Compensation Legislation Amendment Bill 2014[6]) proposes opening up the national Comcare scheme to a far greater range of 'national' employers, thus enabling businesses to shift away from more expensive state-based compensation schemes that provide greater support to injured workers. If the bill were passed, a much greater share of the Australian workforce would come under the Comcare provisions than is currently the case. Schedule 7 of the accompanying legislation (the Safety, Rehabilitation and Compensation Amendment (Improving the Comcare Scheme) Bill 2015[7]) would amend the Act so as to suspend compensation payments by Comcare when an injured employee leaves Australia for non-work related reasons for six weeks or longer. The intention of the provision is to stop malingering workers from holidaying overseas at Comcare's expense, when they should be attending rehabilitation therapy or returning to work. But the implications for injured workers on temporary visas are obvious and ominous. If, like Claire Hewitt, a 457-visa holder (or working holidaymaker or international student) suffers a long-term or lifetime disability in a workplace accident, then two consequences logically flow from this. Firstly, the migrant worker will almost certainly have to leave Australia when their temporary visa expires, because the injury is likely to render them ineligible for permanent residency as a skilled migrant. Secondly, once they are forced out of Australia, any compensation payments that they would be entitled to receive in Australia will be stopped after just six weeks. The injured migrant worker will be forced to rely on the support of family and whatever government disability support or charity services may exist in their home country. The ACTU describes it as a catch-22 situation; foreign workers must stay in Australia to be eligible to receive compensation *for* their injuries, but they are ineligible to stay in Australia *because* of their injuries.[8]

Injured New Zealanders may find themselves caught in a perversely opposite bind—they may have to remain in Australia in order to keep access to their compensation payments, even if they have good reason to move back across the Tasman to be close to family or other support networks. Either scenario is blatantly unfair and fails to meet the test of migrant workers being afforded equal terms and conditions and the same basic rights and protections in the workplace as Australians.

Chris Johnston is a migration lawyer who advised Claire Hewitt. He says that while her situation was unique, the predicament she found herself in was not exceptional. 'Most of our legal and institutional structures are based on an assumption that if you are not a short-term visitor to Australia, then you are either a citizen or a permanent resident,' he says. 'But there are an increasing number of migrants living and working in Australia on a long-term but temporary basis who do not fit these categories.' Johnston says sometimes unscrupulous employers will exploit the gaps in the system to their own advantage. 'Unfortunately,' he says, 'I have seen a pattern over time, where a small percentage of employers use the finite nature of a temporary visa to try to avoid obligations they would otherwise have to meet.'

Claire was caught in the gap between the old system of permanent settler migration and the new reality of Australia's hybrid system. Our administrative, legal and regulatory systems have not been designed for a situation in which a significant and growing proportion of the population consists of people like Claire Hewitt—new *metics*—long-term temporary migrants with work rights. Such people cannot be simply and neatly defined. They are resident in Australia, but they are not, legally speaking, residents. It is the visas they hold that define their status, and since there are a range of different long-term temporary visas that come with permission to work, different cohorts within this group enjoy (or lack) different rights and entitlements. What can be said in general about this group is that they are not quite Australian. As the number of these new *metics* grows, more will be caught in legal and bureaucratic traps that were not previously apparent.

When Tony Abbott was employment minister in the Howard government, he set up GEERS—the General Employee Entitlements and Redundancy Scheme. Its creation followed the collapse of a string of high-profile companies including One-Tel, HIH, Ansett and National Textiles (a company run by John Howard's brother Stan that went bust, leaving 342 workers out of pocket). GEERS is now known as

FEG—the Fair Entitlements Guarantee—but its function remains essentially the same. It is a scheme to cover the unpaid wages and holiday entitlements of workers whose employer goes bankrupt.

In May 2013, the Swan Services Cleaning Group went into administration owing $2.3 million in unpaid wages and $7.2 million in annual leave entitlements to around 2,500 workers.[9] Many if not most of those workers did not qualify for payments under the FEG, however, because to be eligible a person must be 'an Australian citizen or, under the *Migration Act 1958*, the holder of a permanent visa or a special category visa'.[10]

A large proportion of the Swan Services workforce—about half of its staff in Victoria—was made up of international students. Many were left with up to three weeks' worth of unpaid wages and some were owed close to $3,000.[11] They had fallen into a regulatory crevice where the government assistance extended to Australian workers does not reach.

Again, the public-policy assertion that temporary migrants should enjoy the same workplace rights and entitlements as their Australian colleagues proved hollow in practice. Any rule-of-thumb application of the principle of fairness would lead to the conclusion that the *Fair Entitlements Guarantee Act 2012* needs to be amended so that international students, 457-visa holders and other temporary migrants with work rights are offered the same protection as Australian workers when a company goes bust.

The gaps that can trip up temporary migrants extend well beyond workplace issues like compensation rules and unpaid entitlements, as New Zealanders discovered during the devastating floods that hit Queensland in the summer of 2010–11. To help people get through the worst of the crisis, the federal government authorised emergency funds for affected households of $1,000 per adult and $400 per child under the Australian Government Disaster Recovery Payment scheme. To be eligible for such payments, however, a person had to meet the definition of 'Australian resident' under social-security laws. Many long-term New Zealander residents were denied the emergency assistance because they had settled in Australia after 26 February 2001, when the *Family and Community Services Legislation Amendment (New Zealand Citizens) Act 2001* came into force. The Act changed 'the definition of *Australian resident* for the purposes of the social-security law' with the specific intention of 'restricting access to social-security payments' for New Zealanders.[12]

The flood-payments issue caused considerable controversy and media comment, as New Zealanders who had bought houses, had children and established businesses in Queensland were denied the same assistance as was offered to their Australian neighbours. Many felt that they were being treated as 'second-class citizens'.[13] A more accurate—though less catchy—complaint would have been that they were being treated as second-class permanent residents, since they have the right to reside and work indefinitely in Australia, but do not have access to the same entitlements as other permanent residents.

Perceptions of Australian meanness at a time of need were amplified a few weeks later by the New Zealand government's response to the 2011 Christchurch earthquake: Australians resident in that city were offered the same emergency and unemployment benefits as New Zealand citizens.[14]

The outcry on both sides of the Tasman about the flood payments and official lobbying from Wellington eventually pressured the federal government into providing 'ex gratia assistance payments' to New Zealanders who could demonstrate that they had been working in Australia for the previous three years.[15] This appears to have set a precedent that is now routinely repeated in response to other disasters. Similar ex gratia payments have subsequently been made available to otherwise ineligible New Zealanders who were affected by the 2013 floods in Queensland[16] and New South Wales,[17] and by bushfires in October 2013 in New South Wales[18] and in January 2014 in Western Australia.[19]

Despite these case-by-case responses, the situation as it stands is that eligibility for Australian Government Disaster Recovery Payments is restricted to those who qualify as residents for social-security purposes and that excludes New Zealanders who arrived after 26 February 2001. This is in line with the intention of the 2001 amendments to the Social Security Act. Yet because the implications of this arrangement are politically and diplomatically unpalatable, the federal government feels compelled to repeatedly patch the system by applying the bandaid of ex gratia payments. As the lobby group Oz Kiwi comments, the Australian government 'appears confused in its treatment of New Zealanders, leading to confusing and inconsistent results'.[20]

The intricacies of the post-2001 rules mean that New Zealanders can also find themselves in trouble when they unwittingly sign up to superannuation schemes and life insurance policies that use the legal definition of 'Australian resident' as one of the fine-print criteria for determining eligibility for payouts or access to funds. In 2013, for example, the Superannuation Complaints Tribunal considered the case of a New Zealand truck driver who had moved to Australia in 2006 when in his late twenties. When he started work in Australia his employer enrolled him in a superannuation fund that came with a $250,000 life insurance policy built in. In late 2008 the man returned to New Zealand and died two months later. The insurer, however, refused to pay out the death benefit to the man's beneficiary, his elderly mother, because its policy of 'worldwide cover, 24-hours a day' had an exclusion clause—it did not extend to a person 'who is not a permanent Australian resident' unless this had been agreed in writing before the person departed Australia. In the end the tribunal overturned the insurer's decision and the money was paid. In determining that the behaviour of the insurer was not 'fair and reasonable', the judgement noted that on commencing work in Australia, the truck driver had received a letter from the fund 'which included account information under the heading "Residency Details" that stated he was an Australian resident for tax purposes'.[21] Given such mixed messages and confusing language, it's not hard to see how easily New Zealanders could be confused about their rights and entitlements in Australia.

Another example of a system that has failed to respond coherently to the rapid rise in long-term temporary migration to Australia is the childhood immunisation program. I have a friend who is a community nurse and midwife working in local government. Over dinner one night in 2013, she voiced her distress that public-health staff in her unit had been instructed not to give free vaccinations to the babies of 457 migrant workers, international students and other temporary-visa holders. Instead, they were instructed to tell temporary-visa holders that they should take their baby or child to a general practitioner for immunisation. While international students and 457-visa holders are required to take out private health insurance that may refund the cost of vaccinations (at least up to the level of the standard Medicare rebate), my midwife friend was concerned that this restriction may result in immunisations being postponed or missed.

When I checked with the relevant authorities, I found that the boss who gave the instruction not to provide immunisation was indeed implementing official policy. The Australian government's program of free childhood vaccinations against a wide range of communicable diseases is restricted to citizens, permanent residents and other people eligible to hold a Medicare card (so all New Zealanders qualify).[22]

In early 2016, over another dinner, my midwife friend told me happily that the policy at her workplace had been revised and that all children under 10 were now to receive free vaccines, regardless of their visa status. A visit to the Victorian health department website confirmed the change. When I checked in 2013, the Victorian guidelines stated that you needed to be eligible for a Medicare card to get your children immunised for free,[23] whereas in 2016, the Victorian rules were that *all* children under 10 'can receive the National Immunisation Program vaccines'.[24] Yet at the federal level, the policy had not changed. When I called the federal government's Immunise Australia Information Line, the helpful young man who took my call assured me that the rules were the same as when I originally inquired in 2013. Reading from a written document, he told me that you had to be 'eligible to receive Medicare benefits' in order to get free vaccines under the National Immunisation Program, which means that the children of most 457-visa holders and international students miss out. So Victorian health authorities say one thing and federal health officials apply another. What is going on here? The answer, it appears, is that the Victorians are pushing definitional boundaries.

In 2015, the federal government was so concerned at the growing gaps in comprehensive childhood immunisation in Australia that it put in place a 'no jab, no pay' policy, which means that parents who fail to fully immunise their children are no longer eligible for family assistance payments including the Child Care Benefit, the Child Care Rebate and the Family Tax Benefit Part A. This stick was accompanied by a carrot: to encourage parents to fully immunise their children, the federal government introduced a 'catch-up' program for all states and territories to distribute 'free National Immunisation Program vaccines for all children under the age of 10 that require catch-up'.[25] In the Victorian government's interpretation, any child under 10 who is not fully immunised, including newborns, requires 'catch-up', regardless of their parents' visa status. In short, Victoria has used the catch-up program to extend the federal government's free immunisation program to the children of all temporary-visa holders.

The ingenuity of state public servants in stretching the interpretation of federal funding guidelines is admirable, because, in the field of immunisation, even a small percentage increase in population coverage produces very significant gains for public health. It is difficult to work out whether other states and territories are following Victoria's lead or sticking to a narrower interpretation of the federal government's rules, because public resources like health-department websites offer little, if any, detail on eligibility for vaccines by visa status. Even if other states and territories do adopt Victoria's more liberal interpretation of federal rules for under-10s, the teenage children of temporary-visa holders are still ineligible for free vaccinations rolled out through schools. The overall result is an unclear mess of different policies and approaches across the nation—hardly an ideal situation in a crucial area of public-health policy.

According to the National Centre for Immunisation Research and Surveillance, migrants and culturally and linguistically diverse communities are regarded as one of the 'special-risk and under-served populations' for immunisation.[26] The National Health

Performance Authority says tracking the percentage of children who are fully immunised is more difficult in areas with large immigrant populations.[27] While immunisation providers are expected to have a comprehensive understanding of the eligibility rules for access to free or subsidised vaccines, the Centre for Research Excellence in Population Health warns that 'differences in eligibility by vaccine and visa class add complexity and act as a barrier to the provision of catch-up immunisation' in communities that are 'particularly vulnerable to under-immunisation'.[28] Excluding a proportion of that migration population from free mass immunisation schemes on the basis of their visa status serves to further complicate an already complex situation.

Like many other administrative and legal systems, immunisation programs have failed to keep pace with the shift from permanent to temporary migration. Policy and practice neglect the growing cohort of twenty-first-century *metics* who are not quite Australian, because of a flawed assumption that people are either citizens or permanent residents. This is an oversight that could come at significant cost. As one public-health official put it to me privately, 'I don't know too many infectious diseases that distinguish between who is a Medicare holder and who is not.'

Requiring the children of 457-visa holders to pay fees to attend state schools is similarly short-sighted and unfair. This is not a uniform national practice but one that varies between jurisdictions, and it represents, if not a gap in the system, at least a glaring inconsistency across state boundaries. New South Wales charges 457-visa holders $5,000 per annum to send a child to school up to the end of year 10, and $6,000 per annum to attend in years 11 and 12. The money must be paid in advance, either annually or in two six-month instalments.[29]

The Australian Capital Territory charges $10,400 for primary school, $13,600 for junior high school and $15,200 for years 11 and 12. The full fee is due in the first week of March, and late payments incur a $600 penalty.[30] Since the beginning of 2015, Western Australia has charged $4,000 per year for the children of 457-visa holders, although there is an exemption for families earning less than $75,000 per annum and fees can be paid in instalments.[31] South Australia is following suit: it plans to introduce a 'public education contribution' of $5,100 for each primary student and $6,100 for each secondary student from the start of 2017. The fee will only apply to families with an income of more than $77,000 and will be discounted for second and subsequent children.[32] Queensland and Victoria do not charge school fees for the children of 457-visa holders.

Apart from revenue raising, it is hard to see what justification there can be for charging school fees for the children of 457-visa holders, given that at least one parent in the family must be working and paying income tax. As political philosopher Joseph Carens points out, most government-funded or government-subsidised services are available regardless of an individual's visa status. You do not need to prove residency to drive on roads, catch public transport, use a library or call on the help of police or the fire brigade. Carens argues that the fundamental entitlement of school education should be treated in the same way: 'Every democratic state has a system of free and compulsory public education, and again, temporary workers have a right to this education for their children if their children are present.'[33]

On face value Carens' argument would also extend to the children of international students. While not all international students pay income tax, since not all work, many do, and with the fees they pay and through other activities they are making a valuable contribution to the Australian economy and government revenue. Yet all states and territories routinely charge fees for international students to send their children to state schools. In the Australian Capital Territory and New South Wales the fees are the same as for the children of 457-visa holders, although for some inexplicable reason, the fees are much higher in New South Wales if the parent is studying in a private-sector vocational college rather than at TAFE or university. Victoria charges $8,159 for primary, $10,783 for junior secondary and $12,095 for senior secondary school.[34] Fees in Western Australia are steeper still—$11,370 for primary, $13,490 for junior high school and $14,800 for years 11 and 12—but with a waiver for parents undertaking a research masters or a PhD.[35] Queensland charges similar rates, with a similar exemption.[36] (The children of New Zealanders on special category visas do not have to pay fees to attend state schools.)

As well as paying upfront for fundamental entitlements like schooling and health care, international students and 457-visa holders are denied access to settlement services, including English-language classes that are provided to permanent migrants. It would make sense to extend these services at least to the spouses and children of temporary-visa holders. There are tens of thousands of people living in Australia as family members of 457-visa workers and international students, yet we know very little about their lives, since they are not the subjects of any kind of systematic data collection. A spouse, labelled a secondary visa holder in immigration department terminology, does not have to meet the same language requirements as the primary visa holder in order to enter Australia and so may have more limited English. While secondary visa holders generally have the same work rights as their partners, they are not necessarily working. As a result, they may not enjoy the social interaction or have access to the community of a workplace or an educational institution. In cases where a couple has children (who are also categorised as secondary visa holders), the partner is almost certain to be spending more time at home. This can leave partners isolated and vulnerable; they may find it difficult to make contacts, face barriers to finding employment (and if they do get a job, be unaware of their rights and entitlements), and struggle to make sense of Australian society. The Migration Council Australia argues that extending settlement services to the spouses and dependents of temporary migrants 'would improve labour-market participation rates'.[37]

The wider public benefits of generating economic activity and government revenue may well outweigh any upfront costs involved, but even if they did not, the proposal has merit for another reason: since a significant proportion of temporary migrants go on to become permanent residents, it is logical to help their partners and children to settle into Australian society as quickly and as completely as possible. As the Migration Council has pointed out, the best time to provide services to help migrants settle is soon after they arrive. So if we are shifting to a two-step model—of migrants initially coming to Australia on temporary visas and only later becoming permanent residents—then we need to reassess when, how and to whom we provide settlement services.[38]

A more pressing issue affecting the wellbeing of the spouses and children of temporary-visa holders is the government's inadequate response to family violence in temporary-migrant households. If the primary visa holder, usually a man, is abusive, then his partner and children have very limited options: because they are not citizens or permanent residents, they will generally find that they are not eligible for public housing or income support (such as special-benefit payments), free legal advice or other forms of government assistance. Crisis services, like refuges, are only funded to provide short-term assistance to victims of domestic violence, but often women on temporary visas have nowhere else to turn—unless they go back to an abusive partner.

Migrants on temporary visas make up around a third of the clients who approach InTouch, Victoria's only multicultural service for victims of family violence,[39] yet women may be reluctant to come forward at all because of what the Judicial College of Victoria calls 'visa dependency'. The college provides education for judges and magistrates. Its online *Family Violence Bench Book* advises that visa dependency can be 'a critical barrier in accessing the justice system in family violence situations' because temporary migrants fear they will be forced to leave Australia if they bring attention to the problem.[40] This is not an unrealistic concern—a secondary migrant's right to stay in Australia depends entirely on 'their genuine and continuing relationship with a primary visa holder'.[41] If their relationship breaks down, the secondary visa will be cancelled. FECCA—the Federation of Ethnic Communities' Councils of Australia—argues that the primary visa holder can use this dependency 'to control and manipulate' partners and children, by threatening to withdraw sponsorship.[42] FECCA's Pallavi Sinha points out that the pressure can be greater on women who would be forced to return to a homeland where they may suffer alienation and shame for ending their marriage.[43]

A temporary migrant who is here on a partner visa—that is, on the basis of a marriage-like relationship with an Australian citizen or permanent resident—has a way out of this dilemma through the family violence exception in migration law. The exception enables a person to be considered for permanent residence even if their marriage or de facto relationship breaks down as a result of violence by their Australian partner (who is also the sponsor of their visa). The Australian Law Reform Commission has recommended against extending the family violence exception to the partners and children of temporary migrants, however, for fear that this could create a perverse incentive 'to claim family violence' as a back-door route to residency.[44] What the commission recommended instead was that the Australian government create an alternative temporary visa for victims of family violence that would enable them to 'access social-security benefits and entitlements' and give them 'the time and resources to access support services'. This would make it possible for them to 'leave a violent relationship with the knowledge that they can take measures to protect their safety without being removed from Australia immediately'.[45] The recommendation has not been acted upon.

It is fundamentally unfair that children should be punished for the actions of their parents. Yet another administrative trap for temporary migrants produces exactly this effect and can result in child and parent being forced to live in different countries. In this case, the gap in the system is the lack of a clear pathway to permanent residency for the foreign parents of children who are Australian citizens. While this is a small group, the inadequacy of policy in this domain can have devastating emotional and psychological consequences.

If a temporary migrant and an Australian have a child together, then that baby is an Australian citizen from birth. If the couple stay together, they can apply for a partner visa. In the ideal scenario this leads to permanent residency for the foreign parent, and mother, father and child live happily ever after. If the pair breaks up without first applying for a partner visa, however, the situation is much more fraught and complicated. In the worst-case scenario, after years of expensive bureaucratic and legal wrangling, the foreign parent will be forced to leave Australia. This will either entail separating from the child, or it will mean taking the child overseas and away from the Australian parent.

In the case of Solomon Islander Francesca Teua both these things happened: after being refused a visa to remain in Australia, she returned to her homeland, leaving behind her nine-year-old Australian son Kamoa, and taking her two-year-old Australian daughter Alexandra with her. (The children have different fathers.) This meant Kamoa was separated from his mother, and Alexandra was separated from her father, Brian Tait, and from her grandparents, Michael and Judy Tait.

Michael and Judy were heartbroken. Before she left Australia in March 2015, Alexandra would spend most weekends with her grandparents at their home on Bribie Island in Queensland, walking on the beach, swimming and building sandcastles. 'We were looking after her, mainly on the weekends, so her mother could work,' Michael told me.[46] 'So we grew very attached to her.' The way Michael Tait sees it, his granddaughter, an Australian citizen, has been deported by proxy.[47] 'You can't send really young Australian kids overseas to third-world countries,' he says. 'They are citizens. What does citizenship mean? Not much in this case.'

It might come as a surprise that the parent of an Australian child does not have an automatic right to live in Australia. Given the federal government's professed focus on the importance of the family unit, and the view that it is in the best interests of the child to have both a father and a mother (an oft-repeated objection to same-sex marriage), it would seem logical to assume that Francesca Teua and others in similar situations would be able to traverse a fairly short and straightforward path to a permanent visa (barring any serious security concerns or a record of criminal violence). But the opposite is the case. The foreign parents of Australian children often have very limited options for seeking a permanent visa.

'If they are not in a continuing relationship with the other parent of the child, their only options are through Australia's skilled-migration visa programs,' explains Bruce Wells, principal solicitor with Brisbane's Refugee and Immigration Legal Service. 'There is no way that they can rely on the family relationship in order to achieve a visa outcome.'

Being the parent of an Australian child is not enough to provide a pathway to permanent residency. There is no way for an Australian child to seek a visa for a foreign parent, even when that parent is their primary carer and has been granted custody by the Family Court. Generally, the only viable route to a permanent visa runs via the minister's office, and the way through that bureaucratic-legal terrain is tortuous, costly and protracted. The nature of the journey is apparent from its very first step: Francesca Teua's only option was to apply for a refugee visa—a visa both she and her lawyers knew she was not entitled to and that was certain to be refused. Applying for protection as a refugee in the full knowledge that your claim lacks merit might sound like an abuse of the system, but it is Australian migration law that forces such perverse legal contortions.

In mid-2015, there were more than 700,000 international students, 457-visa workers and working holidaymakers present in Australia. So we should not be surprised that sometimes one of these temporary migrants ends up in bed with an Australian citizen and that, on occasion, such liaisons produce a baby. If the couple's relationship does not last, then the foreign parent will usually have little choice but to embark on a long, expensive and uncertain legal journey if they want to maintain a close relationship with their Australian child.

Solicitor Sean Stimson, who runs a weekly clinic for international students at the Redfern Legal Centre in inner Sydney, says cases like this are 'happening more and more'. Immigration lawyer Carina Ford, who runs a busy private practice in Melbourne's west, also says she's advising an increasing number of foreign parents seeking a visa to stay in Australia with their Australian child.

One of her clients is an overseas student who fathered a child with his Australian girlfriend. The child is now three years old. 'As a student, the father had a legitimate visa to stay in Australia, and so the couple did not get around to putting in a partner visa,' says Carina Ford. 'But now the father has finished his studies, the relationship has fallen apart, and he no longer has any legal right to remain in the country and maintain a relationship with his child.'

If the couple had submitted an application for a partner visa before they split up, then the father would still have had a pathway to permanent residency. But it is not unusual for couples, particularly students, to delay applying for a partner visa, either because of volatility in the relationship, or because of cost: the base application charge in 2015 was $6,865, and that is before paying for advice from a migration agent or associated costs like health and police checks.[48] If the relationship breaks down before a partner visa has been lodged, then the only option for the foreign parent of an Australian child is to seek the personal intervention of the immigration minister. But getting the minister's attention is no easy matter, because ministerial discretion can generally only be exercised after every other possible avenue of application and appeal has been exhausted.

Migration lawyer Bruce Wells explains the steps: 'You find a visa that you can validly apply for, you make an application, that application will usually be refused,' he says. 'Then you seek review of that decision through the merits review tribunals—the Migration Review Tribunal or the Refugee Review Tribunal—and then after a tribunal has looked at it you can then seek the intervention of the minister.'

In other words, an applicant has to attempt to jump through every legal and administrative hoop, in the full knowledge that she or he will fail at every stage, before the minister can consider the case and decide whether to intervene and grant a visa.

'And they are considerable hoops,' says Bruce Wells. 'Processing times vary, but they are usually in the order of months. Review at tribunals takes many more months. So before it even gets to the minister, usually a year would have passed with the person just going through the visa application pathway.'

After reaching the minister, the timeline is still indefinite, says Wells. 'Again, it's a non-compellable power, so it can take as long as the minister considers appropriate, and it's not unusual for it to take many years.'

It's a huge waste of resources and time, not only for applicants and their legal advisers, but also for the immigration department, the tribunals, the minister's office and, ultimately, the minister. In addition, it usually involves twisting Australia's refugee protection system to another purpose. A protection or refugee visa is often the only visa for which a foreign parent can lodge a valid application. It is also the cheapest visa to apply for.

Francesca Teua was not an asylum seeker or a refugee. The only reason she was in Australia was to try to resolve questions about the custody and care of her nine-year-old son, Kamoa, who, like her daughter Alexandra, is an Australian citizen. Kamoa was born in Solomon Islands in 2006 to an Australian father. After that relationship ended, Kamoa's father returned to Queensland. He missed his son, though, and in 2008 Francesca brought him to Australia to visit, travelling on a tourist visa.

A dispute over custody ensued and, since it is illegal for a parent to take a child out of Australia without the approval of the other parent, Francesca was in an impossible position. She only had permission to stay in Australia temporarily, but if she went home she would have to leave her son behind.

In the end it was determined that Kamoa's best interests would be served by Francesca sharing custody with his father. 'On the basis of that she made an application to the minister to remain in Australia so that she could maintain that bond with her child,' explains Bruce Wells, who represented her. 'That application took many years to be resolved. In the course of that time she had another relationship which resulted in another child, so she had two Australian-citizen children.'

When I spoke to Francesca Teua by phone in early 2015, not long before she left Australia, I could hear her daughter chattering away happily in the background. 'She's trying to catch a butterfly,' Francesca explained. Although she was still waiting on a final decision from the immigration minister, Francesca was readying herself psychologically to return to Solomon Islands, expecting that she would take Alexandra with her but leave Kamoa behind in the care of his father. She was deeply concerned about the pain this would cause all around. She predicted, accurately, that Alexandra's grandparents would be very sad and upset. When she discussed the impending separation with a distraught Kamoa, she told him that he was a big boy and would have to accept that she must leave him behind in order to look after his little sister. 'I told him we would keep in touch by Skype,' she remarked forlornly.

Cases involving foreign parents with Australian-citizen children are often messy and complicated, and this was true in Francesca's situation.[49] But human lives are like that. People end up in circumstances they didn't plan or anticipate, and they don't always fit neatly into the categories of our system for selecting migrants. This is why the Migration Act provides for ministerial discretion. The minister's 'public-interest powers' are based on an understanding that the 'structured and transparent statutory framework for the implementation and management of Australia's migration and humanitarian program…cannot address every situation where there may be compelling reasons for a person to enter or remain in Australia'.[50]

But the public-interest powers are non-delegable, non-compellable and non-reviewable. In other words, the minister alone can make such decisions; he or she cannot be forced to consider any particular case; and no decision made in this way can be challenged in any court or tribunal. Questions of natural justice don't arise. The immigration department says ministerial intervention is not 'an extension of the visa application or review process', but rather 'a safety net' for 'a relatively small number of cases where the circumstances are unique or exceptional'.[51]

In an effort to ensure that the safety net works in a consistent manner, there are guidelines to advise officials as to which 'unique and exceptional circumstances' warrant bringing a case to a minister's attention. Two of the examples cited on the immigration-department website in 2015 were particularly relevant to Francesca Teua and her children. The first involved 'circumstances that may bring Australia's obligations as a party to the Convention on the Rights of the Child into consideration'.[52] Article 9 of the Convention says that children should not be separated from their parents unless it is for their own good, and that, when the mother and father have split up, children have the right to stay in contact with both parents. According to the 2015 version of the ministerial guidelines, the best interests of a child are 'a primary consideration' in cases raising obligations under the Convention. (It is worth noting that any references to children, their rights or the Convention have since been removed from the guidelines of website.[53]) In the second example, the unique and exceptional circumstances were those that 'would result in irreparable harm and continuing hardship to an Australian citizen or permanent resident'.[54] Severing the bonds between a parent and a child would appear to fit squarely into both categories.

The sole requirement for ministerial discretion to be exercised is that 'the minister thinks it is in the public interest to do so'. When the powers are exercised, the minister must table a statement of reasons in parliament. But if the minister decides *not* to exercise discretion, then no reasons need be given. (Labor's immigration minister Chris Bowen initiated a biannual statistical bulletin on the use of the public-interest powers, but this lapsed after the Abbott government took office.)

Francesca Teua's file shows that the immigration department advised the (Labor) minister in May 2012 that Francesca 'met health requirements and does not have any character concerns that would preclude a visa grant'. Ultimately, however, Immigration Minister Peter Dutton decided that it was not 'in the public interest' to grant her a visa to remain in Australia with her children. Bruce Wells was surprised, since the ministerial guidelines had not changed and, in the past, ministers have tended to intervene to protect the right of an Australian child to have access to both parents. 'We are a very small community legal centre and we don't take on cases where we don't think there is reasonable prospects of success,' he says. 'We had been assisting Francesca for a number of years, so we had invested significantly in that case on the basis that we thought it was quite clear where the best interests of the children and of the Australian community lay.

'The best interests of her children were clearly not considered sufficient to override other considerations,' he adds.

Since the minister will not comment on individual cases, we can only speculate as to what those 'other considerations' might be. One possibility is that the government is keen to send out the message that getting pregnant is not an automatic route to permanent residency. This was certainly the view put to me privately by a senior government adviser. 'You have to be very careful what visa products you put on the market,' he said. 'People will try to exploit those loopholes.'

Bruce Wells says he has not seen any evidence of temporary migrants deliberately having a child in order to secure a visa. In any case, irrespective of the motivations of the adults involved, he says the interests of the child should be a primary consideration.

Carina Ford agrees: 'I don't see how it can ever benefit a child to not have both parents nearby, unless there are reasons determined by the Family Court that it's not appropriate,' she says. 'I think that the long-term damage to children, particularly where there is not an amicable relationship and therefore they are losing part of their culture from that foreign-born parent, is concerning.'

Ford points out that removing a parent from the child can impose costs on the Australian community, because trying to enforce maintenance orders overseas is extremely difficult. 'If maintenance orders aren't able to be paid, then that child is also at a disadvantage,' she says. 'So I think once you have a situation where children are born, something needs to be done to make sure they do have access to both parents.'

If the number of temporary migrants living in Australia continues to increase, and there is every indication that it will, then more foreign parents of Australian-citizen children will be forced to travel a long and tortuous path to seek the intervention of the immigration minister, chewing up scarce administrative, legal and political resources and causing unnecessary distress to children, parents and grandparents along the way. Unless, of course, there is some clear thinking and a change of policy to resolve the issue—but there is little sign that anyone in government is even thinking about it.

Similar concerns apply to the other gaps identified in this chapter. These gaps arise because so many of our legal and administrative systems operate on the assumption that migration is a permanent thing, and are out of step with the new reality of extended temporariness. The confused and confusing array of services and entitlements or fees and charges that do or do not apply to Australia's *metics* across state and federal jurisdictions reveals the lack of a coherent approach to temporary migration. Instead of considered policy, we have arbitrary and ad hoc responses. As one former immigration bureaucrat put it to me, 'the department is basically making shit up as they go along'. He describes the cumulative result of two decades of temporary migration as 'a grab bag of different policies, eligibilities and visas that doesn't quite fit as a holistic system'.

Addressing these concerns will require thoughtful policy

measures, and may impose costs on government or require politically unpalatable changes. It may involve state governments forgoing the revenue from the school fees paid by 457-visa migrants, for example, or a small increase in costs to provide free vaccinations. It may require the federal government to spend more on English-language classes or domestic-violence support services, so that temporary migrants, particularly women, do not suffer from isolation or abuse. At the very least, it requires a new visa category to enable foreign parents to stay in the same country as their Australian children.

Either we think that the benefits of temporary migration outweigh these costs, and make change worthwhile, or we think they do not, in which case we might argue that temporary migration itself should be wound back. To accept the status quo is to ignore the problem, which amounts to confirming that temporary migrants are less deserving of certain fundamental rights and protections than Australians, and that they should be treated like the *metics* of ancient Athens, present in the city, but not accepted as members of the polis. The most acute expression of such a dismissal of temporary migrants would be to allow their temporariness to become permanent. Yet, in stark contradiction to the image of Australia as an inclusive, multicultural society bound together by a shared sense of belonging, that is exactly what we are at risk of doing.

4 | Indefinitely Temporary
Barriers to Becoming Australian

Ilaria De Fusco is not an impatient woman, but her tolerance is being sorely tested. 'We paid for a service and we are entitled to understand when we are going to get that service,' she says, with a look of disbelief.

At issue is not the service of the staff in this tiny Glebe cafe, where the arrival of the vivacious Italian elicited cheerful greetings and rapid-fire exchanges in her native tongue. Ilaria is frustrated because her attempt to become an Australian is going nowhere. Her application for permanent residence has been in the system more than five years, yet neither the immigration department nor the minister can give her any indication of how much longer it will take to get a decision.

When she applied in late 2009, Ilaria paid thousands of dollars in government visa charges. She spent thousands more getting advice from a registered migration agent to make sure the department had all the information it needed and that all the details were correct. The marketing specialist and her tradesman partner exceeded the relevant score for permanent residence under Australia's skilled-migration points test, ticking all the boxes in terms of qualifications, work experience, language proficiency, health status and character. Although Ilaria was advised it would take two years at most to get a decision, when we meet in March 2015, the Department of Immigration and Border Protection is yet to begin looking at her application.

Originally from Milan, De Fusco has been living in Sydney since 2001 and definitely calls Australia home. 'I've been here almost half my life,' she says. She loves Australia, but doesn't feel completely welcome. 'It's very sad,' she says. 'This is such a great country.'

It is not as if the immigration department has lost her file. Quite the opposite: it has deliberately placed her application at the very bottom of the heap. So she remains in Australia on a bridging visa that grants her the right to work but doesn't allow her to build a life here.

Ilaria De Fusco and thousands of others like her have been disadvantaged by a system of officially organised queue jumping called priority processing. Before 2009, skilled-migration applications were dealt with in the order in which they were lodged. An application for permanent residency lodged in January, for instance, would take precedence over one lodged in February, regardless of the type of visa. In 2008, though, the Rudd government faced a massive backlog in valid applications for permanent residency that threatened to overwhelm Australia's skilled-migration program. It introduced priority processing to triage this unprocessed mountain of paperwork, and effectively put Ilaria's life on hold.

The bureaucratic backlog built up after the Howard government unwisely linked permanent residence to successful study in Australia, including vocational courses. In 2005, amid continuing business complaints about skills shortages during Australia's longest boom, 17 extra categories were added to the official list of occupations in demand, all but guaranteeing residency to anyone who obtained the relevant qualifications.

This lit the fuse for an explosion in vocational courses, especially in cookery, hairdressing and accountancy, often run by quickly established private colleges. The best of them offered high-quality training; the worst were shop-front visa factories. The number of foreign students undertaking these vocational courses rose dramatically. As they completed their studies and lodged valid applications for permanent residence, they created a huge bulge in the migration program and a serious pile-up in the visa-processing queue. In 2009, when Australia's annual skilled-migration intake was capped at 108,000 places, 170,000 people lodged valid applications for permanent residence under the program. The backlog of applications grew to 145,000, including 12,000 applications from cooks. (To put this figure in perspective, there were only around 36,000 cooks employed in the Australian economy at the time.) An even larger number of accountants were waiting in the pipeline.

In government, Labor weakened the nexus between study and permanent residency and introduced a priority system to manage the tens of thousands of unprocessed applications. Now, the immigration minister can instruct the department 'to consider and finalise visa applications in an order of priority that the minister considers appropriate'.[1] The minister can modify these priorities as industry demands different skills or the economic climate changes.

On the path to permanent residency as a skilled migrant, express lanes are now reserved for applicants who have been nominated by an employer. The top category for processing is the Regional Sponsored Migration Scheme, which encourages migrant settlement outside high-growth metropolitan areas. (The department's novel definition of regional includes all of Australia except the Gold Coast, Brisbane, Newcastle, Sydney, Wollongong and Melbourne.[2]) The second category is the Employer Nomination Scheme, which does not impose geographical limits. Both these routes are potentially open to 457-visa holders living in Australia who have worked for the same employer for two years or more, and employers can also use them to recruit permanent migrants directly from overseas. In the third category for priority processing are applicants endorsed by a state or territory government agency, and fourth in line are applicants who apply independently and have a qualification on the government's Skilled Occupation List (an official index of job categories deemed to be in short supply in the Australian economy). All other applications fall into priority group five—the last category for processing. Group five includes people like Ilaria De Fusco, and her lane on the path to permanent residency seems to be barely moving at all.

The immigration department tells applicants in priority groups one and two that they can expect their cases to be resolved in less than eight months. For group three it's up to a year and for group four it's up to 18 months. Those in priority group five receive no guidance on timelines beyond being told that assessments will commence when all the cases in higher-priority groups are finalised.[3] This means that every new application lodged at any time in any of the four higher-priority groups adds to the numbers ahead of group five in the queue.

When Ilaria inquires about the progress of her application, the department tells her it is too busy to look into individual cases. The same message—effectively, 'don't call us, we'll call you'—appears on the department's website. The blunt instruction to applicants in priority group five is 'do not contact us to enquire about the progress of your application'.[4]

'The government has taken their money and not given them anything in return,' says Grant Williams, a Sydney-based migration agent with almost twenty years' experience. 'I don't know in what other world you could get away with that.'

The money in question is not insignificant. When she adds the cost of skills certification, health checks, police clearances and language tests to the migration agent's fee and the government's visa charge, Ilaria calculates that her application set her back close to $15,000. But money is not at the heart of the issue. 'This is not just about my application,' she says. 'It's about the whole concept of it. The ethics behind it are just not right.'

Ilaria is not the kind of person to sit still and let life push her around. Driven by outrage at the way she and others were being treated, she set up a Facebook page for the forgotten visa applicants of priority group five. Within six months it had gained close to 500 members. Their posts revealed the intense feelings of confusion, anguish and anger arising out of their uncertain and precarious circumstances.

Grant Williams received similar responses from applicants stuck in priority group five who read his blog on migration matters. 'Sometimes they just need to sound off because they feel like no one is listening to them,' he says. 'A lot of these people came to Australia as quite young students and have spent a lot of their formative years here. The government seems to take the attitude that they are sort of collateral damage to changes in policy.'

Williams points out that he has no clients who are in priority group five, so he has no financial interests at stake and no personal axe to grind. He speaks and writes about the issue because he thinks the treatment accorded to the group is immoral.

He wonders whether the government is unaware of the level of distress that the policy is causing, or whether the unstated policy is 'to starve them out'—to make them so discouraged that they give up any hope of building a life here and withdraw their applications. Sandi Logan, a former spokesman for the immigration department, certainly believes this is the intention. When I wrote about Ilaria and the frustrations of other group-five members for the online magazine *Inside Story*,[5] he tweeted in response to the article, 'Without doubt Grp5 exists to wear down applicants; why else?'[6] In the case of a woman as determined and passionate as Ilaria, this does not strike me as a successful strategy—the longer she waits for an answer, the more determined she becomes to achieve what she sees as a fair outcome.

According to immigration-department statistics, in March 2015 there were more than 20,000 people in priority group five who had waited more than four years for an answer on their applications for permanent residency. These are people who have found that the goal posts shifted after they started playing the game. Like Ilaria De Fusco, close to 3,000 of them had already established lives in Australia and were attempting to build a future here. The other 17,700 applied for permanent residency from overseas. Generally, these people are not yet in Australia, but in many cases they, too, have put crucial life decisions on hold while they await a decision on their visa applications.

Sometimes the onshore and offshore groups overlap. Julio Martinez and Marta Saldana* came to Australia from Colombia to study in 2008. In 2010, while briefly back in Colombia, they lodged an offshore application for permanent residency, even though they were already living in Australia on their student visas.

'We had more than enough points to qualify for permanent residency,' says Marta. 'We were told it would take maximum eight months to one year for the visa to come through.'

When the visa failed to materialise, the couple extended their stay in Australia by applying for other temporary visas. First Julio got an 18-month 485 graduate-work visa. When that expired, Marta returned to study, embarking on a two-year MBA. When we spoke in March 2015 she had nearly finished her course, and her student visa, which includes Julio and their two-month-old baby, was due to expire in a few months' time.

Because their application for permanent residency was lodged offshore, Marta and Julio do not qualify for a bridging visa. So with no apparent progress on their case, Julio was now considering returning to study once more. While this might benefit his career in the long term, the immediate purpose would be to enable the family to remain in Australia by securing yet another student visa. The couple could return to Colombia to wait for their permanent visas to come through, but Julio says they have good reasons not to.

'We've been living here for seven and a half years and we are settled here,' he explains. 'Most of our productive work life has been here in Australia and all our connections, all our experiences, have been gained here. We feel like going back to Colombia would be

---
* Not their real names

almost like having to start all over again.'

'We never thought the process was going to take that long,' adds Marta. 'We were always waiting, waiting, waiting, and now it is too late.'

Julio points out that he and Marta have been paying Australian taxes for more than seven years, yet they don't have access to Medicare or to any government benefits, such as assistance with the high costs of child care. They have paid their way through higher-degree courses but find it difficult to advance their careers in line with their qualifications, because many companies refuse to hire staff on temporary visas. Marta has been in the same job for five and a half years but remains a casual employee. 'I'm not able to become permanent because I don't have permanent residency,' she says. 'I have been deeply affected by the whole situation.'

Ilaria De Fusco has been deeply affected, too. She first visited Australia in 2000 when she was 19. Having just finished secondary school, she was following a family tradition, begun by older siblings, of coming to Sydney to stay with her Australian uncle and cousins, have a holiday and improve her English.

She liked Australia so much that after returning to Italy she applied for a student visa. She completed a pre-university preparatory course followed by an undergraduate business degree, and then successfully applied for a graduate work visa that enabled her to live and work full time in Australia for another 18 months. She went back to study to complete a masters degree and applied for permanent residency based on her skills and experience. For the past four years she has worked as the marketing manager for a small accounting firm.

In the meantime, Ilaria has settled down with her partner, Antonio Lovisi, who is also Italian and who also came to Australia on a temporary visa. The couple met here and have been together for eight years, but they feel like their lives are on hold. 'You can't really think bigger,' says Ilaria. 'To buy a house, invest, even starting a family would be an issue.'

Her partner Antonio is a master painter and decorator who runs a successful small business and engages four other people as subcontractors. He would like to enlarge the business and take on full-time staff, but with his long-term right to stay in the country so uncertain he doesn't want the responsibility of being a direct employer or the risk associated with borrowing or investing capital. If Ilaria's visa application were rejected, she and Antonio would have to pack up and leave Australia within 28 days.

Life on a bridging visa is full of complications. Some are minor irritations: for example, Ilaria must renew her driving licence every year and she cannot get a mobile-phone plan. Other barriers to a full life in Australia are more substantial. She cannot travel overseas without getting permission from the immigration department, which proved a problem in 2011, when Ilaria's grandmother turned 100 and she wanted to go back to Italy to join in the family celebrations. In order to ensure that she could return to Australia after the trip, Ilaria had to apply for another bridging visa, called a Bridging Visa B (for which the fee is currently $140[7]). Initially, the immigration department turned her down on the basis that the explanation she gave on her application form did not amount to 'substantial reasons for wanting to leave and return to Australia'.[8]

As there is no definition of 'substantial reasons' to be found on the immigration-department website, the assessment appears to be at the discretion of the officer who handles the file. 'Staff at immigration go out of their way to help people generally,' says migration agent

Grant Williams, 'but any subjective system is subject to arbitrary outcomes.'

On immigration chat sites, some other bridging-visa holders report having had no trouble in getting permission to take overseas holidays. Yet in Ilaria's case it appears the desk officer refused to take her word for the fact that she had a grandmother turning 100. Two weeks before she was due to fly out, with flights booked and paid for, she was required to furnish copies of both her grandmother's and her mother's birth certificates to prove the veracity of her claim. Given that her grandmother lives in a remote village in Tuscany with no fax machine, this was no small task. Her family in Italy had to drop everything to get the documents to her in time.

The experience added to an overall sense of being treated unfairly. 'You follow the rules, you try to do things the right way, and you just get stuck,' Ilaria says. After more than five years of limbo, she is deeply aggrieved at her treatment, but she is concerned not to be seen as a troublemaker. She feels her arguments are reasonable and the government has a case to answer. In her letters to immigration ministers and to other federal parliamentarians, she makes her arguments in polite and moderate, if resolute, language.

Ilaria has heard stories of migrants successfully cheating the system—engaging in fake marriages to get a visa, for example. In her work she has come into contact with skilled migrants who have only been in Australia a few years, whose English is poor and who are not integrating well, yet they have jumped past her in the queue for residency and have secured a permanent visa (generally via some form of employer or state sponsorship that is accorded higher priority for processing).

Adam Gaster,* originally from Israel, shares Ilaria's frustration at being overtaken in this way. 'What's annoying me,' he says, 'is that I see all the people around me who are getting their PR [permanent residency] with the new system and they don't work in the skill they applied for. I meet people that came here years after me, accountants, architects and more, who got their PR and work in general jobs, not in their skills.'

Adam first came to Australia as a student in 2008 and qualified as a pastry chef. Since then he has worked continuously in his trade and feels like he has made a substantial contribution to Australian society. 'I was involved in the training of young Australian apprentices who are now great pastry chefs,' he says. 'I was involved with charities such as Challenge—helping kids with cancer—using my skills to give back to the community.'

Adam lodged his application for permanent residency in 2010. He understands that changes had to be made to manage the backlog that built up in the permanent skilled-migration program, but after five years at the back of the processing queue, he feels like he is being punished for the mistakes of the system.

All the applicants I spoke to in priority group five are skilled migrants sponsored by a family member who is an Australian citizen. This was possible under the 886 and 176 visa subclasses, which have since been closed to new applicants. Ilaria's sponsor is her Sydney-based uncle. An Australian cousin sponsored Julio Martinez and Marta Saldana. Adam Gaster is sponsored by his sister.

Before the rules changed, it made good sense to apply for this visa category, because sponsorship earned the applicant additional marks

---

* Not his real name

in the migration points test. Under the conditions of the visa, the sponsor guarantees to help his or her migrant relative for up to two years with such things as accommodation, financial assistance, child care and advice. In theory, the visa should ensure that new migrants settle more easily in Australia, and have family resources to draw on if things go pear-shaped.

In reality, Ilaria, Adam, Julio and Marta haven't needed this kind of help. They have established successful careers in their chosen professions and built self-reliant lives. They have been caught out by changes to the system that were totally beyond their control. In some cases, they received poor (and expensive) advice from migration agents. If they had applied under a different category—such as the 885 or 175 skilled-independent visa programs—then their applications would almost certainly have been finalised by now.

They could potentially cut their losses and apply for a higher-priority visa—for example, by switching to a 457 temporary skilled-work visa and then asking their employer to sponsor them for permanent residency under one of the employer-nomination schemes. But the transition from one visa pathway to another would be an expensive, complicated and risky business. Their existing applications cannot be transferred and would have to be abandoned, but none of the money already paid would be refunded. So they would need to spend thousands more dollars on new government charges and fresh migration advice. They would have to repeat bureaucratic procedures they have already completed, such as getting new health and police checks and passing a new English-language test. And if they wanted to apply for employer sponsorship on a 457 visa, they would first have to work for this same employer for at least two years.

Understandably, people in priority group five are fearful that if they did switch streams from one visa category to another, they might just find the rules being changed on them once again. 'I've seen many people who've spent large amounts of money trying to transition and then been kicked in the head,' says Grant Williams. 'They end up tearing up money.'

The migration agent says that since the people in priority group five are not voters, 'no one really cares whether they just keep getting shuffled to the back of the queue'.

The backlog of visa applications that built up prior to the introduction of priority processing in 2009 has been substantially reduced. But this is of little comfort to the applicants still stuck in priority group five, because the government can offer no reassurance that any decision will ever be made in their cases. They have essentially been confined to the status of being indefinitely temporary, forced to put crucial life decisions on hold and denied the capacity to truly settle in their new country. They are not quite Australian.

'Surfing is my passion,' says Adam Gaster. 'I follow the footy. Most of my friends are Australians. I am up to date on Australian politics, history, culture and current affairs. I can say that I feel like this is home for me.' Yet when he writes to politicians about his situation he rarely gets any acknowledgment or response. 'I find it hard not to get cynical,' he tells me.

'We are in oblivion,' says Marta Saldana. 'They have forgotten about us.'

'By the look of it we will never get our applications processed,' says Julio Martinez. 'They charge the money and offer a service, but they are not delivering what they promised. So in my opinion that is fraud.'

'I'm not asking for any favours,' says Ilaria De Fusco. 'I just want an answer. I think I deserve an answer. I want someone to look into my application and say "yes, you can stay" or "no, you can't stay".'

Chances are that if they are willing to hang out in the queue long enough, and withstand the distress and the anxiety caused by an indefinite wait, then the temporary migrants stuck in priority group five will eventually have their applications dealt with and be granted permanent residency. In July 2015, Ilaria sent me an excited email saying she'd finally been allocated a case officer by the immigration department; this means that after living in Australia for the best part of 15 years, and living at the back of the permanent-migration queue for five and a half years, her application is at last being processed. But this raises a question of reasonableness. How long is it reasonable to have someone live in this country, work, support themselves, pay taxes and abide by the law, and yet keep them at arms length—deny them full acceptance as members of society? The answers we give to such questions will reveal much about us as a nation, including what practical content we really give to terms like fairness, multiculturalism and equal rights.

These questions will remain relevant even though the massive backlog of valid skilled-migration applications that built up during the Howard era is unlikely to be replicated. There are two reasons for this. Firstly, there are fewer applications entering the system since the Rudd government dramatically weakened the nexus between study in Australia and permanent migration. (This marked a bureaucratic and political victory for immigration over a much larger and generally more powerful education department that did not want to disrupt the inflow of fee-paying foreign students.) Secondly, the system of selecting and processing applications for permanent skilled migration has been fundamentally redesigned.

From 1 July 2012, the immigration department began rolling out a new mechanism called SkillSelect. It's an innovation as novel as the points test was when it was introduced to Australia in 1979. Under SkillSelect, instead of applying for a substantive visa and paying thousands of dollars in upfront fees, prospective applicants first lodge an online 'expression of interest', in which they provide all their details—occupation, qualifications, work experience, age, language skills, family status and so on. The SkillSelect system allocates them a score under the skilled-migration points test. For example, you get 20 points for 'superior' English (level 8 or above in all written and oral categories of the International English Language Testing System, IELTS, which is very hard to achieve), 10 points for proficient English (IELTS level 7) and zero points for competent English (IELTS level 6).[9] If prospective candidates meet the pass mark (between 60 and 70 points at the time of writing, depending on the visa category and subject to change by the minister[10]) then they go into a pool and wait for an invitation to apply for a visa. Invitations are issued in monthly batches and go to the highest ranked candidates first—so a migrant with a score of 70 on the points test will receive an invitation before a candidate with a score of 65. When candidates' scores are equal, the invitation goes to the candidate whose expression of interest was lodged first. Employers can also use SkillSelect like a labour brokerage, trawling the talent pool for prospective workers with the skills they are seeking and then offering to sponsor them for a visa.

For the immigration department, the new regime has significant advantages over the old system based solely on the points test. Under the old system, anyone who reached the pass mark in the points test could lodge a valid application for a visa. That is why the numbers blew out so dramatically when study in Australia was directly linked to permanent residency. Under SkillSelect such blowouts won't happen, because the government can limit the number of applications it receives for points-based skilled migration by controlling the numbers of invitations it issues in response to expressions of interest (or by raising and lowering the pass mark on the points test). It does not, of course, prevent a backlog of expressions of interest in the SkillSelect system, but an expression of interest is just that. Unlike a substantive application for permanent residency, it imposes no obligations on the government—it does not have to be considered or processed. Nor does an expression of interest give candidates the capacity to extend their stay in Australia (via a bridging visa), if, for example, they have recently graduated and their student visa is about to expire.

SkillSelect essentially embeds a system of priority processing into the migration program at a much earlier stage, with scores in the points test providing the ranking mechanism. Under SkillSelect the government also imposes occupational ceilings, restricting the number of invitations that will be issued in particular sectors. In 2015–16, for example, there was a ceiling of 2,525 invitations for accountants and a ceiling of 2,475 invitations for chefs.[11]

In its 2012–13 annual report, the immigration department described the move to SkillSelect as 'a change in program delivery processes to a just-in-time system for the best and brightest applicants, rather than the previous reliance on a large pipeline of those able to meet minimum requirements'.[12] Stripped of management speak, this means the department can now forestall a backlog of visa applications by only 'inviting' as many applications as it wants to process in any given year. So no queue builds up and the time between a visa application being lodged and processed is reduced.

SkillSelect was developed under former Labor immigration minister Chris Evans, who conceived of the immigration department as 'the job-matching agency for the nation'.[13] He said the old points-only system was 'like pulling a ticket number from the dispenser at the supermarket deli counter', with everyone served in turn. In theory, anyone who amassed a sufficient score in the migration test got a ticket and would eventually get 'served' with a permanent visa. Evans claimed the supermarket-deli model was 'delivering self-nominated migrants from a narrow range of occupations with poor to moderate English-language skills who struggle to find employment in their nominated occupation'.[14] (The example often given of this scenario is a taxi driver with an accounting degree.)

Evans suggested that a better model for selecting skilled migrants was the university-entrance process. 'What do universities do when admitting students?' he asked. 'They work out ways of selecting the best from those putting themselves forward.'[15] SkillSelect is intended to replicate this process. Places are limited, so they are offered first to those most suitable and best qualified rather than those who meet a threshold standard and have waited the longest.

In many ways, Evans ushered in a more stable, predictable and rational system for selecting skilled migrants. (People like Ilaria, who got stuck at the back of the queue in priority group five, were casualties of the transition to this new system.) The reforms confirmed and entrenched the ongoing shift from a supply-driven to a demand-driven migration program. Temporary migration is an integral part of this shift: the 457 visa, in particular, provides a mechanism for business to rapidly import workers to meet its emerging demand for particular skills (and equally makes it easier for business to dispense with those workers if their skills are no longer required). In the realm of permanent migration, Evans sought to build a system in which the demand for particular skills prompts employers and governments to select and sponsor precisely the skilled migrants they need, rather than having a supply of skilled migrants putting themselves forward to be future residents of Australia. This was a significant refinement of the bias towards skilled migration that has characterised Australian policy since the late 1980s, and one of the most far-reaching changes in the permanent-migration program in decades.

But while SkillSelect should prevent another blowout in skilled-migration processing queues, it will not prevent the phenomenon of indefinite temporariness, particularly if policymakers continue to expand the range of temporary visas on offer.

When I meet Belinda Pei[*] I gain the impression of a guarded young woman whose experience of the world has taught her to proceed with caution. There is also an evident resolve about her: I have the sense of a person who stands her ground, determined not to let the vicissitudes of circumstance push her off course or force her into moral compromises.

In an email exchange prior to our meeting, Belinda has admitted to googling me after I first got in touch, to check out who I am and where I am coming from. Her online research brought up some of my writing on temporary migration, and it struck a chord with her. 'This is the beginning of my thirteenth year in Australia, which marks a point where I have lived, studied and worked here as a temporary resident for more than half my life,' she wrote. 'Having been in Australia for so long, and experiencing firsthand the difficulties and

---

[*] Not her real name

frustrations with trying to gain permanent residency and work here, the issues you talk about speak to me quite strongly.'

So Belinda agreed to help me put a human face to temporary migration. I catch up with her when my work takes me to Sydney for a week, and she tells me her story over cups of tea in a Glebe cafe.

It begins in September 1994, when the town of Rabaul in Papua New Guinea was destroyed by the eruption of a volcano. Belinda was four at the time and her parents both ran small businesses. 'Everything was destroyed,' she says. 'The stock that they had ordered in for Christmas was not paid off so they were left with huge debts.' The family took refuge in Port Moresby until the volcano settled down again. Belinda's parents were among the first to return, rebuild and start over. 'Rabaul was like a ghost town,' she says. Most residents never came back. Rabaul's population today is less than a quarter of what it was before the disaster. 'The economy was shattered, everyone had left,' says Belinda. Her father's attempts to revive his trade store failed and he eventually found work as an accountant with a law firm. Her mother started up a uniform shop, catering to small schools that were overlooked by the bigger stores.

Belinda describes her heritage as 'Papua New Guinean-Chinese, mostly Chinese'. Her family history is full of migrations, both forced and voluntary. Her mother grew up in southern China, but the family had to move to survive the Cultural Revolution. There was already a family connection to Papua New Guinea. Belinda's great-grandfather had been recruited to work in New Guinea when it was still a German colony prior to World War I. He had married three days before he left China, but in New Guinea he took a second wife. They had a child together, Belinda's maternal grandfather, and he was sent to southern China to study, which is where he met her grandmother.

Her grandfather returned to Papua New Guinea to escape the deprivations of the Cultural Revolution and brought the rest of the family out after him, including Belinda's mother. Belinda's father moved from Hong Kong to Papua New Guinea around the same time, but for different reasons. 'Dad ended up in Papua New Guinea just before independence [in 1975],' she explains. 'There was a lot of economic activity, a lot of opportunities. He went with his brother and fell in love with the place, impressed with the people and their passion for the country.' Her parents met in Rabaul, married, and built their lives there.

Belinda says it's typical for Chinese-Papua New Guinean families to send their children to Australia for high school. Her mother's youngest sister had been the first to go, encouraged by an Australian family friend. Belinda's older brother followed and completed an engineering degree. So, in 2002, at the age of 12 Belinda was sent off to school in Sydney. She lived with her aunt, studied through to the end of year 12 and went on to university, completing a double degree in commerce and science.

Towards the end of her undergraduate course it dawned on Belinda that her temporary visa would expire when she finished her studies and that she needed to start thinking seriously about her future. By this stage she could not see herself going back to Papua New Guinea. There was no work in Rabaul. She would have a better chance of finding a job in Port Moresby, but living alone in the capital as a young woman was not attractive or advisable. 'I don't look local,' she says. 'I would be a very clear target.' Besides, Belinda now felt as much at home in Australia as in Papua New Guinea. She spent her entire honours year applying for graduate intake positions with Australian accounting firms, banks and management companies, and mostly receiving standard rejection emails. 'I was looking, looking, looking,' she says, 'but I only had two interviews. It was very disheartening.' Belinda realised that the odds were stacked against her; in the graduate recruitment stakes, many employers will not even consider an applicant who is not a permanent resident or citizen. 'If you are not permanent', she says, 'then you have to be Olympic standard to qualify.'

Belinda did not need just any job: she needed a job with an employer who would sponsor her to remain in Australia, at least temporarily, probably on a 457 skilled-worker visa. She realised that she had chosen the wrong degree after finishing high school; her qualifications did not position her well in the employer-sponsored visa stakes. It was not something she'd taken into consideration when choosing her uni course. 'As an eighteen-year-old year twelve graduate, you don't think, "Okay, I might need to look at the SOL [Skilled Occupation List] to see what job I'm going to do,"' she says. But even if she had, it would have been a bit of a lottery. 'You can apply for a degree because it's on the SOL and then the SOL changes,' she points out. 'By the time you finish it might not be on there any more.'

As Belinda approached the end of her honours year with no prospective employer to sponsor her for a job, she decided reluctantly that she would have to keep studying in order to stay in Australia. 'I didn't want to do a masters, because of the cost to my parents,' she tells me. 'But for the sake of getting a visa I found the quickest and easiest masters course that would get me onto the SOL.'

So in 2013 Belinda commenced a masters in early childhood education. 'It ended up being a really good course, with a great cohort, including several other international students,' she says. 'I think we all chose the course for the same reason.'

Her mother had joined her in Australia early that year, just before the semester started. 'She had a lump in her pancreas,' Belinda explains, 'so she flew into Sydney for a follow-up check-up.' Then, in the first week of the semester, as Belinda was celebrating her birthday, her father suddenly and unexpectedly passed away from an unknown illness. 'He was in Papua New Guinea all alone and he had to be buried the very next day, because the hospital morgue was not working,' she says. 'The community stepped in and organised everything for us.' Belinda's mother was too unwell to travel home in any case. A short time later, she was diagnosed with pancreatic cancer. 'Most people die of that within three to six months,' says Belinda. 'Mum lasted a year.' There were major operations, relapses, hospital admissions, constant visits to specialists and everything else that goes with a terminal illness. An added stress was her mother's visa status. She had arrived on a tourist visa that had to be converted into a medical-treatment visa. Ironically, Belinda had to worry both about her mother dying and about her pulling through, because she was anxious about how she would be able to keep her mother in Australia if she did recover. 'She could not have passed any kind of medical clearance for a visa application,' says Belinda. In the end that was not an issue. The family was about to apply for an extension of the medical-treatment visa when Belinda's mother passed away.

'It was just insane,' says Belinda, recalling that year. She and her brother are still caught up in selling their parents' house and business in Rabaul—a protracted process in Papua New Guinea—but luckily her father's insurance policy paid out just enough to cover the fees for the final year of Belinda's masters. 'His final gift to me,' she says. As she approached graduation in 2014, Belinda once again began assessing her options. Not only did she see no future for herself in Papua

New Guinea, she no longer had any family to return to there. This raised the possibility of an application for permanent residency as a 'remaining relative' under a migration category called 'other family'.

Of the more than 60,000 places in the family stream of the migration program, about 80 per cent go to partners (mostly the spouses and fiancés of Australian citizens and permanent residents). Four out of five of the remaining 13,000-odd visas go to children and to 'contributing parents'—that is, parents of Australian citizens or permanent residents who are willing and able to pay more than $20,000 to secure a visa.[16] (This is essentially another form of organised queue jumping, justified on the basis that 'many families wanted a faster visa process and were prepared to pay a higher contribution towards their family members' health and welfare costs in Australia'.[17]) This leaves a few thousand visas for non-contributory parents (who could not afford a 'faster' process and must anticipate a wait time of 30 years[18]), carers and 'remaining relatives'—the subsection of the 'other family' category for which Belinda, as the last non-Australian member of her family, could now apply. (Her aunt and her brother are both Australian citizens.) In 2013–14, a total of 182 'remaining relative' visas were granted. When Belinda looked into the detail, she discovered that if she lodged a valid application in 2014–15, she could expect it to take 'approximately 56 years to be released for final processing'.[19] In other words, by the time her visa was issued, Belinda would be more than 80 years old.[20]

If Belinda had applied, she would, at best, have been granted a bridging visa, putting her in the same position as Ilaria and others stuck in priority group five. She would have had no access to any kind of social security or public health care, she would have had to apply for permission to travel overseas and her career prospects would have been limited by her visa status. She would have been present in

Australia, but not included in the life of the nation. She would have been indefinitely temporary.

Belinda took a different tack: she searched for an employer who would sponsor her for a 457 visa. The timing was tight; after receiving the letter of completion for her masters in November 2014, Belinda had until early March 2015 to find work with an approved employer who would lodge a 457 application before her existing student visa expired. 'If I was a citizen or had permanent residency I could have shopped around more,' she says, 'but I settled for good enough.'

When we meet, Belinda is a few weeks into the six-month probationary period for her job in a privately run day-care centre. It seems to be working out okay so far, but she has reservations and is acutely aware of the constraints of her position. She would be concerned, for example, about making a complaint about conditions or taking industrial action for fear of getting on the wrong side of her employer. 'You have to pick your battles carefully,' she says, noting that if she loses her job, then she has only 90 days to find an alternative employer to act as her visa sponsor. 'That leaves me very vulnerable to exploitation,' she says. 'They have a lot of power.'

Belinda has realised that many things that she took for granted as a high-school student, and that many Australians continue to take for granted, are really luxuries. It is a luxury to be able to have choice in the course you study or the job you go for. It is a luxury to decide to take a gap year between school and further study. It is a luxury to feel secure in your membership of Australian society. 'After twelve years' living in Australia, I'm still jumping through hoops,' she says.

Belinda says most people assume she is Australian when they meet her, because she sounds and acts like an Australian. 'They are genuinely surprised that I am not Australian, especially when they find out how long I've been here,' she says. 'Culturally I feel very comfortable with Australia; I fit in very, very easily and quite happily, but I can never feel one hundred per cent Australian because of the constant reminders—like having to pay full fare [on public transport] as a student.' So while Belinda might blend in, she often feels excluded. 'I've never been able to feel Australian because of all the barriers and all the closed doors,' she says. 'It makes me feel a bit alienated and like an outsider.'

Belinda can be reminded of her outsider status in unexpected and hurtful ways. At a family gathering, for example, her aunt's partner launched into a tirade about foreign workers being brought in as cheap labour on temporary visas. 'He's an electrical engineer who had just been made redundant from a telecommunications company,' she explains. 'He was extremely bitter about it and his sentiment was that someone on a 457 visa had taken his job.' As he fumed about Indians with dodgy qualifications, Belinda kept quiet. Her own 457 visa had been confirmed just a few days earlier.

'That's the general sentiment among the general public,' says Belinda. 'They don't put a face to migrants. They are just foreigners, ignorant of Australian culture, not as skilled, not as competent.'

'I'm not here to steal jobs, use up your Medicare or go on the dole,' she says. 'I'm here to fulfil my parents' dream of having better opportunities than they ever had. My mother grew up in the Cultural Revolution and lived an extremely difficult life. She worked and worked and worked. She would open her shop at seven in the morning and be on her feet all day. She would stay up until one the next morning sewing clothes. She never got to enjoy life up until her death. Her priority was giving me the opportunity that she never had.'

Stories of mothers and fathers devoting their lives to securing their children a brighter future in a new land are central to the universal narratives of migration. In Australia, our assumption has long been that such parental privations lead to security for the next generation—at least in terms of their membership of the new society. But in the twenty-first century, this assumption is questionable.

Like all the case studies in this book, Belinda's story is unique, but that does not make it exceptional, particularly as we peer into Australia's future. Chinese-Papua New Guinean families are not the only ones packing children off to high school in Australia. Indeed, high-school education is being actively marketed as a new growth area for Australia's international education industry, particularly in China. After visa rules were relaxed in 2014, the number of new school enrolments from China jumped by 20 per cent, leading Quentin Stevenson-Perks from the Australian Trade Commission to enthuse about the 'go earlier' strategy evident among Chinese parents sending their children to Australia for schooling. He told ABC Radio's *PM* program: 'I think they're seeing that the benefits of their children gaining English language or foreign language studies earlier, becoming more settled in their country which they wish to study in, and also the prospects of higher education provides a pretty good package for the Chinese parent.'[21]

A government discussion paper on the future of Victoria's international education industry also argued that the state needed to be prepared to take advantage of what it termed the 'go younger' trend. It noted that Chinese parents in particular were 'seeking to send their children abroad to study from a younger age, to help them build their English-language skills, build friendships and networks, and acclimatise so that they are a step ahead of the competition when they are entering university'.[22]

In other words, children as young as 12 or 13 are being sent to study at Australian secondary schools in the full expectation that they will then go on to study at Australian institutions of higher education. In 2013–14, almost 10,000 subclass 571 visas were granted for international pupils to study at Australian schools, about 40 per cent of them applicants from China.[23] If Australia proves successful in 'growing' this 'market', then we can expect those numbers to climb.

The push to recruit younger international students is one example of ongoing efforts to expand the education export industry. Another is the redesign of the subclass 485 post-study work visas, which makes it much easier for international students to remain living and working in Australia after completing their studies.[24] Changes to the 485 visa were made in March 2013. Previously, it was limited to graduates with a qualification on the Skilled Occupation List, and granted them an 18-month stay in Australia to undertake an approved post-graduate professional year at a university, improve their English skills or gain work experience in their profession. The revamped 485 visa is far more generous: it is available to all international students graduating from an Australian university, regardless of course and qualification. It grants a minimum two-year stay, with full work rights, to any student who has completed either a bachelors degree or a masters degree by course work. Students who complete a masters by research qualify for a three-year work visa, while those who complete a doctorate get four years. Applicants do not need to be qualified for one of the jobs on the Skilled Occupation List, nor is there any requirement that they work in the professional field in which they studied. They can work in any field, for any employer. Any graduate who is under 50 years of age and has competent English is eligible for a 485 visa, as long as their first visa to study in Australia was granted on or after 5 November 2011.[25]

The visa changes were driven by a desire to make Australian universities more attractive to full-fee-paying overseas students, following the sharp drop-off in enrolments after racist attacks on international students, the rise in the value of the Australian dollar and the Rudd government's breaking of the close link between study in Australia and permanent residency. A review of Australia's international education industry declared in 2011 that 'the absence of clearly defined post-study work rights entitlement puts Australian universities at a very serious disadvantage compared to some of our major competitor countries' and concluded that an expanded work visa was essential to 'the ongoing viability of our universities in an increasingly competitive global market for students'.[26]

The announcement of the revamped 485 visa was greeted with enthusiasm by interested parties. Glenn Withers, chief executive of Universities Australia at the time, said that the 'breakthrough' proposal was as good as or better than the work rights on offer in Canada and the United States.[27] Higher-education sector modelling suggested that by 2018 there could be more than 200,000 international student graduates working in Australia on the revamped 485 post-study visa.[28] This would be significantly more than the number of 457-visa holders present in Australia in December 2014.

The question is whether anyone involved is thinking critically about what happens at the end of this process; about the future generations of young adults caught in situations similar to Belinda's. Belinda's case was complicated by the sudden and unexpected deaths of both her parents, leaving her essentially homeless in her homeland of Papua New Guinea. But even when student graduates have homes and families to return to in other countries, having spent their formative years in Australia they may well feel themselves more at home here. What happens if there is no place for them in our permanent-migration program? Can we honestly describe a student graduate who has lived, studied and worked in Australia for half her young life (or more) as a foreigner? As Belinda pointed out to me, by the time she graduated her parents had paid hundreds of thousands of dollars in fees for her education. She has also worked and paid taxes, and continues to do so on her 457 visa. Are such people—Belinda and others like her—nothing more than 'temporary migrants' who have no further claims upon us?

Perhaps readers will feel that I am exaggerating the problem, that cases like Belinda's will be few and far between, that they will get sorted out one way or another. But bear in mind that Australia's permanent-migration program has an annual cap, while temporary migration is open-ended. For me, this conjures up the image of a funnel: the wide opening at the top is temporary migration; the narrowing at the neck represents the permanent-migration stream. Granted, many temporary migrants leave Australia after a relatively short stay, but growing ranks of international-student graduates and 457-visa holders are trying to pass through the funnel in order to achieve the status of being fully Australian. Meanwhile, a range of powerful actors and interest groups are constantly seeking to expand the opening at the top and feed more temporary migrants into the funnel, as indicated by the enthusiastic recruiting of international secondary-school students and the 485 visa changes. Since temporary migrants cannot vote, and since business has nothing to gain from turning temporary migrants into permanent settlers, there is no similar political pressure to broaden the channel that runs from temporariness to permanence.

In this context, it is increasingly likely that large numbers of student graduates will find themselves unable to gain a permanent visa, and will seek to extend their stay in Australia on some kind of temporary visa instead, such as a 485 or 457 visa. The potential for a growing number of them to become indefinitely temporary is evident.

It is, for example, entirely conceivable under our current arrangements that a student might arrive at age 16 to complete the final two years of secondary school in Australia, then go on to do a three-year undergraduate degree, a year of honours and a two-year masters before working for three years on a 485 post-study employment visa. At the end of this period the student graduate will be 27 and will have spent 11 formative years in Australia. Their family will have invested tens if not hundreds of thousands of dollars in education fees, and the student will very likely have paid tax as a worker, but he or she will not necessarily be any closer to becoming an Australian resident. Success in the permanent-residency stakes will depend to a considerable degree on the mix of skills and occupations that employers and policymakers deem essential for the Australian economy at the time of application, which might differ from the mix of skills and occupations that was in demand when the student first embarked on a university course. It might also depend on the political climate and popular opinion about immigration and population growth.

If the pathway to permanency remains closed, then this contemporary *metic* might seek to jump to yet another temporary visa. The next step could be a 457 skilled-worker visa or even a working-holiday visa. This would extend their precarious state of temporariness for a few more years, while simultaneously deepening their connection to Australia.

After many years of writing about migrant and refugee flows to Australia, and watching the ways in which the complexity of human lives interacts with bureaucratic systems, I am constantly coming across new examples of people ending up in situations that were never conceived of or contemplated by policymakers and public administrators. The available mechanisms for extending a stay in Australia are likely to be used in ways that may appear surprising to those who put the rules in place, but are entirely logical and reasonable from the perspective of the temporary migrant who wants to remain in Australia and for whom permanent residency remains out of reach. In 2013, for example, at a seminar at Swinburne University, I met a young woman from China, who told me how five years of living and studying in Australia had fundamentally altered the way she approaches the world. She thought differently, her values had changed, she had become a Christian and she had a close network of friends in Melbourne. She found it very difficult to contemplate returning 'home' because she felt like she belonged more in Australia than China. At the same seminar was a young Pakistani national, who was born and grew up in one of the Gulf States, where his parents had worked as temporary migrants. His father was still working in the Gulf, but as an independent adult, the son could no longer rejoin him there as a family member. His mother was back in Pakistan, where he had hardly ever lived; she was imploring her son *not* to return there, and to do whatever he could to stay away, because the situation in the country was so dire. Siblings Phillip and Amy Choi, aged 20 and 18 respectively, are South Korean nationals who have spent most of their lives in Australia (Amy was born here and Phillip first came as a baby). They lost their right to stay, however, when the immigration department refused to renew their father's business visa. 'We are Australian. This is our home,' says Phillip.[29] 'Phil and I grew up here,' says Amy. 'It's so absurd that they'll send someone away from their home.'[30]

If we create systems that enable migrants to extend their stay in Australia by moving from one temporary visa to another, then I predict that this is what a significant number of them will do. If the pathway to permanent residency is too restricted, and the duration of temporary stay stretches into years, then this presents a challenge for a nation that claims to hold dear core principles of liberal democracy—such as the right to have a say in the formation of laws by which you are governed, the right to be involved in choosing the government, the right to be politically represented, the right to have a voice and the right to be treated equally with others in society. The moral issues at stake are compounded when a migrant arrives as a child and spends their formative years in Australia.

In opening up the potential for migrants to be indefinitely temporary, Australia is moving away from these principles. Some of the most glaring evidence of this shift is right under our noses, but rarely gets noticed: it is to be found in our treatment of New Zealanders.

5 | New Zealanders
A Special Category

In the exotic-foods section of my local supermarket is a set of shelves catering to the particular tastes of New Zealanders: bottles of L&P (Lemon & Paeroa) soft drink and packets of Bluebird green onion chips sit below Black Knight licorice twists and Arataki clover honey. Around the neighbourhood I regularly come across Kiwis: the cheerful barista at the corner coffee shop, a Polynesian woman on the supermarket checkout, the Pākehā (New Zealanders of European descent) couple running the local clothing-alterations store. We've had Māori carpenters build us a new fence, and I have had my hair cut by a young man newly arrived from a small South Island town, who was blown away by the delights of big-city Melbourne.

Frequently encountering New Zealanders should come as no surprise, since there are lots of them in Australia—654,000 as of June

2015. Around 100,000 are on short holidays or brief work trips,[1] but the rest are longer-term residents.

The history of people moving back and forth across the Tasman has its roots in the early colonial era and predates free trade in goods. The first overseas military expedition by Australians was to the Māori land wars: between 1845 and 1872 more than 2,500 volunteers served with British forces in New Zealand.[2] Australia's first Labor prime minister, Chris Watson, grew up in New Zealand and came to Australia as a young adult. Until the mid-1960s, the number of people moving in both directions was roughly equal. In most years since then, however, there has been a clear bias towards migration from east to west.

Much of this movement is circular or repeat migration.[3] A Kiwi might come to Australia, work for a few years, then go home again to a better job or because an elderly parent needs care. If circumstances change, they might then come back to Australia a few years later. Some New Zealanders might spend the bulk of their working life here, but still choose to go 'home' in retirement. Many, however, do settle, even if that was not their original intention. The rate of arrivals fluctuates with the relative economic fortunes of each country, but since the late 1960s, faster growth, higher wages, greater job opportunities and a stronger dollar have been an economic magnet drawing New Zealanders across the ditch. The simple mathematics of the trans-Tasman equation is that Kiwis have been steadily adding to Australia's population through net migration: since 2001, the average annual increase has been more than 28,000 people per year.[4] (The end of the mining boom and a slowing of the Australian economy have broken this trend in recent years, with fewer New Zealand citizens departing for Australia and more returning home. In 2014–15, the net loss of New Zealanders to Australia was only 6,000 people.[5])

New Zealand-born people comprise the second largest overseas-born group in Australia (after those born in the United Kingdom),[6] but New Zealand is less discussed as a major source of migrants to Australia than India, China and the United Kingdom. In part, this is because New Zealanders arriving under the Trans-Tasman Travel Arrangement are not counted as part of Australia's official immigration program.[7] We also tend to treat New Zealanders as if they come from interstate rather than overseas, accepting them as de facto Australians. When I talk about my work on temporary migration and add Kiwis to a list that includes international students and 457-visa holders, people often think that I'm joking. But since 2001, New Zealanders in Australia have found little to laugh about. Their official treatment has become a source of growing anger, frustration and resentment.

Since the 1920s, Australian and New Zealand governments have made agreements to facilitate cross-border movement—although for decades, travel 'without the formalities of passports or permits' was restricted to white Australians, Indigenous Australians, white New Zealanders and Māori.[8] In the era of White Australia and White New Zealand (which, like Australia, passed legislation restricting immigration in the late nineteenth and early twentieth centuries), people of Asian or Pacific Islander descent were not welcome in either country.[9] As historian Paul Hamer documents, the situation with Māori was more complex, because of the hope that New Zealand would join the Australian Federation.[10] The *Pacific Labourers Act 1901*—designed to remove blackbirded 'Kanakas' from the Queensland cane fields (and elsewhere)—specifically exempted Māori from being expelled from Australia.[11] Unlike any other 'aboriginal native of Australia

Asia Africa or the Islands of the Pacific', Māori were also entitled to have their names on the Australian electoral roll.¹² This more generous treatment of Māori did not sit comfortably with many Australian politicians. In 1948, for example, Arthur Calwell tried to prevent a Māori ex-serviceman from settling in Australia with his Australian wife.¹³ Reflecting marked differences in relations between the colonisers and the colonised on either side of the Tasman, New Zealand prime minister Peter Fraser responded fiercely, saying that 'any hint of discrimination against our Māori fellow citizens would be indignantly and bitterly resented as an unforgivable insult to our country and every one of us'.¹⁴

As late as 1971, the McMahon government rejected New Zealand's proposal to extend free movement across the Tasman to citizens of non-European descent. As Paul Hamer has documented, immigration minister Jim Forbes warned cabinet that such a reform might encourage the arrival of New Zealanders of Pacific Island background, who he believed were 'unsophisticated' and 'quite unsuited to settlement in Australia'.¹⁵ This concern has continued to animate the thinking of Australian politicians and bureaucrats up to the present day.

In the face of Australian opposition to the free movement of non-Europeans, New Zealand acted unilaterally in 1971 to allow the entry of all Australian citizens, regardless of race. Australia eventually followed suit, abolishing racial restrictions under the 1973 Trans-Tasman Travel Arrangement. The arrangement was based on an agreement between prime ministers Gough Whitlam and Norman Kirk that 'citizens of each country and citizens of other Commonwealth countries who have resident status in either Australia or New Zealand should henceforth be able to travel between Australia and New Zealand, for permanent or temporary stay, without passports or visas'.[16] It is not a binding treaty, but a set of procedures embedded in the immigration policies of each country, given additional force by the Closer Economic Relations Trade Agreement between Australia and New Zealand, which specifically endorses the idea of a free flow of people for work and social purposes.[17]

The practical operations of the Trans-Tasman Travel Arrangement have changed since its inception. Since 1981, for example, all travellers from New Zealand have had to carry a passport to enter Australia, and since 1994, when Australia introduced a universal visa requirement for all non-citizens entering the country, New Zealanders have needed a visa, too—although this special category (or subclass 444) visa requires no paperwork, attracts no fees and is issued automatically to all New Zealanders on arrival (unless there are health or character concerns).

These amendments since 1973 have not changed the fundamental role of the arrangement to facilitate free movement in both directions, thus allowing Australians and New Zealanders to live in each other's countries indefinitely. (Australia extends this right only to New Zealand citizens, whereas New Zealand also allows Australian permanent residents to settle, even if they are not citizens.) Yet the arrangement is silent on the entitlements that accrue with time, such as access to welfare or the right to vote. Australians who move to New Zealand quickly gain similar rights and responsibilities as those of New Zealand citizens. They can enrol to vote after just one year of residence; they become eligible for welfare payments, including unemployment benefits and student allowances, after two years; and they can become citizens after five years.[18] Since 2001, the treatment of New Zealanders in Australia has been far less generous.

For a long time, New Zealanders in Australia were classified as 'exempt non-citizens',[19] which, if they intended to stay permanently, essentially gave them the same status as permanent residents, including full welfare entitlements on arrival. In 1986, in response to the popular myth of the 'Bondi bludger'—New Zealanders scrounging off the Australia taxpayer—a six-month waiting period for access to social security was introduced. In 2000, this waiting period was extended to two years, essentially putting New Zealanders on the same footing as other permanent migrants.[20] New Zealanders could then, after the required length of stay, convert their Australian residency into Australian citizenship, and so participate in elections as voters or candidates, get a job with the Australian Public Service or join the Australian Defence Force.

Since 2001, however, things have been different. New Zealanders can still stay and work in Australia for as long as they like, but their rights and entitlements remain restricted, no matter how many years they live here.

Although it has no time limit and never expires, the special category visa granted to New Zealanders on arrival is viewed as a 'temporary' visa.[21] This is nonsensical. The Migration Act defines a 'temporary' visa in three ways: as a visa to remain in Australia 'during a specified period', 'while the holder has a specific status' or 'until a specified event happens'.[22] Since a New Zealander's right to stay is open-ended, the visa is clearly not temporary in the sense of being for a 'specified period'. It is equally ludicrous to say that the special category visa is temporary because it is linked to the 'specific status' of being a New Zealander, since New Zealand citizenship is, for all intents and purposes, a permanent condition. The only remaining interpretation is that the special category visa is temporary because it expires when a 'specified event happens'—the 'event' in question being the visa holder leaving Australia. This appears to be the logic of the government's position,[23] but it is a hollow, self-serving logic, since a New Zealander who returns to Australia the very next day will be granted a 'new' special category visa identical to the one that just expired.

Despite treating the special category visa as temporary, the Department of Immigration and Border Protection continues to refer to New Zealanders as 'permanent settlers' in many of its publications.[24] The Australian Bureau of Statistics classifies the special category visa as a permanent visa in its calculations and special category visa holders are also considered permanent residents under the *Income Tax Assessment Act 1997*.[25]

However contorted and contradictory the bureaucratic reasoning may be, the effect on New Zealand migrants is very real: they are rendered indefinitely temporary, and like temporary migrants on other types of visas, they suffer from many disadvantages that attend to such a status. The only way New Zealanders who arrived after 2001 can become permanent residents of Australia—and subsequently citizens—is by making the often difficult, and always expensive, leap to a different visa category. If they are in an ongoing relationship with an Australian citizen, for example, they can apply for a partner visa. If they have a qualification that is in high demand, then they can apply for permanent residence as a skilled migrant. If, however, they build fences, cut hair, work on a supermarket checkout or make coffees, this route will almost certainly be closed to them.

On average, two-thirds of Australia's overseas-born population have taken out Australian citizenship and one-third have not.[26] In the case of New Zealanders, these ratios are reversed.[27] Only one-third of

Kiwis counted in the 2011 census were citizens, which gives them one of the lowest take-up rates of any migrant group. Prior to the changes introduced in 2001, the explanation for this was that New Zealanders had little motivation to become citizens, because they received all the benefits of permanent residence in any case. Removing those benefits should, in theory, have prompted an increase in citizenship take-up rates after 2001, but instead the trend went in the opposite direction: ever fewer New Zealanders became citizens, because after 2001 most new arrivals could not qualify for a permanent visa, which is the necessary precursor to citizenship.[28] In the four years to 30 June 2014, close to 150,000 New Zealand citizens settled in Australia under the Trans-Tasman Travel Arrangement, but fewer than 10,000 were granted permanent residence.[29]

According to Paul Hamer's research, when the 2001 restrictions were being planned, Australian officials calculated that less than half of all future New Zealander arrivals would qualify for a permanent visa.[30] History has proved them largely correct: in 2014, the federal government acknowledged that perhaps as many as 60 per cent of special category visa holders would 'not be able to meet the requirements for a permanent visa'.[31] By this time it was estimated that the 2001 changes were disadvantaging around 200,000 New Zealanders living in Australia,[32] and with the number continuing to rise the issue had become a persistent and growing irritant in trans-Tasman relations.

In February 2016, after a meeting with his New Zealand counterpart, John Key, Prime Minister Malcolm Turnbull offered what he hoped would be the soothing balm of a 'new pathway' to citizenship for New Zealanders. The new pathway—available from July 2017—is based on taxable income, rather than skills and qualifications, and will make it easier for some relatively affluent New Zealanders to gain the same rights and entitlements as Australians. Yet tens of thousands of New Zealanders will still be excluded: they will remain in a 'special category'—permanent settlers on temporary visas.

There was no change to the Trans-Tasman Travel Arrangement itself in 2001; New Zealanders could still freely enter Australia to live and work. What changed were their entitlements after arrival. Crucially, the Howard government amended the definition of 'Australian resident' in social-security laws to exclude New Zealanders arriving after that time.[33] New Zealanders who arrived before the change came into effect on 26 February 2001 are described as 'protected' special category visa holders and continue to receive essentially the same entitlements as permanent residents. Later 'unprotected' arrivals do not qualify as Australian residents, and so are denied access to a range of government payments, including unemployment benefits, youth allowance, sickness benefits, sole-parent payments, carer payments and special benefits. (New Zealanders may be eligible for a one-off series of payments for up to six months if they have lived in Australia for at least a decade.) The state- or territory-based rules for housing assistance also generally exclude New Zealanders who arrived after 2001, which means that they are not eligible for public or community housing schemes.[34]

The situation was compounded in 2005, when the government tightened eligibility for the Higher Education Loan Program (HELP), the concessional scheme that enables Australian citizens and permanent residents to avoid paying upfront fees to study at university, and only requires them to start repaying their student debt when their earnings cross a certain threshold. Nor are New Zealanders eligible for the Commonwealth's vocational education loans program (VET FEE-HELP) that was introduced in 2009. (In most of Australia, but not Western Australia, New Zealanders qualify for vocational training supported by state governments under skills-guarantee schemes.) Most New Zealand-born children who want to go on to further study after school and mature-age New Zealanders who want to upgrade their qualifications must therefore pay upfront fees. Fees are charged at the same rate as domestic students, not at the much higher commercial rates paid by international students and the children of skilled workers on 457 visas, but for many people the financial barrier to study is nevertheless insurmountable. Since 1 January 2016 there have been some limited exceptions to this rule: a New Zealander can access the HELP and VET FEE-HELP loans scheme if they arrived in Australia as 'a dependent child aged under 18' and 'have been ordinarily resident in Australia for the previous 10 years'.[35] This still means that any Kiwi school leaver who moved to Australia after the age of nine will have to pay upfront fees or defer further study until they pass the 10-year threshold.

New Zealanders are also required to pay levies for the National Disability Insurance Scheme, but will not have access to any of its services. As Kiwi advocate David Faulkner explains, *eligibility* under the NDIS is determined by the definition of 'Australian resident' used in the Social Security Act (which excludes New Zealanders), while the definition of 'Australian resident' used to work out who has to *pay* the levy comes from the Health Insurance Act (which includes New Zealanders).[36]

On the upside, all New Zealanders who provide evidence that they are living in Australia—such as an electricity bill or a lease agreement—can access Medicare, regardless of when they arrived.

All New Zealanders, regardless of date of arrival, are also eligible for family-assistance payments, child-care benefits, a health-care card, a senior's-health card, parental-leave pay, free school education and even first home buyer grants. Australia and New Zealand have reciprocal arrangements in place for payment of the aged pension, disability support and carer payments for the severely disabled.

Overall this might sound like a pretty good deal, and in many ways it is, particularly in comparison to other *metics*, long-term temporary migrants in Australia—like international students and 457-visa holders—who receive no government payments or services of any description. But without a clear pathway to permanent residency, the indefinite right to remain in Australia presents a curious and potentially cruel kind of trap for New Zealanders. Australia may well be their home; they may have lived here for 10 years or more, they may have grown up here from a very young age and they may assume that they have similar rights and entitlements to Australians, yet when trouble hits they can suddenly discover that there is no safety net, and they must get by without any form of support.

Let's return to my neighbourhood, where there is a crisis centre for people who are homeless or in other kinds of difficulty. When an Australian citizen or resident turns up and asks for help, they can be provided with emergency accommodation, given an appointment with a special Centrelink homelessness team to fast-track access to benefits and be referred to other service providers for long-term assistance. 'Unprotected' New Zealanders don't get any of this.

'We see them when things go pear-shaped,' says Richard Sherman, a social worker with years of experience at the crisis centre. 'Domestic violence, retrenchment, unemployment—that's when the horror hits for them.' Often all Richard can do is assist them to return to New Zealand. 'You sit opposite them and give them the information and you see their faces drop.'

In these circumstances, women leaving abusive relationships will not infrequently decide that their best option is to go back to their partner. 'To get accommodation you have to have an income,' says Richard. 'Without access to benefits, they have no income, so they return to the violence and we see them again six months later.'

Gae Old, another seasoned worker at the centre and a New Zealander herself, says women often turn up with young children in tow, after exhausting the generosity of friends and family by couch surfing for a few weeks. 'We try to make the best of the situation,' she says. In effect, this means that when a woman has run out of other options and decides to return to her partner, the crisis centre helps her to develop a 'safety plan'—strategies to manage potentially violent scenarios. 'She won't leave, because she knows she can't,' says Gae. 'The only reason she's staying is because she does not have the financial independence to go.' Sometimes women also come to Australia with their children to escape domestic violence in New Zealand, only to find themselves stranded, without practical support or access to services.

Even when there is no family violence involved, New Zealand women can find themselves facing very difficult choices. One of Richard's regular Kiwi clients is a mother of three who is an established resident of a town in regional Victoria. Since her husband lost his job, leaving the family with no income, she has been coming to Melbourne on Friday nights to work as a prostitute. Richard knows this because she asks him to look after her bags while she turns tricks on the street. She says it's the only way her family can get by.

Another group at risk are adolescents. 'Families come here when their kids are six or seven years old,' says Richard. 'Then as teenagers they get in trouble and get tangled up in the justice system and become estranged from their families, but they've got no entitlements.' The Department of Human Services will only step in if a child is 16 or younger. Richard says that if a kid is 17 and in trouble, then sometimes the only safe option is to sit at the police station overnight.

Richard is authorised to cobble together funds from a variety of relief agencies in order to provide these young people with a plane ticket 'home' to New Zealand, where they can access government benefits. With no connections and little sense of belonging in New Zealand, many turn down the offer. 'So instead they live the homeless life and end up doing more crime,' he says.

Under the UN Convention on the Rights of the Child, Australia promises to protect the rights of children within its jurisdiction 'irrespective of citizenship status or nationality'. The National Welfare Rights Network argues that the post-2001 policy puts Australia in breach of this international obligation. It cites several examples, including the case of 'Toby', who came to Australia with his family, aged 14:

> Two years later he left his family due to family violence and moved into a refuge. As he is here on a New Zealand passport he is not residentially qualified for Youth Allowance or Special Benefit. If he were living with an adult, that adult could claim Family Tax Benefit on his behalf, but it cannot be paid to him directly and in the absence of such an adult in his life, it cannot be paid at all. He is surviving only with the assistance of Mission Australia and is falling behind at school. It is not

reasonable to expect him to return to New Zealand as he is still only 16 years old and is not mature enough to effect the move and resettle alone.[37]

Data from other welfare agencies supports these anecdotes about New Zealanders. New Zealanders make up 13 per cent of the overseas-born clients who seek assistance from specialist homelessness agencies—a much larger proportion than those born in any other nation outside Australia. In part, this might be explained by weight of numbers, given how many New Zealanders live in Australia—but if sheer numbers were the only factor, then one would expect the United Kingdom-born to figure even more prominently in the statistics, and they do not. (There are more United Kingdom-born than New Zealand-born residents in Australia, but they account for only seven per cent of clients.[38]) As Tamara Walsh from Queensland University has documented, in 2013–14 more than 40 per cent of the vulnerable New Zealanders seeking support from welfare rights centres in Brisbane and Sydney were parents of dependent children (and anecdotal evidence suggests many were women experiencing domestic violence).[39]

The social vulnerability of New Zealanders is particularly evident on the Gold Coast, where about one in 10 people are Kiwis. This compares to about one in 30 people in my local government area and about one in 50 Australia wide.[40]

It's a hot and humid December day when I visit the Nerang Neighbourhood Centre in the Gold Coast hinterland. A power outage means the air conditioning is not working, and the converted weatherboard cottage is sticky and close. Coordinator Vicky Rose is apologetic when she realises that she cannot even boil the kettle to fulfil her welcoming offer of a cup of tea.

It's a busy time at the centre: the start of the rainy season means a drop-off in building work, so many casually employed locals find themselves with no income in the run-up to Christmas. The dominance of the tourism, hospitality and construction industries on the Gold Coast gives the region higher levels of part-time and casual work than the Australian average. 'We have a large population of working poor here,' Vicky tells me. The neighbourhood centre offers interest-free loans, financial counselling, social-work services, and legal, migration and tax advice. Unlike at Centrelink, there are no eligibility requirements—there are no questions asked about visas and residency status. 'One of our services is to provide fifteen-dollar food hampers to anyone who needs it, and in December and January, we just get hammered,' says Vicky. 'More than half of our inquiries are from Kiwis.'

Vicky is Ngāi Tahu, South Island Māori. She moved to the Gold Coast in 2007 with her husband, a Kiwi of Samoan background, and their two daughters, Jennesia, then aged 12, and Gracyn, six. When she started work at the Neighbourhood Centre Vicky had no idea about the many ways in which things could go wrong for New Zealanders in Australia. 'Nothing I researched before we came over alerted me to this stuff,' she says. 'We looked at schools, at employment prospects, at house rental prices. We didn't look at what happens if your husband leaves you, if you have a baby with a disability, if you get cancer. No one thinks about stuff like that. I've never been on a government benefit in my life, so it's not something that even entered my thinking. The job was a process of discovery.'

Vicky was particularly upset by cases of domestic violence

involving children: just like the partners of 457-visa holders and international students, New Zealand women who flee abusive partners find themselves with nowhere to go and no support. Often, they cannot return to New Zealand, because it is illegal to take a child out of Australia without the approval of the other parent. 'Some men will refuse to give their partner permission to take the kids back to New Zealand,' says Vicky. 'They will drag out the process of conciliation to try to force the woman to come back to them.'

If the matter has to go to court then it can take months to get in front of a judge. 'The worst case ever was one where the mother was going to leave her toddler with her violent ex-partner so that she could go back to New Zealand and fight for custody from there,' says Vicky. 'She was living in a car and child protection were sniffing around. So you have a situation where a woman is forced to flee violence and live in a car and then ends up with her child taken away.'

The other big shock was what happens to kids who become homeless when family relationships break down. Vicky introduces me to Julius Kuresa, who runs the Nerang Neighbourhood Centre's Youth at Risk Initiative. 'Families come over here for a better life,' he says, 'but then there is a relationship breakdown.' A teenager may leave home to escape violence, or may get kicked out for doing drugs. 'They are not entitled to any benefits and often have no skills, so they can't compete with more experienced applicants for entry-level work,' says Julius. 'They end up doing bad things on the streets just to survive.'

Julius works with 21 homeless young people—all Kiwis, mostly boys, and all from Māori and Pacific Islander backgrounds. 'But it's not just Kiwi kids that do bad things,' he reminds me.

Julius is Samoan, but grew up in New Zealand from a young

age. He meets with his clients individually for about an hour and a half each week, trying to support and mentor them to improve their decision-making skills. 'It's not enough to keep them on the straight and narrow,' he says. Julius can provide these young people with food parcels, but otherwise the only practical assistance he can offer is to help them to apply for a passport and then scrape together enough money from other welfare organisations to buy them a one-way ticket 'home' to New Zealand.

Julius has organised four passports in the six months he's been in the job, but so far no one has taken up the offer of a plane ticket. 'A lot of these kids have been here for more than ten years,' he says. 'As much as they've got nothing on the streets here, they think that it is more than what they'll get back home in New Zealand. I tell them that they can get financial support and housing assistance but it doesn't get them excited. Many have done all their schooling here in Australia. They have their own clique, their own group and that is family for them.'

His oldest client is 25 and has been living on the streets for five years. His youngest is just 11 and is on the run from the police with his older brother. His clients sleep in stairwells and hotel car parks. They find places to stash their goods, and sniff out homeless services that will give them a free breakfast or dinner a couple of times a week. 'There are places where they can survive and eat,' says Julius. 'These kids are used to having no boundaries and doing as they please.'

They are also vulnerable. Some, girls and boys, end up working as prostitutes. One of the most distressing cases for Julius involved a 17-year-old boy who was enticed to move in with an older man by the older man's promise to find him work. 'He was giving the boy money, buying him clothes, putting a roof over his head. But he was also abusing him.' To cope with his distress, the boy turned to drugs and developed a serious substance-abuse problem.

The young people Julius works with often end up in the juvenile justice system, and this is when he sees that progress is possible. 'Kids engage in juvie,' he says. 'There are no distractions. There are boundaries. Positive stuff happens. They have a roof, they have food, they're drug free and they respond to the programs being run there.'

When they get out, however, and have no ongoing support, it all falls apart again. 'Four kids have been released from juvie in the past couple of weeks,' he says. 'Two of them have already been arrested again.' Eventually, when they become adults, repeated arrests and convictions are likely to lead to criminal deportation; they will be forced back to New Zealand and prevented from ever setting foot in Australia again.

One of Scott Morrison's final acts as immigration minister was to shepherd through amendments to the Migration Act that require automatic cancellation of the visa of any non-citizen who is serving or has served a prison sentence of at least 12 months (or a series of shorter prison terms that cumulatively add up to 12 months or more).[41] While the legislation barely rated a mention when it was passed in late 2014, its impact in 2015 was dramatic. At the start of the year there were just six New Zealanders in immigration detention; by mid-year there were close to 200.[42] The only country with more of its nationals locked up in Australia was Iran.[43] New Zealanders accounted for more than half of all foreign nationals whose visas were cancelled on character grounds in 2014–15[44] and the number of New Zealanders being deported grew fivefold after Morrison's changes took effect.[45]

Australia's detention and deportation of New Zealanders caused huge anger across the Tasman, particularly as many of the Kiwis in question had lived in Australia since they were children. The issue was a repeated topic of journalists' questions at post-cabinet press conferences in Wellington; the New Zealand media carried headlines like 'Christmas Island: The "Kiwi Alcatraz"';[46] the opposition Labour Party called on the government to refuse to back Australia's bid for a seat on the United Nations Human Rights Council until the policy changed;[47] and Prime Minister John Key's claim that critics of Australia's policy were 'supporting rapists, child molesters and murderers' prompted mass walk-outs from parliament.[48]

In effect, the change brought in by Scott Morrison means that as soon as a non-citizen has served their jail time, they can be deported from Australia or placed indefinitely in immigration detention until they can be deported. Previously, the minister (or a delegate) was required to determine whether or not a visa should be revoked after taking into account a range of considerations. Primary considerations were the protection of the Australian community, the nature and seriousness of the crime, and the risk of the person committing further offences. These were balanced against other important concerns, such as the best interests of any child who might be affected by the decision, the potential impacts of deportation on other family members, and the strength, duration and nature of the visa holder's ties to Australia.

In the case of New Zealanders brought to Australia as babies or young children, this last consideration was often of particular importance. As a senior New Zealand official put it to me, such people are 'Australians in all but passport'. Yet under Scott Morrison's amendments, connection to Australia is not only irrelevant—the law prevents the minister from taking it into account at all. If a non-citizen has a 'substantial criminal record', then visa cancellation is automatic and immediate, regardless of how much of that person's life has been lived on Australian shores.

The threshold of a substantial criminal record is crossed when a person is 'sentenced, cumulatively or concurrently, to prison terms totalling 12 months (whether the sentences were handed down on one or more occasion)'.[49] The NSW Council for Civil Liberties warns that three relatively minor non-violent crimes, including such 'trivial crimes' as shoplifting or graffiti, could lead to deportation.[50] (The minister does have the power to revoke a cancellation, but this power is not subject to natural justice or to any kind of legal review.)

The minister also has broad discretion to cancel a visa on 'character grounds' without any criminal conviction. This happened in the case of a New Zealand army veteran decorated with three medals of honour for service in Afghanistan. Former Lance Corporal Ngati Kanohi Te Eke Haapu, known as Ko, moved to Australia after leaving the New Zealand Defence Force in 2012, and took a fly-in, fly-out job in the mining sector. In November 2015 he was detained while visiting a friend at Perth's Casuarina Prison. Ko had his visa revoked and was placed in solitary confinement on the basis that he was a security threat. It has been reported that Ko was arrested because he is a member of the Rebels outlaw motorcycle club, although the Rebels are not a criminal organisation in Western Australia and Immigration Minister Peter Dutton refused to give reasons for revoking his visa. A spokesman would only say that a person fails the character test if the minister 'reasonably suspects that the person has been or is a member of a group or organisation which has been involved in criminal conduct'. The minister can base such suspicions on secret information from the Australian Crime Commission, the Federal Police and other intelligence agencies. As a result, the minister's decision is very hard to challenge.[51]

In a submission to a Senate committee, the Australian National University's Migration Law Program warned that the amendments were blurring the boundaries between criminal law and migration law:

> Having one's visa cancelled for failing the character test because of having a substantial criminal record effectively means permanent banishment from Australia... This serious and life-time immigration consequence of having received a 12-month sentence is disproportionate. It amounts to a secondary punishment on the offender. The sentence imposed by the court is the penalty for the crime. Banishment is a harsher and additional penalty.[52]

The ANU submission argued that the amendments would create situations in which 'the Australian community is being protected, by banishment, from persons who are themselves products of our society'.

Melbourne migration lawyer Carina Ford agrees. 'Do we not have some form of obligation to people who have grown up here?' she asks. Every year Carina's firm represents between 20 and 40 people facing criminal deportation, most of them young New Zealanders. 'If we had the resources we could take on a lot more than that,' she says. Many lack the funds to pay for a lawyer and legal aid is not available in such cases, so Carina often acts pro bono or for a reduced fee. Some of the cases are brought to her attention by prison guards. 'We've had corrections officers bring us files because they think, well, who else is there to help these young guys?' she says.

Carina is not a soft touch. She recognises that, sometimes, criminal deportation is the appropriate sanction. Most of the cases she sees, however, are far from black and white, especially when the offenders have children living in Australia. 'Removing a parent completely from Australia means that relationship is completely gone,' she says. She thinks the knee-jerk response of automatic visa cancellation and deportation for offenders who have grown up in Australia from a young age belies 'a lack of belief in the capacity of the justice and corrections system to rehabilitate'.

For most New Zealanders Carina sees, their original crime was linked to drug and alcohol abuse. 'Many of these young people will grow out of their offending,' she says. 'If they were released in Australia they would have to keep to their parole conditions. In New Zealand those conditions don't apply. They are released without any reporting conditions and no rehabilitation, like drug and alcohol programs, that would have been required in Australia.' (In November 2015, as a matter of urgency, the New Zealand parliament passed legislation enabling the government to monitor criminal deportees as if they had been released on parole from an Australian prison. This followed an information-sharing agreement reached between Australia and New Zealand in September 2015, which should mean that New Zealand authorities receive advance notice of a deportee's criminal history, physical health and mental wellbeing.)

While the Howard government's changes apply to all New Zealanders who arrived in Australia after 2001, the stories that I hear from Vicky Rose, Julius Kuresa and Carina Ford underscore the fact that it is Kiwis of Māori and Pacific Island background who are most likely to be adversely affected.

The New Zealand-born Māori population in Australia grew about 80 per cent in the 10 years to 2013. Around one in six of all Māori live in Australia, including 50,000 Māori living in Queensland—that's more Māori than live in 10 of New Zealand's 16 regions—though it is also important to note that one in three Māori in Australia were born here. These figures come from Dr Tahu Kukutai, senior research fellow at the National Institute for Demographic and Economic Analysis at the University of Waikato. When we meet at her office at the university in Hamilton, Tahu describes how obvious the exodus of Māori is in her 'culturally traditional' hometown of Ngāruawāhia, about 20 minutes' drive away. 'What's been amazing in the last ten years is that there's probably not a single family that hasn't got at least one family member living in Australia,' she says. 'One member will go, and then a cousin will go or a sister will go, then a grandparent will go as well and so you're getting *whānau*, which is the Māori word for family, *whānau* chain migration.' Tahu worries, however, that a lot of Māori pack up and go to Australia without understanding what could happen if they run into problems.

She says Māori in Australia are hit harder by the 2001 changes than Pākehā New Zealanders, because they are less likely to be able to navigate the more restricted path to permanent residency. 'When you look at the occupational structure of Māori in Australia, the vast majority of them are just not going to have the skills that would enable them to get a skilled-migrant visa,' she says. 'So it's not direct discrimination, but it's an indirect and disproportionate disadvantage that Māori will experience.'

Tahu does not think the 2001 changes have deterred Māori migrants from crossing the Tasman or encouraged them to return in large numbers; she thinks people will be drawn to Australia as long as there are jobs available offering higher wages than in New Zealand. 'We also can't overlook the fact that Māori are still very much second-class citizens in New Zealand, as are all Indigenous peoples in developed settler states,' she says. 'There's also a sense of escaping and perhaps liberation that Māori feel. It might not necessarily drive Māori to Australia—I think Māori are going there for economic reasons just like other New Zealanders—but being in Australia, being free from the racial dynamics that still very much prevail in New Zealand, becomes part of the reason for staying. Being a voluntary minority in Australia is different from being an involuntary minority in your homeland.'

Despite the potential social and economic advantages of moving to Australia, Tahu Kukutai is concerned about the vulnerability of New Zealand-born Māori in Australia post-2001. Her research shows that Māori take out Australian citizenship at a much lower rate than any other ancestry group, with the exception of the Japanese. Japanese-Australians are far fewer in number, and their low rates of citizenship are explained by Japan's strict ban on dual citizenship. Māori migrants also have substantially lower rates of citizenship than other New Zealanders—at the 2011 census, only 16.6 per cent of Māori migrants had Australian citizenship, compared to 38 per cent for non-Māori. Significantly, since the 2001 changes narrowed the pathway to permanent residency, the take-up of Australian citizenship has dropped even further among New Zealanders, both Māori and non-Māori.[53]

Tahu Kukutai says that the figures on citizenship 'do not augur well for the future security of New Zealand-born Māori in Australia, nor by association their Australian-born children'. Another New Zealand researcher, Victoria University's Paul Hamer, has described New Zealand-born Māori as 'the most disenfranchised "ethnic" immigrant group in Australia'.[54] He warns that 'there is a significant overhang amongst the New Zealand-born population in Australia of people who do not have a secure footing and could potentially return to New Zealand en masse if the Australian economy worsens'. Vicky Rose puts it in more colourful terms: 'If all of us here in Australia packed up and went home, New Zealand would sink.'

For Vicky Rose and Julius Kuresa, the issues affecting New Zealanders who arrived in Australia after 2001 are personal.

Although his parents and siblings are all New Zealand citizens, Julius holds a Samoan passport. (He was away when the rest of his family applied for citizenship.) Julius is married to a New Zealander and so lives in Australia on another subclass in the bewildering array of temporary visas.

Known as the 461 or New Zealand Citizen Family Relationship (Temporary) visa, Julius's visa permits the close family of New Zealanders who are not New Zealand citizens themselves to live in Australia. Unlike the special category visa, however, the 461 has to be renewed every five years, a process Julius was working his way through when we met in Nerang: filling out forms, organising and paying for medical examinations and police checks, and stumping up the visa charge of $325. Julius's daughter finished school in 2012, but she's not eligible for federal government support to continue her studies. 'She's applied for a personal loan to do a TAFE course that costs thirteen thousand dollars,' he says. Julius's life is in Australia. He has settled, to the extent that he can, but he and his family remain indefinitely temporary.

When Vicky Rose and her then husband left New Zealand in 2007 they were looking for a bit more space. 'You get enveloped in a Pacific Island family, and we left to be just us,' she says. She didn't realise how important the embrace of family could be as a source of support. 'I never understood how much I valued security until I didn't have it,' she reflects ruefully. Some years after she arrived in Australia Vicky's marriage ended, and she is now a single parent providing for two teenage daughters. After she finished school, Vicky's older daughter Jennesia was accepted to do a dual diploma at TAFE, but then Vicky's marriage broke down and she could not afford the fees. Luckily, Jennesia has found a job with a registered training organisation that will put her through the diploma for free. Vicky describes her younger daughter, Gracyn, as 'a little nerd' who is destined to go to university, but she worries that she cannot afford to support her to study in Australia. 'I have a full-time job, but no assets, and rent to pay,' she says.

The chances of Vicky converting to permanent residency seem remote. So after seven years, Vicky Rose, winner of a Queensland Inspiring Woman's Award, is contemplating moving back to New Zealand. She knows the idea will come as a shock to her daughters. 'All their friends are here. My older daughter has a boyfriend here. The thought of going back to New Zealand is just not an option for them.'

When I arrived at the Nerang Community Centre to meet Vicky the sun was shining down from a cloudless blue sky. As I drive away, a threatening mass of battleship-grey thunderheads has gathered, and it is clear we are in for a deluge. I reflect on how quickly bright prospects can darken, and how vulnerable people can be to unexpected change when they lack the shelter of a permanent visa.

6 | Fear in the Family
Australia's Conflicted Relationship with New Zealanders

In February 2011, when prime minister Julia Gillard became the first foreign leader to address the New Zealand parliament, she said, 'Australia has many alliances and friendships around the world, economic and defence partnerships of every kind; but New Zealand alone is family.'[1] A week later, when an earthquake destroyed Christchurch, Gillard reaffirmed that view: 'Today our family are suffering a very devastating blow.'[2] Soon after taking office in late 2013, prime minister Tony Abbott echoed his predecessor's sentiments, telling his New Zealand counterpart John Key that 'New Zealand is family in a way that no other country on Earth is'.[3] In October 2015, newly installed Prime Minister Malcolm Turnbull chose New Zealand as the destination for his first overseas trip and declared: 'We are in every respect family.'[4]

So if New Zealanders are family, why is our embrace half-hearted? We count New Zealand-made programs as Australian content under television quota rules, but deny support to New Zealand children with a disability, even when they've grown up here. We happily accept the taxes Kiwis pay, but deny them essential government help in times of need. We allow any New Zealander to live in Australia indefinitely, but only allow a select group to become full members of the political community. Without citizenship, New Zealand-born Australians cannot vote, run for office, sit on juries, work for the federal public service or join the defence force.

Part of the explanation is fear, although there seems to be persistent confusion about the exact nature of the threat. Sometimes the core problem has appeared to be that New Zealanders work too hard, and so threaten to 'steal Aussie jobs'; at other times the fear is that New Zealanders are too lazy, and threaten to sponge off the generous and unwitting Australian taxpayer. Both myths—of job-thieving Kiwis and Bondi bludgers—have roots that reach decades into the past.

From the mid-1980s until the early 1990s, there was a strong current of concern that New Zealanders were displacing locals in the labour market. The wool industry came in for particular scrutiny, with the Australian Workers' Union claiming in 1992 that more than 40 per cent of the Australian clip was being shorn by New Zealanders, while half of all Australian shearers were out of a job. 'How are we supposed to find work when our government encourages outsiders to come and take it from us?' complained the union in a press release.[5]

In that same year, Labor backbencher Clyde Holding (who had briefly been immigration minister) circulated a paper in federal caucus which argued that New Zealanders were 'over-represented' in the Australian workforce and holding down 'close to 190,000 jobs...

which in almost all instances can be performed by Australians'. (He also noted that New Zealanders were 'over-represented in road fatalities in Australia'.) Holding wanted the government to 'crack down' so that New Zealanders would 'go back to work in New Zealand' and leave 'jobs in Australia for Australians'.[6]

Yet at the same time as they were forcing Australians into dole queues by stealing jobs, New Zealanders were also, evidently, not working hard enough, but instead making wanton use of Australia's welfare system. In 1986, Liberal MP and future foreign minister Alexander Downer used his position on an opposition waste-watch committee to claim that pregnant single New Zealand women were coming to Australia to give birth to their children so that they could get access to the supporting parents benefit. He alleged that they would then return to New Zealand to live on the proceeds. Then social-security minister Brian Howe debunked Downer's claims as a beat-up, pointing out that they defied logic, since at the time New Zealand offered single mothers more generous benefits than those available in Australia.[7]

In 1988, Brisbane's *Sunday Sun* reported on a Liberal Party survey that found that hostility towards Kiwi dole bludgers 'romped in' as the issue of greatest concern to Queensland voters. In November that year, in a live interview from Bondi Beach broadcast on breakfast television, comedian Vince Sorenti joked, 'to all you New Zealanders, there are only twenty-seven shoplifting days left to Christmas'. In 1989, in an aside in parliament, Labor finance minister Senator Peter Walsh accused New Zealand of exporting its unemployment problem to Australia.

The immigration minister at the time, Robert Ray, issued a media release urging his compatriots to 'show Kiwis some respect' and pointing out that, far from being a collective burden on the taxpayer, New Zealanders in Australia were generally 'young, mobile and working'.[8] In Archives New Zealand in Wellington, I came across a 1989 file note in which the New Zealand High Commission guestimated that for every dollar in unemployment benefits paid to New Zealand citizens, the Australian government received more than $10 in tax revenues from New Zealanders who were working.[9]

A similar calculation made today would almost certainly put the Australian government even further ahead, since Kiwis who arrived after 2001 are denied access to most government benefits. Besides, Australian Bureau of Statistics data reveals that New Zealand-born residents are far more likely to be working, and working full time, than the Australian population in general.[10] The age profile of the New Zealanders in Australia also means that there are fewer Kiwis aged under 18 or over 60 than in the population as a whole, so even if New Zealanders were granted access to welfare, it is likely that they would remain net contributors to government revenues overall.[11]

Still the myth of the Bondi bludger refuses to die. In the quiet news week after Christmas 2013, mastheads from the Murdoch stable conveniently rediscovered the pressing threat posed to Australia by people crossing the Tasman. The headlines varied from paper to paper. The *NT News* was concerned about welfare rip-offs: 'Kiwi Layabouts Are Flooding In' it screamed.[12] The *Australian* focused more on the integrity of our borders. It warned of an immigration 'back door'.[13] Beneath the arguably more sober title 'New Zealand Migration to Australia Soars 40 Per Cent', News Corp's online version of the story led with 'Jobless Kiwis are flocking to Australia in search of work—and demanding the dole.'[14]

Tabloid treatment of the issue in the papers inevitably resurfaced on tabloid television. On 13 January 2014, Nine's *A Current Affair* picked up the story. 'They're coming to Australia for our jobs,' ran the teaser. 'Now they're fighting en masse to rewrite our welfare rules. Should you pay so they can stay?'[15]

To be fair, the newspaper pieces and the story on *A Current Affair* also raised concerns about the difficulties faced by many New Zealanders who arrived after 2001, but the dominant message was this: New Zealanders are arriving in record numbers (*A Current Affair* called it 'the Kiwi invasion'), taking jobs and seeking welfare benefits to boot. What is more, a significant proportion of them were not even born in New Zealand, but originally hail from Pacific Island nations and countries in Asia.

This is the 'back door' referred to by the *Australian*'s headline, which often serves as a veiled concern about race. The language is more circumspect, but there are definite echoes from 1971 and immigration minister Jim Forbes' concerns that New Zealanders of Pacific Islander background were 'unsophisticated' and 'quite unsuited to settlement in Australia'.[16]

In a journal article written as the 2001 changes were being implemented, Monash University researchers Bob Birrell and Virginia Rapson argued that while in 'official rhetoric' the sole motive for the policy shift was 'to limit Australia's responsibilities for paying social-security benefits to New Zealand citizens', other important motives were involved, 'notably the Australian Government's desire to limit the influx of people who would not meet the standards set by the official migration program'.[17]

Historian Paul Hamer offers a blunter conclusion. He argues

that there is 'good cause' to believe that one of the reasons Australia has sought to curtail the rights of New Zealanders here is 'Australian dissatisfaction with New Zealand's more liberal rules of entry' for Pacific Islanders.[18] This view was confirmed in my conversations in Wellington with New Zealand government officials who were involved in negotiations with Australia in the lead-up to the 2001 changes, or who have dealt with the fallout since.

At one level, Australia *was* pressuring New Zealand to contribute more to the benefits paid to New Zealand citizens living across the Tasman. Former foreign minister Phil Goff recalls prime minister John Howard 'saying quite clearly' that he expected New Zealand to 'to pick up a welfare bill…that might have amounted to one billion dollars'. But as Goff points out, New Zealanders were also paying taxes. The New Zealand Ministry of Foreign Affairs and Trade estimated that Australia's welfare outlays were more than counter-balanced by $2.5 billion in taxes paid by Kiwis.[19] Another economic study calculated that Australia got a net fiscal benefit of $3,000 for every New Zealander resident in the country.[20] Goff says that New Zealand pointed out to John Howard 'that it was patently unfair' for Australia to benefit from the taxes paid by New Zealanders, and the skills and qualifications they brought with them across the Tasman, and then to expect New Zealand to pick up the tab for income support that people occasionally need if they lose their job or get sick or suffer a marriage breakdown. 'If you get the benefit of their taxation, then you've got to also respond by giving them the same sort of treatment that any other long-term resident in Australia would get,' he told me.

Apart from this point of principle, and the desire to limit budget outlays, New Zealand's Labour government also had domestic political reasons to refuse to pay more. At the height of the negotiations, prime minister Helen Clark bluntly told journalists that New Zealanders in Australia 'would not get a bean' from Wellington.[21] While Australian politicians exploited the myth of the Bondi bludger, their New Zealand counterparts portrayed a move to Australia as unpatriotic. 'Why on earth would we pay money to people who are turning their backs and leaving the country?' Clark asked. She was connecting to a populist tradition stretching back at least as far as Robert 'Piggy' Muldoon (National Party prime minister from 1975 to 1984), who famously joked that New Zealanders moving to Australia raise the IQ of both countries.

The exodus to Oz is also a sensitive political issue in New Zealand because it is used as a rough barometer of economic competence. Whenever departures to Australia rise, the party in opposition will claim that New Zealanders are leaving in droves because the government has stuffed up the economy. So in 2001 the Clark government had good political reasons to publicly discourage emigration from New Zealand. Nevertheless, the final decision to restrict the welfare entitlements of New Zealanders in Australia from 2001 onwards was not the result of a bilateral accord, as it is often portrayed, particularly as the current Prime Minister John Key likes to blame his Labour predecessor for selling out New Zealanders in the negotiations. 'We did not agree to Australia imposing discriminatory measures against New Zealanders,' says former foreign minister Phil Goff, adamantly.

A reciprocal agreement was reached on sharing the cost of pensions based on the years worked and the tax paid in each country. For humanitarian reasons, provision was also made for benefits for people with severe disabilities. Beyond this, New Zealand refused to pay a bean. Goff says the Clark government acknowledged, however, that it was 'up to each country to make its own decisions' about access to its welfare benefits.

When the Howard government restricted welfare access for New Zealanders in Australia, the Clark government initially considered a tit-for-tat response of cutting the entitlements of Australians living in New Zealand. Ultimately it rejected the idea. As one government official in Wellington put it to me, New Zealand feared that putting too much pressure on Australia could backfire and threaten the Trans-Tasman Travel Arrangement—'the fundamental base on which other policies rest'. Since free movement is of greater importance to New Zealand than to Australia, Wellington will not do anything to put those arrangements at risk. As another official commented, New Zealand is 'a bit of a supplicant in the relationship'. Phil Goff has a different take—he says retaliation did not stack up. Australians in New Zealand 'are working hard, they are making a contribution, they are good citizens, why wouldn't we treat them equally?' he asks.

I met Phil Goff, who is still a New Zealand Labour MP, in his electorate in Auckland. His office is located above a tattoo parlour, the Three Kings Automotive garage and a bedding shop. I arrived early, so I strolled around the local shopping centre and ate lunch in the 'Bombay Chinese Indian' takeaway across the road. I was struck by the cultural diversity of the suburb—the preponderance of Chinese, Indian, Māori and Pacific Islander ancestry evident in face and dress. When I remarked on this to Phil Goff, he said he estimated that about half the population in his electorate had an Asian background and that at least 15 per cent were 'Pasifika' (the term used in New Zealand to refer to people of Pacific Island heritage). This was not the New Zealand of the mainstream (white) Australian imagining, nor,

I suspect, is it the New Zealand that Julia Gillard and Tony Abbott have in mind when they talk about New Zealanders as 'family'.

In questions about ethnicity in the 2013 New Zealand census, 15 per cent of the population identified as Māori, 12 per cent as Asian and seven per cent as Pacific peoples. (People can identify with more than one ethnicity.) Pacific, Māori and Asian New Zealanders are on average much younger than European New Zealanders—the median age for Europeans is 41, compared to 31 for Asian, 24 for Māori and 22 for Pacific peoples.[22] The 2013 census also revealed that more than a million people—a quarter of the people living in New Zealand—were born overseas, and that they are now more likely to hail from countries in Asia than from the United Kingdom and Ireland.[23]

New Zealand is not only a country of large-scale immigration, but also a country of large-scale emigration. Since 2013, improved economic conditions have resulted in the number of long-term and permanent arrivals significantly exceeding the number of long-term and permanent departures, with New Zealand's annual net gain of migrants hitting new records.[24] In earlier years, however, the gap between the two was often quite small and sometimes departures exceeded arrivals.[25] In such circumstances, it is hardly surprising that a growing proportion of the New Zealand citizens coming to Australia were not born in New Zealand.

Yet in the late 1990s, Australian government officials became alarmed at the increasing amount of such 'third country' movement, as the share of 'non-natives' in the flow of New Zealand migrants to Australia climbed from 24 per cent in 1995–96 to 30 per cent in 1999–2000. In late 2000, immigration minister Philip Ruddock, spurred on by the Labor spokesman on population, Martin Ferguson, released figures showing that the number of New Zealand citizens not born in New Zealand migrating to Australia had increased tenfold, from 958 in 1990 to 9,744 in 1999. Mr Ruddock said Australians would be 'uncomfortable' about migrants entering the country via New Zealand when they would not have met the selection criteria if they had applied directly to Australia.[26]

This is the 'back-door' migration referred to by the *Australian*. Birrell and Rapson call it 'third country movement' and say that it made Australia 'hostage to the vagaries of the New Zealand immigration selection system'.[27] They weren't the only academics to surmise that this was the substantive issue lurking behind the publicly canvassed issue of welfare payments when Australia changed its policy towards New Zealanders in 2001. As another group of researchers put it, the Australian government was concerned not so much 'with the volume of immigration' from New Zealand as with 'the mix of people who were entering…especially Pacific Islanders, people from countries in Asia, and refugees accepted by New Zealand from Africa and the Middle East'.[28]

Several contemporary factors influenced these concerns, but when I did some digging around in Archives New Zealand in Wellington, I found indications that they have a longer history.

Firstly, there was a view in the 1990s that New Zealand's business- and skilled-migration rules were much more lax than Australia's, with particular concern about the suitability of migrants entering New Zealand from Hong Kong. Such concerns were not new. In July 1988, the acting head of Australia's Department of Immigration, Local Government and Ethnic Affairs, Tony Harris, raised the issue with New Zealand's deputy high commissioner to Australia, Priscilla Williams. She summarised the conversation in a file note:

> Australian immigration officials in Hong Kong report that they have had comments from Hong Kong Chinese to the effect that it does not matter whether or not Australia turns them down for business migration because they can easily obtain entry to New Zealand and can, from there, cross the Tasman. The Australians' concern in this area seems to be based on rather shaky ground. First we would presumably screen out undesirables and only take those who would be valid nominees under our business migration policy… Secondly, such people cannot cross the Tasman readily until they are New Zealand citizens, which involves a minimum of three years 'good behaviour'…I told Harris I was surprised there should be concern on this point.[29]

The same issue arose in another guise four years later, when New Zealand was considering offering visa-free entry to tourists from Hong Kong and Taiwan. In May 1992, Australia's high commissioner in Wellington forwarded a letter from immigration minister Gerry Hand to his New Zealand counterpart, Bill Birch. In the letter, Hand linked the visa question with the debate in Australia about the New Zealand shearers, who were allegedly stealing Australian jobs. (It should be noted that a significant proportion of those New Zealand shearers were Māori.) Hand also indicated that he was more than willing to use the threat of revoking the Trans-Tasman Travel Arrangement as a political lever:

> As you will appreciate, the business of Government frequently links somewhat disparate issues. I would be less than frank if I did not therefore refer to the situation the Australian government is currently confronted with in relation to New Zealand shearers. There are very strong

pressures to apply some form of controls on New Zealand shearers. This is bringing into question in some quarters the whole question of trans-Tasman movements. Against this background, I could not predict the reactions on this side to what might be perceived as a further opening of New Zealand's borders.[30]

Gerry Hand was the Labor immigration minister who first conceived of and implemented the policy of mandatory, indefinite detention of asylum seekers coming to Australia by boat. He was grappling at the time with the so-called 'second wave' of boat arrivals—15 boats that made it to Australian territory between 1989 and 1992 carrying a total of 654 mostly Indochinese asylum seekers.[31] Hand was apparently worried that if New Zealand granted 'visa-free' entry to visitors from Taiwan and Hong Kong then this could produce another kind of refugee 'crisis'. The deputy secretary of his department, Wayne Gibbons, conveyed the minister's concerns to the New Zealand High Commission. Again, there was a veiled threat to the future of the Trans-Tasman Travel Arrangement, with a warning that 'the linkage between the current shearers/TTTA problem and the visa-free proposal could become public in a way which would be embarrassing…' According to a High Commission record of the meeting, Gibbons complained that New Zealand 'did not understand the problems which Australia already confronts (with 23,000 illegal arrivals each year who claim refugee status)'.[32] The New Zealand officials questioned the relevance of this linkage, pointing out that short-term visitors from Taiwan and Hong Kong would not be able to cross the ditch under the Trans-Tasman Travel Arrangement. But Gibbons insisted that New Zealand could still be used as a 'back door…for illegal immigrants':

> ...he outlined his scenario that NZ would inevitably be deluged with Chinese nationals on false (probably Taiwanese) passports if we were to eliminate the visa requirement. On arrival they could claim refugee status under the UN Convention in such numbers that our ability to process claims would be overwhelmed. The likely outcome would be an amnesty and granting of NZ citizenship opening the way for this group to then move to Australia.[33]

The unnamed author of the memo comments dryly: 'We found Gibbons' assertions somewhat colourful'.

Alongside 'back-door' migration from northeast Asia, Australia was also concerned about 'back-door' migration from the Pacific. Since 1970, New Zealand has had an annual quota for migration from its former colony of Western Samoa, which allows up to 1,100 Samoans to be granted permanent residence in New Zealand (above and beyond any Samoans who might move to New Zealand through other migration channels). The people of the Cook Islands (population 20,000), Tokelau (population 1,400) and Niue (population 1,600) are automatically entitled to New Zealand citizenship. Former New Zealand immigration minister Anthony 'Aussie' Malcolm recalls that during his stint in government (between 1977 and 1984), his Australian counterparts were troubled by these links. They 'would tell him, informally, that they had no problem with white New Zealanders settling in Australia, but that Māori and Polynesians represented a significant problem to them'.[34] Aussie Malcolm (who was born in Australia) told Paul Hamer:

> They had...a stereotype in their head that a Kiwi was a white guy like an Aussie. And when New Zealand started producing these Polynesians, who weren't like Aussies,

but who were New Zealanders, that rattled them. No two
ways about it.[35]

In 2000, New Zealand announced an amnesty for visa overstayers, enabling about 7,000 people—about half of them originally from Tonga and Samoa—to regularise their status and obtain two-year work permits as a stepping stone to permanent residency. Applicants had to be 'well settled' to qualify—which meant they had to have been living in New Zealand for five years or more, be in a genuine stable relationship of at least two years' standing with a New Zealand citizen or permanent resident or be the parent of a New Zealand-born child.[36] Australia's immigration minister Philip Ruddock publicly criticised the amnesty, saying it would allow back-door entry to Australia by people who have broken immigration law in another country.[37] As a New Zealand immigration official recalls, 'The Australian government was very pissed off.'

At the time, Ruddock rejected suggestions that his concerns had anything to do with race, but again, there is a longer history of Australian anxiety about 'back-door' migration from the Pacific Islands in general, and Samoa in particular. A New Zealand High Commission file note from August 1989 records a discussion with Philip Ruddock when he was shadow immigration minister. The note says Ruddock 'inquired about immigration into NZ from the South Pacific' and noted that there had been a lot of violent incidents in his electorate involving 'Samoans'.[38]

A year earlier, in a memo summarising talks with their Australian counterparts, New Zealand immigration officials noted:

> The one area in which some officials may have concerns
> for the future, although they are very cautious and

sensitive in discussing it, relates to the special quota from Western Samoa. They were asking questions about the sort of person we were getting and we explained that while we were not selecting people for their skills we did take only good quality people who were making a good contribution to NZ.[39]

Again, New Zealand officials found Australia's concerns about 'back-door' Pacific migration to be poorly based. For a start, the numbers are small. Of the 600,000 New Zealanders present in Australia in June 2011, only about 21,000, or 3.5 per cent, were born in Pacific Island nations. Secondly, as New Zealand officials explained to me in Wellington, the Samoan quota does not mean open-door access. Primary applicants must speak English, be aged between 18 and 45, and satisfy health and character checks to qualify. They must also have the offer of a job in New Zealand, which will pay a salary adequate to support themselves and their dependents. (The cap of 1,100 visas includes accompanying family members.[40]) The same rules apply to the Pacific Access Category, which was introduced in 2002 and which offers 75 residence visas to citizens of both Kiribati and Tuvalu and 250 residence visas to citizens of Tonga.[41] They must become New Zealand citizens before they can migrate to Australia under the Trans-Tasman Travel Arrangement, which now requires five years 'good behaviour' in New Zealand.

It seems perverse that politicians and immigration officials in Australia, a country where more than a quarter of the population is born overseas, should be so concerned about 'back-door' or 'third country' migration via New Zealand. It should be publicly offensive—reflective of a 'we grew here, you flew here'-type racism—to suggest that an Australian who swore an oath of citizenship as a migrant somehow had a lesser or more dubious standing than someone who just happened to be born with that status. Yet this double standard often hides behind the 'back-door' migration argument, which seems to be based on an archaic (or perhaps always mistaken) notion of what New Zealand is and who New Zealanders are. The widespread assumption that Pacific Islander migrants to Australia have used New Zealand as a stepping stone is in most cases likely to be simply wrong, since about two thirds of New Zealand's 'Pacific peoples' are New Zealand-born.[42]

When the legislation to restrict welfare access for New Zealanders passed the Australian parliament in 2001, only one MP, Democrats Senator Andrew Bartlett, raised significant concerns, noting that changes could leave some New Zealanders worse off than migrants from other countries.[43] He foresaw, for example, that a woman who left an abusive relationship could find herself stranded. Bartlett warned his fellow senators that a 'woman in that circumstance will not qualify for any income support',[44] foreshadowing a scenario that has today become a reality for community workers who are left to pick up the pieces, like Vicky Rose and Julius Kuresa at the Nerang Neighbourhood Centre in the Gold Coast hinterland.

Bartlett pointed out that the bill would 'ensure that people who live, work, pay taxes and raise children in Australia will never be entitled to social-security income support because they were born in New Zealand, unless they take the previously unnecessary step of obtaining permanent residence'. They would be unlikely to do this, he argued, because apart from the change to social-security law 'there is no need or purpose for them to do so'.[45]

The senator did not quite see the whole issue: it was not just a question of whether or not New Zealanders would *have reason* to take out permanent residence, but whether they would *be able* to do so, since the new regime made this much more difficult for them. There are no qualification requirements for New Zealanders to enter the Australian workforce, but if Kiwis aspire to become permanent residents then they must jump through the same skilled-migration hoops as entrants from other countries (unless they can access the limited 'new pathway' announced by Malcolm Turnbull in early 2016). If New Zealanders are on low incomes and do not have a profession that is in short supply—if they are bus drivers or cleaners, for example—then they are highly unlikely ever to become residents. If they are over 50, they will almost certainly be considered too old to ever become Australian. If they are in casual work, then there is no chance of getting employer sponsorship for their migration application. Long-term employers have little incentive to sponsor New Zealanders either, since they can stay indefinitely and so there is no risk of losing that worker because their visa expires. As a result, New Zealanders like the young Māori guy who built our fence will not only be denied access to government benefits, but will never be able to vote or stand for election.

In 2001, as New Zealand's foreign minister, Phil Goff publicly expressed his doubts 'about the fairness of the situation for future taxpaying Kiwi migrants who lack permanent residence in Australia'. Goff presciently suggested that this was 'something Australia may find it has to grapple with further down the track'.[46] As the numbers have swelled, the inequity that Goff warned about has become ever more apparent. Federal government bureaucrats realise it is an issue that cannot be ignored forever. We know from documents released under freedom of information that in 2009–10 considerable effort was put into an interdepartmental 'thought paper' investigating the possibility of creating a 'pathway' to permanent residency for New Zealanders, outside the existing options already available under the migration program.[47]

In August 2013, David Drummond, the public servant who oversaw that work, told a meeting organised by Oz Kiwi that they had been considering 'a time-based visa—so that anyone who had been in Australia for a certain period of time would qualify' for permanent residency.[48] New Zealand Prime Minister John Key publicly suggested eight years' residence in Australia as an appropriate threshold. Creating a pathway to permanent residency (and ultimately citizenship) was one of the recommendations put forward in the joint report on the trans-Tasman relationship published by the Australian and New Zealand Productivity Commissions in 2012. The idea was dismissed in the joint response to the report from the Australian and New Zealand governments, which stated curtly that it is 'not expected that existing arrangements will be changed in the near future'.[49] Hopes among New Zealanders that the issue might be put on the table in February 2013 as part of the annual leaders' meeting between prime ministers Julia Gillard and John Key were dashed. In his stint as prime minister, Tony Abbott dismissed any discussion of changes, despite early post-election speculation that his New Zealand-born wife, Margie, might influence his views on the question.[50]

Then in February 2016, after a trans-Tasman meeting in Sydney, prime ministers Malcolm Turnbull and John Key announced 'a new pathway' to citizenship for New Zealanders who had lived in Australia for at least five years. The move caught everyone by surprise, and at first blush it looked promising. At last there was some official recognition of the inadvertent trap created by the combination of the 2001 changes and the Trans-Tasman Travel Arrangement—a situation that condemned New Zealanders to live in Australia 'in a particular category that hasn't allowed them to become Australian citizens', as John Key put it at his joint media conference with Malcolm Turnbull.[51]

The fine print of the deal revealed, however, that far from offering a comprehensive fix to a messy and unfair area of migration policy, Turnbull had added yet new layers of complexity and discrimination. From July 2017, New Zealanders wanting to become permanent residents will no longer have to jump over the same hurdles as other migrants by proving that they have a qualification listed as a skilled occupation in demand in the Australian labour market, or by finding an employer to sponsor them for an ongoing skilled job. Instead, they can gain permanent residence if they can demonstrate that they have paid tax on an annual income of at least $53,900 for the previous five years. The sum is based on the TSMIT, or Temporary Skilled Migration Income Threshold, which is the legislative instrument used to set the minimum salary that can be paid to a temporary migrant worker on a 457 visa.

While this sum is significantly lower than average annual full-time earnings in Australia (around $78,000), it is much higher than the minimum full-time wage (around $34,000). The 'occupation matrix' in the Department of Employment's annual overview of the labour market, *Australian Jobs 2015*, shows that the median full-time salary for many occupations falls below the TSMIT of $53,900.[52] A quick scan of just the job headings from A to C reveals that New Zealanders who work as bakers, bar attendants, baristas, beauty therapists, bricklayers, cafe workers, car detailers, care workers (in child, aged, disability, personal or nursing care), checkout operators, cleaners, clothing-trade workers and cooks may all struggle to meet the required salary threshold for Turnbull's new path to residency.

In other words, a taxable income of $53,900 per year for five years is a threshold that many Kiwis will fail to cross, particularly if they are in casual or part-time work, or if they have had any time out of the labour force due to ill-health or temporary unemployment. What the new policy does is penalise New Zealanders engaged in low-paid or precarious work and those who do not work full time, usually women caring for family members. The immigration department says that it may vary the income requirement when a person falls below the income threshold because they were on parental leave after the birth of a child and that it will consider 'limited exemptions' for particularly vulnerable New Zealanders.[53] (The sort of case that might fit such an exemption is a mother who has primary care of her children, but who cannot take them home to New Zealand because of a court order requiring that they have access to her estranged partner in Australia.)

In general, those who don't earn enough to walk down the new pathway to permanent residence are more likely to be of Māori or Pacific Islander heritage than Pākehā. An analysis of the 2011 Australian census by University of Waikato researchers Tahu Kukutai and Shefali Pawar shows, for example, that less than half the New Zealand-born Māori in Australia of 'prime working age' (between 25 and 54 years of age) had successfully completed year 12.[54] These are markedly lower figures than for Australian-born Māori or New Zealand-born non-Māori. Since education levels are correlated with earnings, they are also more likely to be on low incomes. The labour-market participation rate of New Zealand-born Māori is high—for

Māori men, the employment rate was nearly three per cent higher than the Australian average—yet Māori are disproportionately concentrated in lower-skilled jobs, with four out of 10 working as labourers, machinery operators or drivers.[55] The intent of the new visa pathway may not be discriminatory, but its effect almost certainly will be.

The health requirements will exclude people with a disability or chronic illness. In its report on the Turnbull–Key announcement, New Zealand's *One News* profiled Sydney Kiwi couple Kirk and Angela Bensemann, whose seven-year-old Australian-born son Toby has been diagnosed with autism.[56] Although they have lived and worked in Australia since 2007 and meet the $53,900 earnings threshold, the Bensemanns anticipate that their son's disability will render them ineligible for permanent residence on health grounds.

The immigration department says that the additional visa pathway to permanent residence is for New Zealanders who have 'shown a commitment and contribution to Australia'.[57] The implication of this statement is that child-care workers or single parents who work part time and earn less than $53,900 per year, or families like the Bensemanns with a disabled child, are somehow lacking in commitment to Australia or failing to make a contribution to the nation.

In an email exchange after the Turnbull–Key announcement, Vicky Rose from the Nerang Community Centre described it as 'a token gesture and still sends the message that Australia only wants "the performers" and those that will continue to "perform" down the track'. Vicky told me that she could pass the income threshold, but fears she would stumble on the health criteria due to a medical condition. As a result, she probably will not even apply, because she does not want to risk thousands of dollars in fees only to get rejected. 'I cannot afford to throw $6,000 away like that,' she wrote.

The visa application charge under the new pathway is $3,800 for the primary applicant, plus an additional $1,800 for a partner and for each dependent child aged over 18, and an extra $900 for children aged under 18. (So the charge for Vicky and her two daughters would be $6,500.) These significant sums are another barrier to New Zealanders becoming Australian citizens.

Age may also prevent New Zealanders accessing the new visa pathway. There is no mention of age limits in the information so far released by the immigration department, but it does say that the pathway 'will be made available within the Skilled Independent category of the General Skilled Migration (GSM) stream of Australia's annual Migration Programme'. Under current rules, any applicant for skilled independent migration (visa subclass 189) must be under 50 years of age.

Curiously, the new pathway has been limited to those who were already living in Australia at the time of the announcement on 19 February 2016. Turnbull says that New Zealanders who arrive in the future who 'wish to become Australian citizens, have got many other visa categories to use'.[58] Put plainly, this means that future settlers from New Zealand will be subject to the same rules that have applied since 2001 and so will risk being caught in the same trap identified by John Key as the source of the problem Turnbull was supposedly seeking to address: they will be living in Australia 'in a particular category' that does not allow them 'to become Australian citizens'.[59]

Key anticipates that up to 100,000 New Zealanders living in Australia could benefit from the new visa pathway;[60] the Department of Immigration and Border Protection offers a more sober estimate of 60,000 to 70,000 people.⁶¹ Even if Key's more optimistic prediction is correct, this means that more than half of all New Zealanders currently living here will still be indefinitely temporary and not quite Australian.

Australia's approach perplexes Phil Goff. He thinks that denying New Zealand migrants 'a fair go' not only damages them, but also damages Australia. 'It's not in the interests of Australia to have a subclass of people who don't have equal opportunity and the chance to make the most of their lives and to make the best contribution they can to Australia,' he told me during our Auckland meeting. 'I would have thought that was self-evident, but apparently not to a generation of Australian politicians, who have kind of pretended that New Zealanders are guest workers; they come to Australia for a while and they go back home.'

One potential response to Phil Goff—and to others who demand a better deal for New Zealanders in Australia—is to argue that we should get rid of the Trans-Tasman Travel Arrangement altogether. In his lobbying against New Zealanders in the early 1990s, Labor MP Clyde Holding called it 'an anachronistic hangover'. He was right in the sense that Australia's 'special' relationship with New Zealand has its roots in the days of Empire. As the Department of Foreign Affairs and Trade points out on its website, the indefinite right to live and work in Australia 'is a benefit not conferred on any other nation'.⁶² It is without doubt a discriminatory policy, and the people of other countries, particularly a former Australian colony like Papua New Guinea, might reasonably argue: if them, then why not us, too? But migration policy is never drafted on a clean slate; it is overwritten on the accretions of the past, both the historic injustices and biases of the White Australia policy and the economic, personal, social and cultural ties that have built up over time. Cancelling the Trans-Tasman Travel Arrangement would cause major disruption and seems unlikely to happen, particularly given the mutual commitment by governments in Canberra and Wellington to creating a single economic market. 'There are industries here that would collapse if all the New Zealanders went home,' says Vicky Rose bluntly.

In the end, the push to further integrate New Zealand and Australia economically is incompatible with the continued denial of core entitlements and rights for long-term migrants from across the Tasman.

In 2001, the public justification for changing the status of New Zealanders was a desire to reduce welfare expenditure. It is axiomatic that this goal will have been realised, though the cost savings involved would be modest. Figures mentioned at the time of the changes were in the order of $100 million per year.[63] Since New Zealanders, like other permanent migrants, were already required to wait two years in order to qualify for working-age benefits, the idea that they were attracted to Australia by a welfare honey pot was a myth. Those who chose to come and to stay would have been largely self-reliant. Of course, it is possible that the changes meant that New Zealanders did return home in greater numbers when they fell on hard times—but it is hard to find evidence that this has been the case.

When the planned change to social-security entitlements was first revealed in October 2000, it did appear to generate a 'substantial spike' in travel from New Zealand to Australia, as people tried to get in before their access to welfare was curtailed.[64] This 'artificially high' level of movement was followed by a sharp drop in numbers, because potential migrants had brought their plans forward.[65] In subsequent years, migration from New Zealand to Australia first returned to, and then surpassed, its previous levels, before declining again recently. Australia's welfare settings are far less influential in migration decisions than other factors, like job opportunities, levels of pay and exchange rates.

The other objective of the changes—less spoken about but extending back through time in bilateral negotiations over trans-Tasman travel—was to 'place obstacles in the way of…less skilled movers from New Zealand', including 'third country' migrants from Northeast Asia, the Pacific and elsewhere.[66] It is hard to assess whether or not this aim has been realised, but it seems unlikely. Between 2006 and 2011, 24 per cent of the New Zealand citizens moving to Australia were born outside New Zealand—down from the 30 per cent that alarmed Australian officials in 1999–2000, but still a significant proportion.[67] The rationale for restricting 'back-door' migration, if there ever was one, has in any case disappeared, since, with the exception of the small Samoan and Pacific Access categories, New Zealand is just as tough in its selection of migrants as Australia.

So rather than deter migration by certain categories of New Zealanders—whether potential welfare recipients or 'back-door' migrants—the 2001 changes have instead created new inequities that affect all New Zealanders in Australia, making their lives more precarious because they are more vulnerable to the vagaries of existence, like illness, relationship breakdown, accident and unemployment. Malcolm Turnbull's new pathway will benefit a specific cohort of New Zealanders on relatively comfortable incomes who were already living in Australia on 19 February 2016—but it will be of no assistance to low-income earners or to those who move to Australia after that date.

Nor does it alter the underlying realities that could turn the undercurrent of concern about Pacific Islanders and Māori into a self-fulfilling prophecy—in the sense that a generation of New Zealand citizens raised in Australia feel disenfranchised and disconnected as their life prospects are curtailed. 'This is not a cultural issue, it's a socio-economic problem,' says Julius Kuresa of the Nerang Neighbourhood Centre. 'There is an underclass developing. Something's gotta change one way or another, either by giving New Zealanders residency rights or by limiting their numbers.'

I am surprised that he even raises the prospect of a cap or quota for New Zealand entry to Australia—and even more surprised when his boss, Vicky Rose, also canvasses the idea: 'What the Australian government has done so far is half-arsed and it's creating an underclass,' she says. 'Australia needs to swing either one way or the other.' By this, Vicky means that Australia must either take the 'risk' of offering all New Zealanders a pathway to permanency, or give up the benefits that flow from maintaining free trans-Tasman travel.

'Perhaps,' she says, 'Australia has to man up and say to Kiwis, "you know what, you're not family after all".'

7 | Asylum Seekers and Refugees
Temporary Protection, Permanent Rejection

Sherene* is staring down at her lap and winding the strap of her bright orange handbag round and round one hand as she listens to the lawyer. She is hearing everything he says twice. First in English, a language she has learned to speak with remarkable fluency after just three years in Australia, then again in her native tongue, Hazaragi, a minority language of Afghanistan, as the translator interprets for her mother, Sima.

By rights Sherene should be in school, sitting a test and preparing for her final year 11 exams. Instead, she has accompanied her mother to this essential but ultimately devastating meeting at the community-based Refugee and Immigration Legal Centre (or Refugee Legal).

---

* The names of Sherene and other members of her family have been changed to protect their privacy.

In the waiting room a few minutes earlier, Sherene was telling me how much she misses the kebabs her father, Ali, makes and excitedly anticipating the huge feast he will prepare for our families to share when he is finally able to join them in Australia. Now the country's leading refugee lawyer, Refugee Legal's principal solicitor David Manne, is spelling out the brutal reality: there is no way that they can bring Ali to Melbourne—at least not until government policy changes. 'The law is very clear,' he tells Sima. 'Your husband can't come to Australia.'

Sima whispers 'very bad, very bad' and wipes a tear from the corner of her eye. Sherene's head sinks lower, anxious hands contorting her bag strap with increased intensity—winding and unwinding, folding and unfolding. The rest of Sherene's body is perfectly still and I sense that she is controlling her frustration. Lively, inquiring, intelligent and opinionated, Sherene wants to engage David directly in English, to argue with him, ask why, explore other possibilities. David has insisted, properly, that Sherene speak only through the translator, so that he can be sure that Sima, who is the family's primary applicant for refugee status, also understands everything that is being said.

It is a heartbreaking two hours. David knows that he must be absolutely, clinically honest in laying out the family's limited options so as not to give them false expectations. I wonder at his ability to remain calm and professional, when he must have to convey similar messages time and time again. I want to short-circuit the process, to jump in and offer solutions. But I bite my lip and stay quiet, because, as David has patiently pointed out, neither he nor I can tell the family what to do. We can only explain the facts of the situation so they can make their own decisions. Besides, it seems there is no way to unpick the knot. I begin to wonder whether I did the right thing in encouraging Sima and Sherene to attend a meeting that has only served to confirm their worst fears. The faint hope that they brought with them into David's office may have been illusory, but even that scrap of optimism is now gone.

Afterwards, as we walk past the boutiques and crowded cafes, Sherene tells me that inner-city Fitzroy reminds her a bit of Damascus, where her family lived before coming to Australia, because the streets are lined with shops and lively with people. It is a happy memory. In Syria, she says, people have a lot more time for each other; they go out just to walk and talk, or to sit and chat over coffee. Australians always seem to be rushing about, staring at their phones, too busy to interact. Describing that fragment of a lost life lifts Sherene's mood. Not for the first time, or the last, I marvel at her resilience.

In the car, as I drive Sherene and Sima back home to Melbourne's outer west, a pair of motorbikes with brightly coloured petrol tanks power past us and disappear into the distance. Sherene admires the way they cut through the traffic and tells me that after she has learned to drive a car, she wants to get a motorbike licence and buy a bike like that. It is an incongruous and appealing image—slight, modestly dressed Sherene, headscarf under helmet, fearlessly tearing off on a Kawasaki.

Sherene subsequently asks me what kind of engineering degree I think she should study. 'If I go back to Afghanistan I want to do something good for my people,' she says. I'm at a loss to advise her. 'Civil engineering,' I offer tentatively, 'so you can help build important infrastructure like roads and bridges?' Sherene had been thinking nuclear, so she can help Afghanistan develop an atomic bomb—not because she relishes war and destruction, but because she hopes to end it. 'If my country had a nuclear weapon, then Pakistan, Russia,

Iran and the United States would leave us alone,' she says. 'If I could make a nuclear weapon then I would have enough power to control my country, to defend my country.'

Sherene's other idea is that she should become a politician. 'Because of the experiences I've been through,' she explains. 'I've seen the conditions people live in, how they drown at sea, and it makes me angry, really angry, so it would be good to go through politics and change the policies.'

I begin to appreciate that Sherene's dream of riding a motorbike does not represent freedom to do what she likes so much as autonomy—the possibility of setting her own direction, taking charge of her destiny. 'You have to have power,' she says. 'I need power.'

Power is what Sherene and Sima lack. They are subject to a merciless policy that sees splitting families as an acceptable element of deterring boat arrivals. The separation of child from parent violates the most cherished human bond and a fundamental, universally agreed human right. A temporary visa in Australia may provide physical protection from persecution and armed conflict in countries like Syria and Afghanistan, but it cannot be said to offer safety in any meaningful sense if it leaves vulnerable people tortured by uncertainty and plagued with doubts about the future. Sima and Sherene worry constantly about Ali, who has been separated from his wife and children for more than three years. In this unsettled state they are unable to put down roots and have no place to call home.

Sherene refers to Afghanistan as her country, but she has never set foot there. Neither have her brothers, Mohamed and Khalid, who are also in Australia. As we drive, I piece together the family's story. Sherene, sitting next to me, responds directly to some of my questions, but more often she translates them for Sima to answer from the back seat. Sima tells me that Ali left Afghanistan for Iran as a teenager in the mid-1980s, and that she moved to Iran a couple of years later. The couple were married in Iran when Sima was just 14. After this has been translated to me, Sima says, in English, 'Too young!' and gives an embarrassed laugh. 'In Afghanistan, women have no rights,' adds Sherene, matter-of-factly. Sherene, who is 17, was born in Iran, as was her brother Mohamed, who is one year older. When they were still very young, the family moved to Syria and settled in Damascus, where Sherene's younger brother Khalid was born. He is now 12.

Sima says life in Iran was always difficult. As undocumented migrants and members of Afghanistan's persecuted Hazara ethnic minority, she and Ali suffered discrimination and harassment and could only get menial, poorly paid work. By contrast, all the family have fond memories of life in Damascus. Ali had a good job, working as a chef in a big hotel, cooking meals for huge sittings of pilgrims touring Syria's holy sites. Sima could move about freely as a woman and the children could all attend school. Despite the many well-documented crimes of Syrian dictator Bashar al-Assad, the family felt relatively secure and accepted under his secular regime. 'We had a good life in Syria,' Mohamed tells me as we talk in the family's lounge room over glasses of hot mint tea. 'We didn't come to Australia to go shopping,' he adds, with a tinge of bitterness. 'We were forced to come here, we were forced to leave.'

The family had been living in Damascus for about 12 years when their troubles started. As the civil war hit the city, extremist Sunni militia groups affiliated with Islamic State targeted the family. (Hazara are Shia Muslims and usually easily identified as an ethnic group by their facial characteristics.) Khalid vividly remembers the last meal they shared with Ali. 'There was shooting going on outside,' he says.

'My father's hand was shaking so much that there was hardly any rice left on his spoon by the time it reached his mouth.' Subsequently their house was burned down and Ali went missing. That was in July 2012.

Fearful of what might happen, and not knowing where her husband was, Sima decided to use their savings to get out. She booked flights to Kuala Lumpur and after a week in Malaysia they were smuggled to Indonesia. They spent about three months in Indonesia waiting for a boat and arrived in Australian waters in early November 2012. They were detained on Christmas Island for 10 weeks and in Darwin for another six weeks before being transferred to community detention in Melbourne. This was a big improvement. Although they were technically still in detention, the family could live in the community, as long as they resided at a designated address and abided by certain conditions (such as returning to the house by a certain time in the evening and reporting regularly to the immigration department).

After 18 months in community detention the family was precipitously released on bridging visas and given a fortnight to find their own accommodation. With no rental history, no references and a very limited income, this was no easy task, but Sima managed to find a run-down house that they could just about afford. 'It was really dirty,' says Sherene. 'The floor vents for the heating were all stuffed with rubbish,' adds Khalid.

The family scrubbed the walls, fixed broken doors and locks, cut down the weeds in the backyard, cleaned out the heating ducts and covered the floor with rugs. The house is now clean and comfortable. 'But it's still freezing cold,' says Sherene.

Nor does it feel like home, because of Ali's continued absence. For almost two years after they left Syria, Sima had no idea what had happened to her husband. She did not know if he was alive or dead, a prisoner of a militia group or stranded in a refugee camp. (I'm not sure if she knows, even now, the full story of what happened when Ali disappeared. As I spend more time with the family, I perceive that there are some protective silences between them—things they choose not to tell one another to spare spreading the pain.) Determined to do everything she could to find Ali, Sima sought the help of the Red Cross tracing service, and discovered that her husband was detained on Manus Island. He had returned to Damascus, learned that his family had left for Australia and decided to follow them. He took the same smuggling route via Malaysia, Indonesia and Christmas Island, but his timing was bad.

Ali arrived in August 2013. Just a few weeks earlier, Kevin Rudd, in his second stint as prime minister, signed a 'regional resettlement arrangement' with Papua New Guinea. On 19 July 2013, in a joint media conference with the prime minister of Papua New Guinea, Peter O'Neill, Rudd declared that from that time on asylum seekers arriving in Australia by boat 'will have no chance of being settled in Australia as refugees'.[1]

Julia Gillard, who was both Rudd's successor and predecessor as Labor prime minister, had already reconstituted the Howard-era policy of offshore detention and processing on Manus and Nauru. Under Gillard, however, it was still possible for people recognised as refugees in Manus and Nauru to be resettled in Australia—eventually. The intention was that the process would take just as long as would have been the case if they had successfully applied for protection via the UNHCR in Indonesia—which could be several years. This was an attempt to enforce the 'no-advantage principle' recommended by an expert panel on asylum seekers chaired by Air Chief Marshal Angus Houston. The intention was 'to ensure that no benefit is gained through circumventing regular migration arrangements'.[2] In other words, it was designed to remove the incentive for engaging a people smuggler to sail from Indonesia.

Gillard's version of 'no advantage' failed to 'stop the boats'. Behind in the opinion polls and with an election less than two months away, Rudd implemented tougher measures. In a policy he declared to be both 'balanced' and 'hard-line', Rudd ruled out any possibility of future resettlement in Australia for any asylum seekers arriving by boat from that time on. 'Our responsibility as a government is to ensure that we have a robust system of border security and orderly migration, on the one hand, as well as fulfilling our legal and compassionate obligations under the refugees convention on the other,' he said. Rudd anticipated that Australians, who he described as people with 'hard heads' but also 'kind and compassionate' hearts, would accept his policy.[3] The subsequent Coalition governments of Tony Abbott and Malcolm Turnbull have continued Rudd's approach.

What this balanced, hard-line policy means in practice is the indefinite separation of a husband from his wife and of a father from his children. The family can speak to Ali briefly on the phone once a fortnight, and by Skype once a month. 'He can see us but we cannot see him,' says Sherene. The connection is precious but tenuous, and long-term separation is taking a toll on them all. The children tell me that Sima is 'sick with stress' and that Ali is suffering from itchy rashes all over his body. Later I learn from Sima that Ali is very depressed and has gone numb down one side. 'He can't feel half of his body,' she says. Whether his symptoms are the result of a physical or a psychological illness is unclear, but Sima worries that he relies heavily on pills to get to sleep at night.

An additional irony of the family's situation is that Ali has already been recognised as a refugee in Papua New Guinea, while, after more than three years in Australia, Sima and her children are yet to have their asylum applications processed. They are not alone: at the end of March 2016, there were close to 29,000 asylum seekers living in the community on a bridging visa E, waiting for the government to assess their claims for protection.[4] Since the Coalition government under Tony Abbott 'stopped the boats' in late 2013, that means that these asylum seekers have already waited two years or more to have their claims for protection heard.

Even when their cases are processed—under a new 'fast-tracked' system—the best outcome that Sima and her children can hope for is to be issued with a temporary protection visa. Not only does this make it impossible to build a secure future, it explicitly rules out the possibility of bringing Ali to join them in Australia.

While Sima and her children are indefinitely separated from their husband and father, Syed Ejaz Hussain Zaidi is indefinitely separated from his wife and children. Syed, who is also Hazara, arrived in Australia by boat at around the same time as Sima, and lives in Dandenong, on the opposite side of Melbourne. He fled his home in Quetta, the capital of Pakistan's Balochistan province that borders Iran and Afghanistan, where the large Hazara community has been targeted by Sunni extremist groups like Lashkar-e-Jhangvi that appear to operate with impunity.

'I had a good life in my city,' Syed told me when we first met in April 2014.[5] 'I earned a good salary and had a small business on the side. I was such a successful person there.' Syed worked in the regional office of a Pakistan government department and was the only Hazara staff member in his section. When five strangers came asking for him in August 2012, but refusing to say what they wanted, Syed's colleagues rang him and warned him not to come to work. After receiving death threats by phone and text, Syed went into hiding and then fled the country. I asked him why he chose to seek haven in Australia rather than some other country.

'Because it was easier and cheaper than Europe,' he told me. 'At that time Australia was a leading country, welcoming refugees and giving them shelter. I was thinking about the future of my children and thinking about the future of my own life.' Syed had hoped to bring his family to join him in Australia. The rules of temporary protection now make that impossible. Syed talks every second day with his wife and five children by Skype or Viber, but he struggles to answer the question frequently posed by his six-year-old daughter, his youngest child: 'Papa, when will you bring us to join you?' The only answer he can give is: 'It is in God's hands.'

When we meet in November 2015, Syed's circumstances are materially much improved compared to our first meeting 18 months earlier. 'I am very busy these days,' he says. 'My financial difficulties are over.' For more than two and a half years after his release from detention, Syed could live in the community on a bridging visa E, but was denied permission to work. Instead, he had to get by on a government payment of about $221 per week, equivalent to 89 per cent of the Centrelink Special Benefit. Using standard OECD measures, the Australian Council of Social Services calculates that the poverty line is $358 per week for a single adult and that anything below this 'equates to a very austere living standard'.[6]

The removal of work rights formed part of the Gillard government's response to the 2012 Houston panel, even though the panel made no such recommendation. According to then immigration minister Chris Bowen, however, preventing asylum seekers from working was 'consistent' with the panel's 'underlying principle' of 'no advantage'.[7]

As we chat in our usual spot, a quiet nook in Dandenong library, Syed tells me about his factory job casting automotive parts. 'It is very intensive,' he says. 'You have to concentrate all the time to keep up with the machine.' Syed's position is casual and insecure. He has work through December, but he knows that he will be one of the first out the door if business slows after that. Yet he feels lucky to have a job at all: some of his friends, also asylum seekers on bridging visas, have had the right to work for six months, but are still unemployed. 'Never in my life have I earned so much money,' he says of his $1,000 per week income. The pay enables him to remit more money to his family in Quetta, a small consolation for the fact that he cannot bring them to join him in Australia. 'I want my children to be proud of me,' he says, 'because I have been able to help them in their lives.'

As welcome as the money is to Syed, the sense of dignity that comes with paid work appears to be just as important. At one of our earlier meetings, Syed told me that being forced to live on government handouts was poisonous—it ate away at his soul and made him feel like a beggar. 'I hated being on Centrelink,' he says. 'If I am healthy, I should try to work. The government should not pay me for doing nothing.' Syed did not want to break Australian laws and work illegally, cash in hand, despite the massive inducement to do so in order to get by and save money to help his family in Quetta.

Being busy with work also means Syed has less time to focus on his difficulties. Before, with nothing to do, he says he used to walk around the streets of Dandenong 'like a mad person', in a state of depression. 'If you have many problems, and if you have too much time, then you cannot get away from your troubled thoughts,' he says. The more hours he can work, the better—not just for the money, but because it exhausts him. He is glad to have a job that leaves him with little time and energy for anything apart from eating, washing and sleeping.

Yet as we talk on this Sunday afternoon, his one day off, Syed's troubles inevitably resurface. He apologises to me for becoming tearful as we speak of his family. 'If I had known the policy would be like this, I would not have come to Australia,' he says. 'I would have tried for some other place, maybe Europe.'

Syed's comments might be seen to lend support to the government's argument that temporary protection visas deter asylum seekers from travelling to Australia without authorisation and so save lives at sea. But past experience challenges that claim. There is no strong evidence that temporary protection visas deter asylum seekers from undertaking risky journeys. As sources close to the action will admit privately, under Howard, as under Abbott, the measure that ultimately stopped asylum seekers from getting on boats in Indonesia was not temporary visas (or offshore detention), but the practice of turning those boats around and forcing them and their passengers back to Indonesia. Temporary protection is not policy as prevention, but policy as punishment. It has been tried and abandoned more than once before.

In August 1998, Howard government health minister Michael Wooldridge launched a GP's manual on refugee health. In his speech he noted that 'creating uncertainty and insecurity…is one of the most dangerous ways to add to the harm that torturers do'. At the launch, the minister attacked the views of Pauline Hanson's One Nation Party for its 'spurious claim…that, at best, Australia should only be a temporary haven for refugees before they are sent back again when "things are better"'. Wooldridge warned that the policies of One Nation would 'continue the suffering of refugees who have been tortured and could well complete the insidious work that torture began'.

Just over one year later, in October 1999, the Howard government made One Nation's 'deeply flawed and dangerous' proposal into official policy for all refugees who arrive in Australia without a valid visa. The regulations could have been disallowed by a combined opposition vote in the Senate. But the federal Labor Party decided to vote with the government, even though Con Sciacca, then shadow minister for immigration, told the ABC's *AM* program that the new measures 'would not stop one illegal immigrant from coming to this country'. He pointed out that Labor had tried a similar approach in government in 1990 and abandoned it as a costly failure. Among other problems, the policy results in multiple handling, because each asylum case has to be assessed repeatedly: first when the applicant arrives in Australia and then again whenever the temporary visa expires. In 2008, in its first budget, the Rudd Labor government abolished temporary protection visas and enabled about 1,000 refugees still on Howard-era temporary visas to gain the security and peace of mind that comes with permanent residence. Then immigration minister Chris Evans described temporary protection visas as 'one of the worst aspects of the Howard government's punitive treatment of refugees, many of whom had suffered enormously before fleeing to Australia'.[8]

The Howard government had introduced temporary protection visas in 1999 in response to a surge in boat arrivals. The aim was to 'take the sugar off the table'—that is, to make Australia a less attractive destination for refugees and asylum seekers and so deter people smuggling. There is evidence, however, to suggest that this backfired. The number of asylum seekers that arrived by boat in 2001 was 50 per cent higher than the number that arrived in 1999.[9]

Not only that, but the introduction of temporary visas for refugees was followed by an increase in the number of women and children attempting to reach Australia by sea. As Mary Crock and Ben Saul documented in their book *Future Seekers*, children made up only 13 per cent of the asylum seekers arriving on boats in 1999. In 2001, after the introduction of the temporary protection visa, the proportion of children on boats rose to more than 30 per cent. While correlation is not causation, the effect of telling refugees already present in Australia that there was no legal means to bring family members to join them may have prompted some men to encourage wives and children to follow them on the boats. It was, after all, the only way to get here. If refugees just setting out on the journey from their homeland or a country of first asylum were made aware of the policy, then the temporary protection visa may have been an incentive for whole families to leave together, rather than men going ahead alone in an endeavour to establish a base for the family first.

In response to continued boat arrivals, the Howard government made the temporary protection regime even harsher. The terms of the policy in 1999 were that after three years of temporary protection, refugees found to be still at risk of persecution were issued with a permanent visa. In the wake of the Tampa affair, the Howard government restricted this pathway to settlement. After September 2001, refugees had to demonstrate why they had been unable to obtain effective protection in any country in which they spent seven days or more while en route to Australia. In other words, they had to demonstrate why they could not seek asylum at the UNHCR office in a transit country like Indonesia or Pakistan. If refugees could not meet this test, then the best they could hope for was rolling renewals of their temporary visas every three years. At the time, immigration minister Philip Ruddock openly acknowledged to ABC Radio National's *Law Report* that this could create 'a permanent population of people who are second-class citizens'. Ruddock said this was justified because these refugees were 'essentially taking places from people who have a more urgent need for a resettlement outcome'.

The latest iteration of the temporary protection regime—initiated under Abbott and continued under Turnbull—is even more punitive. It rules out any future possibility of permanent protection for a refugee who arrived in Australia by boat, regardless of how long they remain here. This means that on a temporary protection visa, there is no way in which Syed can ever become Australian or bring his family to join him in this country.

While individual asylum seekers and refugees pay the acute personal price of a regime that divides families, the experience of the eight-year experiment with temporary protection under Howard is that the policy will also inflict a significant cost on the broader Australian community, because temporary protection visas create a marginalised and distraught cohort of people who live among us, but not with us. As researchers at Curtin University have noted, numerous studies conducted during the Howard era all reached essentially the same conclusion: that temporary protection visas had a 'profound deleterious effect on people's mental health and well-being'. Several factors combined to produce this result, including the uncertainty and insecurity of refugees' status, their fear of being returned to a place of persecution or immigration detention when their visa expired, fears for the safety and welfare of family overseas and the struggle to come to terms with their limited entitlements in Australia.¹⁰ (For example, refugees on temporary protection visas pay international student fees for post-school study and cannot travel overseas except in compelling or compassionate circumstances and with the express permission of the minister.) The predictable effect of treating 'temporary' refugees in this way is that they will become high-demand users of health and welfare services. While they will have access to Centrelink payments, Medicare benefits, 510 hours of English-language classes and some associated services (like help getting a job or short-term counselling for torture and trauma), it is likely, as happened last time around, that state and local governments, charities, community groups and volunteers will have to step in to fill other gaps in necessary support.

Brisbane's Refugee and Immigration Legal Service assisted more than 1,000 refugees on temporary protection visas between 2000 and 2008. It found they were 'often depressed and traumatised' and often 'highly distressed' at being separated from immediate family members who were stuck in dangerous situations back in their homeland or in transit countries. The experience of having to reapply for protection after three years when their first visa expired 're-traumatised' the refugees and created a mountain of work for legal services, government officials, tribunals and courts.[11]

In 2002, in the foreword to a report on refugees on temporary protection visas in the state of Victoria, former human rights commissioner Chris Sidoti asked: 'Is it in our own interest as Australians to have people here for periods of years who are insecure, traumatised... accorded a discriminatory status that inhibits their integration into the broader community, left unsupported by and worried about their spouses and children? Surely and self-evidently it is not.'[12]

The report he was introducing identified 'despair, disillusionment and unusually high levels of anxiety and health disorders' among refugees on temporary protection visas. It documented that the difficulty faced by 'temporary' refugees in finding work was not only due to poor English-language skills and the lack of other training opportunities; even refugees with professional qualifications and fluent English encounter problems, because their insecure residency status makes them unattractive to prospective employers.

Sherene's older brother Mohamed experienced exactly this problem when he applied for a job at McDonald's. Part way through the interview he was asked about his visa status. When he replied that he was on a temporary visa, the interview was swiftly terminated. Even more disillusioning for Mohamed is the likely prospect that he will be unable to continue his education beyond school.

When I first met Sherene and her family, Mohamed was sitting his year 12 exams. Having loved science from a young age, he chose subjects that might help him realise his dream of studying medicine or engineering—advanced maths, maths methods, physics and chemistry. The subject he was most concerned about, however, was English as an Additional Language, because he must pass it in order to get into an Australian university. Mohamed already speaks Hazaragi, Dari, Farsi and Arabic, and his English is quite good, given that he has only lived in Australia for three years, but the year 12 exam will test his language skills to their limit.

An even greater barrier to tertiary education is the cost of study. As an asylum seeker on a bridging visa waiting for his case to be assessed, Mohamed will be treated as an international student, and this won't change even if he is recognised as a refugee and granted a temporary protection visa. In other words, in order to study beyond high school he will have to pay thousands of dollars in upfront fees—something his family could never afford. His only hope of continuing study will be to find a university that offers him a scholarship or a fee waiver. Despite his intellectual capacities, when I first met Mohamed he was deeply disheartened and questioning the point of studying hard for his final exams. 'School is okay,' he says to me, 'but what is the point if I can only go to year twelve?' I could see Sherene, who was studying for her year 11 exams, listening intently. She knew that she would face the same roadblock in 12 months. 'You've got to keep trying,' I told them, 'because you never know what is going to happen or what opportunities are going to come up.' But I felt that my attempts to boost their spirits were lame and inadequate.

On the other side of Melbourne, Syed dreams that higher education could be a way to bring at least one member of his immediate family to Australia. His oldest daughter is studying a bachelor of business at university in Quetta. Syed hopes that if he can keep his job casting auto parts, then he might eventually be able to save enough money to pay for her to do an MBA at an Australian university. At current rates this would cost at least $22,000 in fees (for the cheapest two-year course). His daughter would also have to prove that she could cover her living expenses in Australia, which may require her to show evidence that she has funds of at least $18,600 per year to draw on during her two years of study. If these obstacles can be overcome, Syed hopes that, after graduation, she might be able to transition to permanent residency. It sounds like a logical plan, but I know enough about the way Australia's migration system operates to think that it could be stymied. I feel compelled to tell Syed, as gently as I can, that I have some doubts about whether his plan will work. Because his daughter is a Hazara living in the dangerous Pakistani city of Quetta, where Hazara are routinely persecuted, her application for a student visa will raise red flags in immigration. There is a good chance she will be seen as a high-risk applicant, who is likely to apply for refugee status after arrival. Her prospects of getting a student visa might also be reduced because her father is already seeking Australia's protection as a refugee. 'It's worth a try,' I say to Syed, 'but I would not get your hopes up too high.'

Syed grasps at such straws because his options are so restricted. When he has his claim for protection as a refugee assessed—like Sima and her children, after three years in Australia Syed has not yet been through this process—then he will have to choose between two different temporary visas: a standard three-year TPV (temporary protection visa) or a five-year safe haven enterprise visa, known by its acronym as the SHEV.

The SHEV is the initiative of Queensland magnate and politician Clive Palmer, and at first glance, it would appear to be a better deal—not only does it last an extra two years, the SHEV also opens up at least some prospect of a transition to permanent residency. But the potential opportunity to move from SHEV to permanent residency is, as the government puts it, 'very limited'.[13] A refugee on a SHEV who works or studies in a 'designated regional area' for at least three and a half years, without receiving any government income support during that period, may be able to apply for other permanent visas, including family visas (if they are in a relationship with an Australian, for example) and skilled visas.

While the SHEV is new, former immigration minister Amanda Vanstone introduced a similar residency pathway in 2004, when she enabled the 9,500 TPV holders living in Australia at that time to apply for 'mainstream migration visas'. The take-up rate was, however, very low. A year later, only 34 applications for mainstream visas had been received.[14] The problem is that to get a skilled visa you need specific qualifications in a profession that is in short supply in Australia, relevant work experience and excellent English, as well as meeting age and health requirements. Many refugees on temporary visas simply will not be able to clear this very high bar. Syed, for example, speaks very good English, but does not have a profession that would qualify him for a skilled visa. An alternative route might be for him to move from a SHEV to a 457 temporary work visa, which does not have such stringent skill requirements, and then to seek sponsorship from his employer, but this would add at least another two years to the process.

When we talk in the Dandenong library Syed is confused and anxious about which visa to apply for. He wants more than anything to bring his family to Australia, and is drawn to the prospect—however slight, protracted and uncertain—of moving from a SHEV to permanent residency. Yet he would have to give up his job in Dandenong and move away from a community where he has friends and support. I point out to him that there could be another problem: Syed is already in his late forties. After five years on a SHEV, he will be more than 50 years old—which could render him ineligible for a skilled visa in any case.

In the offices of Refugee Legal, solicitor David Manne emphasises to Sima and Sherene that they should think carefully about whether they want to apply for a TPV or a SHEV. Either way, they also need to be ready to jump through the hoops of the refugee determination process at short notice, since they could be 'invited' to submit an application for protection at any time. Under the Department of Immigration and Border Protection's 'fast-tracked' refugee determination process, asylum seekers who came to Australia by boat—'illegal arrivals' in the blunt official terminology—cannot apply for protection until they are invited to do so.

The public rationale for the fast-track procedures is that they will enable simpler, speedier processing of tens of thousands of pending refugee applications from asylum seekers, who, like Syed and Sima and her children, arrived in Australia 'on or after 13 August 2012'. Refugee lawyers suspect the true intent is to make it easier for government to knock back applications for protection while avoiding legal scrutiny or challenge.

The fast-track process narrowly codifies the definition of a refugee in Australian migration law, by removing most references to the international Convention relating to the Status of Refugees—a convention that Australia has signed and which defines the term 'refugee' in international law. It also makes it easier for immigration department officials to rule people out because their claims for protection are 'manifestly unfounded'. If an application is rejected, there is no longer any right of appeal to a tribunal; a much more limited form of review on the papers, without any kind of oral hearing, may be possible, but only at the minister's discretion. The Law Council of Australia fears that the fast-track procedures 'truncate the refugee status determination process by removing safeguards that operate to ensure each claim is fairly and carefully assessed on its merits'.[15] The UN High Commissioner for Refugees warns that asylum seekers will be denied 'due process and procedural fairness'.[16]

The fast-track procedures, bundled with the reintroduction of temporary protection visas and the Clive Palmer-initiated SHEV, secured passage through the Senate just after midnight on Friday 5 December 2014, in the final sitting of that year. Motor Enthusiast Party Senator Ricky Muir cast the deciding vote, finally overcoming his anguish at making such a decision after the Abbott government promised to release asylum-seeker children from detention, increase

Australia's annual humanitarian intake by 7,500 people and grant work rights to asylum seekers on bridging visas. (So the same piece of legislation that granted Syed the right to work in the car-parts factory also destroyed his aspiration to become an Australian and bring his wife and children to join him here.)

Fast-track refugee processing may be supposed to simplify government administration, but it is doubtful that it will achieve this outcome in practice, since the government has simultaneously cut funding for legal services to assist asylum seekers with their applications. As the Law Council has pointed out, this is likely to be a false economy, since immigration officials 'will be left to make decisions on poorly prepared and incomplete applications'.[17] It is entirely possible that fast-tracking applications will ultimately lead to more delay and litigation, not less. By March 2016, there was little evidence that fast-track processing is fast: 15 months after it was legislated and temporary visas reinstated, only a handful of TPVs and SHEVs had actually been issued.[18] And of course most, if not all, of the asylum seekers who are granted temporary protection visas will have to go through the same process all over again, every three years, putting a huge additional workload on the bureaucracy and the legal system.

Despite losing funding, Refugee Legal and other similar services continue to do their best to provide free high-quality advice to asylum seekers entering the refugee determination process. They now rely on donations, pro bono legal services and volunteers. It is unlawful to provide migration advice without being a registered migration agent, and even legally qualified volunteers need specific induction and training before they can work with clients in the complex and sensitive area of refugee protection.

For asylum seekers themselves, there is certainly nothing simple about the fast-track process. 'You will have to fill out sixty-two pages of forms,' David Manne tells Sima and Sherene. 'That is one hundred and eighty-four questions, all in English, plus a statement about your claim. It is impossible to complete on your own.' On part C of the form, before providing their personal details, applicants are required to sign a 'declaration of truth'. The preamble to the declaration states that 'Australians value honesty and fairness'.

While they wait for their invitation to apply for protection as refugees, Sima, Sherene, Mohamed and Khalid get on with their lives as best they can. Under the Asylum Seeker's Assistance Scheme, Sima receives $1,110 a fortnight, which is equivalent to 89 per cent of a Centrelink special benefit. The monthly rent of $1,240 eats up a bit more than half of this, leaving Sima with about $250 per week to feed and clothe her family, pay their public-transport fares and keep their phones in credit. In one of our chats, 12-year-old Khalid talks about how much he likes playing basketball and how well he played in a recent school tournament. 'Is there a local team you can join?' I ask. 'No money for that,' he says, looking down. 'Can't afford the team fees and the cost of the uniform and stuff.' Despite the tight budget, when I visit Sima always insists on feeding me—delicious meatballs in a sauce of lentils, spiced chicken drumsticks, fragrant rice. She sends me home with extra supplies for my family. On one occasion it is a large tub of homemade yoghurt; on another it is freshly made apple jam.

I am amazed at how well they manage in such straitened circumstances, and at how determined they are to try to build a future when their foothold in Australia is so insecure. Sima is diligent about attending community-run English classes; the children are committed to their schoolwork. Yet the pain of a missing husband and father is never far below the surface and can never be eased.

The cruellest aspect of dividing a family is the corrosive effect that it can have on trust. Cut off in Manus, and sceptical of all the information he is given by the authorities, Ali has begun to wonder whether his wife and children are doing all that they can to help him get to Australia. He has a creeping suspicion that they could do more to get him out of Papua New Guinea. Nothing could be further from the truth. 'All we want is to be safe and to be together,' says Sherene. There is nothing that she or her family can do to bring such a situation about.

The only distant prospect for the family to be reunited appears to be for Ali to accept resettlement in Papua New Guinea, and for his wife and children to eventually join him there. Quite apart from the questionable tactic of Australia offloading refugees on a country that faces challenges of its own, the parameters of what is meant by 'resettlement' remain opaque and uncertain.

At the end of April 2016, 448 of the 905 men on Manus had been found to be refugees and were able to move out of detention and into the East Lorengau refugee transit centre, but only 59 had taken up that option.[19] The majority, including Ali, remained locked up, apparently unwilling to take the first step towards resettlement in Papua New Guinea and holding out for an alternative option. Those who moved into the transit centre found not so much changed anyway. They were still subject to a night-time curfew and unable either to work on Manus or to leave Manus Island to seek work in other parts of the country.[20] In early December 2015, media in Papua New Guinea reported that the government had waived strict protocols and work-permit requirements that had been preventing refugees from entering the job market,[21] and that the human resources company JDA Wokman had been engaged to help them find jobs.[22] According to deputy chief migration officer Esther Gaegaming, however, the refugees would still not be allowed out of Manus until they were employed.[23] In other words, the refugees have to find a job outside Manus in order to settle in Papua New Guinea, but they cannot leave Manus in order to find a job.

By April 2016, only eight refugees had been found jobs and resettled in other parts of Papua New Guinea. Three of them were back in Manus within a few weeks, having found life so difficult in Papua New Guinea's second largest city of Lae that they preferred to return to the restrictive life of the transit centre.[24]

Problems like this were supposed to be resolved under the National Refugee Resettlement Policy, belatedly approved by the Papua New Guinea government in October 2015,[25] but the broad general principles outlined in the 12-page document give rise to exactly these sorts of contradictions that refugees are encountering. The policy document notes, for example, that refugees 'must be able to support themselves' because 'unemployment remains high and Papua New Guinea does not have a comprehensive social-security system'.[26] It adds that if refugees are to be accepted within Papua New Guinea 'they must not be perceived to be provided special treatment or distinct advantages over local people'. So refugees have to get a job, but the government cannot offer them much help to find work because this might provoke a backlash from Papua New Guinea nationals.

The policy document also says that after eight years living in Papua New Guinea 'refugees are able to fully commit to their new home country and take up citizenship'. Once they have 'successfully established themselves and become self-sufficient they are permitted to sponsor their families to join them through regular migration processes'. It is unclear from this whether the eight-year process of achieving citizenship is a necessary part of becoming 'successfully established' and 'self-sufficient', or if a refugee who has established a secure income might be able to bring family to Papua New Guinea sooner than that. Either way, if Ali accepts resettlement in Papua New Guinea, and if the country can find a place for him, it could be a very long time indeed before he is eligible to sponsor his wife and children to join him there.

On 26 April 2016, the uncertainty about Ali's future increased when Papua New Guinea's supreme court declared that Australia's detention of asylum seekers and refugees on Manus breached the constitutional right to personal liberty and was unlawful. The next day, Papua New Guinea's Prime Minister Peter O'Neill declared that the Manus Island detention centre must close. He said any refugees who wanted to settle in Papua New Guinea were welcome to do so, but—recognising that most did not want to—he asked Australia to make 'alternative arrangements' for everyone else.[27] The Minister for Immigration and Border Protection Peter Dutton responded that under the memorandum of understanding signed with Australia, all the asylum seekers and refugees on Manus were the responsibility of Papua New Guinea.[28] He reiterated that none of them would come to Australia. The question of where else they might go remained unanswered.

In September 2015, as the world was transfixed by the plight of tens of thousands of migrants trudging across the borders of Europe from Greece to Germany, the Abbott government outlined the details of its response to the Syrian refugee crisis. Australia would accept an additional 12,000 Syrian refugees—the most vulnerable members of persecuted minorities. On Radio National Breakfast, Foreign Minister Julie Bishop was asked why the government was providing permanent resettlement, rather than offering a temporary 'safe haven' visa until the troubles in Syria eased and refugees could return home, as had happened in the past with people displaced from Kosovo and East Timor. 'The difficulty with the persecuted minorities is that they effectively have no home to return to,' Bishop replied. 'We are talking about people who are being persecuted in the most egregious ways. Their homes are being looted and burned. They are being threatened. If they don't pay taxes to this terrorist organisation they will be killed. They have nowhere to return to…Once people have been brought all the way to Australia, and stay here for literally years, it will be much more difficult to send them home.'[29]

Just after the first Syrian refugees landed in Perth in mid-November, I visited Sima and her family. 'What is the difference between them and us?' an agitated Sherene asked me. 'We are the same, so why won't the government help us?'

Former human rights commissioner Chris Sidoti said in 2002 that the Howard-era refugee policy offered temporary protection and permanent rejection. He described the denial of family reunion as 'a flagrant violation of the human rights of children, the most vulnerable of these vulnerable people'. It is impossible not to reach the same conclusion today.

8 | The Pros and Cons of Temporary Migrant Labour
The 457 Scheme

When Greece played Costa Rica for a place in the quarterfinals of the 2014 World Cup in Brazil, thousands of members of Melbourne's Greek community braved the chill of early morning to watch the nail-biting match live on a huge screen in Eaton Mall in Oakleigh. About half of Australia's 100,000-strong Greek-born community live in Melbourne, and Oakleigh, in the city's southeast, is one of the demographic centres of the Greek community—the place to go if you want to find a good quality baklava or *galaktoboureko*. You might also try Thornbury in Melbourne's north or Doncaster in the city's east. Around each of these suburbs, along with authentic Greek cafes, you will also find a specialist Greek aged-care facility.

Fronditha Care in Clayton is a short drive from Oakleigh's Eaton Mall. When I visit in November 2015, the front half of the property is a construction site as a new residential wing nears completion. The nursing home, dating from the early 1980s, is being completely rebuilt. When the work is finished the facility will have doubled in size to accommodate up to 150 residents. The not-for-profit Fronditha (which means 'care' in Greek) urgently needs the extra space, because Melbourne's Greek community is getting old.

'We are at full occupancy,' says Fronditha CEO George Lekakis. 'If we had another two nursing homes we could fill them up, too.'

At the 2011 census, the median age of Greek-born Australians was 67, compared to a median age of 37 years for the population as a whole. What this means is that in the next couple of decades tens of thousands of Greek-born Australians will enter the frailer stages of later life and need increased care.

Whether they move into a residential facility or receive support in their homes, many of these postwar Greek migrants would prefer to be looked after by someone who speaks their native tongue and understands their culture. Providing language-appropriate care becomes increasingly important for residents with dementia, since many will lose their ability to communicate in English and revert to speaking only Greek. Fronditha has 'memory support units' to provide dedicated dementia care at its facilities. The organisation needs appropriately trained Greek-speaking staff.

'Our workforce is ageing and needs to be replenished and replaced,' Lekakis tells me over tea and *loukoumi* (commonly known to English speakers as Turkish delight). But the demographics that give rise to the spike in demand for linguistically and culturally appropriate care also reduce the chances of finding an Australian workforce with the skills to meet this need. Sure, there are plenty of second- and third-generation Greek-Australians, but their Greek may not be very fluent, and, even if it is, few of them will choose to work as low-paid personal-care assistants or even as better-paid aged-care nurses.

'There is a prejudice and taboo associated with nursing in the Greek community,' says Lekakis, who, having originally trained as a nurse, describes himself as a rarity. 'It is not a preferred career path for young Greeks.'

With few local Greek speakers available to work in aged care, Lekakis decided to look offshore. Here he struck another problem: the Certificate III qualification required to work as a personal-care assistant does not meet the necessary skill threshold for temporary or permanent migration. This appeared to rule out any possibility of bringing in general aged-care staff from overseas. Lekakis found a way around this problem in the form of a labour agreement—a formal arrangement with the federal government that enabled Fronditha to recruit an agreed number of semi-skilled workers on 457 visas.

'I went to immigration and put a case forward,' he says. When Labor was in power the idea languished. (Lekakis claims Labor was 'not predisposed' to a labour agreement because of the influence of the CFMEU in New South Wales and its 'anti-immigrant hysteria'.) After the change of government in 2013, he found an enthusiastic champion in WA Liberal Senator Michaelia Cash, assistant minister for immigration under Tony Abbott. 'I negotiated directly with Cash,' he says.

Although visas granted under labour agreements make up only a small fraction of all the 457 visas issued,[1] the program is seen by trade unions and other critics as one of the most problematic aspects of Australia's temporary-migration regime. One concern is that a labour agreement opens up the potential for employers to bring in overseas workers to take up positions that—with the appropriate investment in training—could be filled relatively easily by Australians. The use of labour agreements has tended to cluster in sectors of the economy with high rates of casual employment and exploitative conditions, such as labour hire, meat processing, tourism and hospitality.[2] The Human Rights Clinic at the UNSW Law School argues that labour agreements 'pose unique risks for temporary migrant workers' because they fall outside the standard regulations of the 457 scheme and are less transparent. Although core obligations remain, such as the requirement to treat migrant workers no less favourably than Australian workers, other details are worked out between an employer and the Department of Immigration and Border Protection and may remain hidden from view as 'commercial-in-confidence'.[3]

The Fronditha labour agreement was the first to bring in temporary workers for the aged-care sector. The deal was discussed with the relevant trade unions and incorporated into the enterprise agreement. Senator Cash hailed it 'as a great outcome for the community' and indicated that she was open to approving similar deals for aged care involving other community languages.[4] As far as Lekakis is concerned, it is the only way that culturally specific aged-care providers can recruit an adequate number of appropriately skilled and urgently needed staff. He anticipates that Fronditha will have hired about 60 Greek-speaking migrants by the time its three-year labour agreement expires. If everything works out—that is, if the Greek-speaking worker likes the job and if Fronditha management is happy with the worker's performance—then after four years Fronditha will sponsor the temporary migrant to shift from a 457 visa to permanent residency.

In practice, Fronditha has not actively recruited personal-care assistants directly from Greece. While it has sourced a small number of highly qualified nurses offshore, it has found most of its personal-care staff among Greeks who were already living in Australia on other temporary visas, mostly as international students.

This is how Evgenia Skandalaki came to work at Fronditha. 'This was a great opportunity for me,' she says with a broad smile. 'I never imagined going to another country and starting from zero without even speaking the language. After three years in Australia, it's like I'm dreaming.'

Before she left Greece, where she originally trained as a nurse, Evgenia worked as a product specialist with a hospital-equipment company. She earned a good salary, but after the firm sacked seven of her colleagues in 2012, she found the work increasingly stressful. The worst of the Greek economic crisis was yet to come; when a younger co-worker died of a heart attack, however, Evgenia knew she had to get out. 'It was now or never,' she says.

She decided to travel to Melbourne to spend time with her great-uncle and cousins, but almost changed her mind at the last minute. Shortly before she was due to depart, her sister gave birth to twins, a boy and a girl, born prematurely. The baby boy died a week before Evgenia's flight.

'It was very difficult to leave,' she says. After arriving in Melbourne, Evgenia felt insecure. 'I couldn't speak the language,' she says. 'I asked myself, have I made the right decision? Should I go back?' She had come to Australia on a tourist visa, but with an open mind about potentially staying on. When she investigated getting her nursing qualifications recognised here she realised it would be a long and hard road, not least because she would need to spend a long time learning English. 'I am thirty-five years old,' she says. 'It is harder to learn a new language when you are older.'

Despite her doubts, she decided to swap her tourist visa for a student visa and enrolled in an English course. At a cost of $13,000 per year, this was a significant investment. When the immigration department asked whether she was studying English because she was intending to stay in Australia—which would have been grounds for refusing her visa application—she said no. She told them that English would benefit her career in Greece because a lot of migrants there don't speak Greek and English would help her communicate with them when they needed health care.

Evgenia studied hard, often until midnight. Most of her classmates—many of them also from Greece—took a much more relaxed attitude. 'They were coming to class only for the attendance,' she says, meaning that they needed to get marked off the roll to show that they were turning up to class in line with the requirements of their visa, even though their major reason for enrolment was not to learn English, but to stay in Australia and benefit from the right to work up to 40 hours per fortnight that comes with being an international student.

Evgenia worked, too—20 hours a week in a Greek cafe in Thornbury—and this eventually led her to Fronditha. A Greek-speaking customer told Evgenia about her work in a nursing home, and gave her information about how to qualify for a Certificate III in aged care. Evgenia enrolled immediately, adding three days a week of vocational study to her language course and her job. Six months later, to complete her qualification, she did an unpaid placement of 180 hours at Fronditha's Thornbury facility. Fronditha then offered her casual work for up to 20 hours per week (the maximum allowed on her student visa). When an ongoing position came up at Clayton, the organisation sponsored her for a four-year 457 visa under its labour agreement.

There was still one hurdle to overcome. To get a 457 visa, Evgenia had to reach at least level five in the nine-level International English Language Testing System. Nine is the 'expert' ranking, while five designates modest users, who have partial command of the language, can cope with overall meaning in most situations and are able to handle basic communication in their own field. Despite speaking no English when she arrived, after spending less than two years in Australia, Evgenia achieved level six or seven in all four components of the demanding test—listening, reading, writing and speaking.

'It wasn't easy,' says Evgenia of her path to a 457 visa. 'It was very hard. But I still feel like I was lucky. If you ask all the Greek newcomers now, everyone is trying to find sponsorship.' I ask if she hopes to become a permanent resident of Australia at the end of her four-year contract with Fronditha on a 457 visa. 'Of course,' she says, with another broad smile.

Evgenia was one of 13 Greek-speaking migrants Fronditha sponsored for 457 visas in the first year of its labour agreement. Another 16 international students were employed casually after completing a Certificate III in aged care, with the intention that they, too, will be sponsored for 457 visas as ongoing positions become available. Three-quarters of the workforce at Fronditha's 120-room Thornbury facility are now Greek speakers. Fronditha is gradually increasing the number of Greek-speaking staff at other sites like Clayton, too, not by replacing existing employees, but by seeking to recruit Greek speakers whenever vacancies arise.

'The results are outstanding,' says George Lekakis. 'We've found excellent people. The climate is happier. Complaints are down because the care is more appropriate to residents. It means if someone needs to go to the toilet, they can tell someone and they don't wet themselves.'

On 25 March, residents and staff dress in national costume and put on a play and a choir performance to celebrate Greek Independence Day. 'That could not have happened without our Greek-speaking staff,' says the CEO. 'It's not just the language; it's the cultural ethos, what you say to people.' He says that Fronditha has also paid for its non-Greek-speaking staff to undertake Greek-language courses, but that this failed to achieve the same result. 'The major part of looking after people is being able to communicate,' he says.

The Fronditha Care labour agreement illustrates that despite the many potential pitfalls of temporary migration, it can work well, delivering positive outcomes for employers, migrants, the community and the nation. Fronditha Care needs workers with very specific additional linguistic skills—workers it cannot find locally. Greeks like Evgenia are looking for opportunities abroad so they can escape the stifling effects of the economic crisis in their homeland. Australia has an ageing Greek-born population, many of whom would like to be cared for by someone who speaks their language and understands their culture. If older Greek-Australians can be cared for in this way, then their later years will be happier and healthier, and their families will have fewer anxieties. Temporary migrant workers like Evgenia make a net positive contribution to government budgets, because they pay tax but are not eligible for government payments or services. What is more, they fund their own training and skills development, and generate jobs and profits in the Australian education sector along the way. 'I call it pay-as-you-go migration,' says George Lekakis.

The rise of the 457 visa over the past 20 years does not just mark a shift in emphasis from permanent to temporary migration; it also signals an equally profound change from supply-driven to demand-driven migration that transfers significant decision-making power in migrant selection from government to employers.

Under what we might call the late-twentieth-century model of skilled migration, the government set an annual quota for skilled migration and applications were assessed on a first-come, first-served basis via the points test, against arguably objective criteria such as English-language proficiency, age, qualifications, work experience and the level of demand for a particular profession in the Australian economy. This system worked pretty well—in fact, Australia was often seen as a world leader in the effective administration of skilled migration—but it still had some weaknesses. As a supply-driven system, it delivered a set number of apparently suitably qualified migrants into the labour market every year, yet some migrants still struggled to find work at a level appropriate to their qualifications and experience. Accountants ended up driving taxis; medical scientists cleaned office buildings. There could be several reasons for this 'human-capital wastage' (to adopt economist-speak). In some cases, discrimination by employers might have been to blame; in others, migrants who, on paper, should have been in high demand, may have lacked some of the 'soft' skills necessary for the relevant job, something the migration points test could not adequately assess. Another factor might have been that migrants had reasons to live in big cities, when the skills shortages that brought them to Australia were located in regional towns or remote areas. Finally, annual government planning and target setting is not very responsive to changes in business conditions that can rapidly reduce or increase the demand for skilled labour in particular sectors or in the economy as a whole.

Australia's hybrid twenty-first-century model of demand-driven migration addresses many of these issues. By giving employers a greater say in the selection of migrants, it enables businesses to seek out the particular combination of hard and soft skills that they need to meet the immediate needs of their enterprise—such as fluency in Greek among aged-care assistants. Rather than moving to Australia and then looking around for a position to suit their qualifications, migrants are recruited directly into a specific job with a specific firm in a specific location. They are employed from day one. Giving employers a bigger role in migrant selection results in better matching of workers to jobs, and this boosts productivity, because skills and experience are more efficiently allocated to the employment needs of the economy. A demand-driven system is also more flexible and responsive to changing economic conditions—employers do not bring in migrant workers to fill an annual quota, but only recruit when they have a vacancy. If business booms they recruit more staff; if it falls away they recruit less.

As a potential stepping stone to permanent residency, the 457 visa also acts as a filter: if migrants prove, for whatever reason, to be ill-matched to the firm or the job or the location, then they will only be temporary until a better match can be found. If, however, a firm sponsors a worker to become a permanent resident, then it is because that person is filling an important and ongoing role in the enterprise. In such circumstances, a migrant's prospects of building a successful life in Australia are good: the Productivity Commission concludes that 'employer-nominated immigrants have, on average, better short- and medium-term labour-market outcomes than independent skilled immigrants'.[5] Economics professor Bob Gregory agrees, and describes recent outcomes for permanent settlers to Australia under the hybrid model of two-step migration as 'phenomenal'.[6]

What is there to criticise in this picture? One concern is that employers will use temporary visas to bring in migrants ahead of employing locals. In theory, a business must test the labour market to see if suitable Australian workers are available before it can fill a position with a migrant on a 457 visa. In practice, labour-market testing is little more than a joke: there are a host of exemptions and, even where labour-market testing does apply, the requirement can be met with online advertisements or social-media posts made over the previous 12 months, regardless of how widely these job notices were seen. In its current form, labour-market testing amounts to a box-ticking exercise. Previous attempts to implement it more rigorously did not work well either: they proved cumbersome and difficult to monitor and enforce.

Employers regard labour-market testing as an unnecessary bureaucratic impediment; the Australian Chamber of Commerce and Industry describes it as 'akin to asking employers to walk through wet cement'.[7] Business argues that there is already a strong incentive to hire Australians first before looking offshore, since it is far easier and cheaper to recruit locally. This argument does not really hold water since many temporary migrants are now recruited locally, too—around half of all 457 visas are granted onshore, to temporary migrants who are already in Australia (as existing 457-visa holders, international-student graduates and working holidaymakers). In such cases, employing a temporary migrant worker instead of a local imposes few additional costs on employers.

The Migration Council Australia argues that the best way to encourage priority recruitment of Australians is through a stronger price signal. It has called for a substantial increase in the fee that a business pays to nominate a worker for a 457 visa. In 2015, this fee was just $330. This is a rock-bottom price compared to the $1,060 visa charge that the migrant must pay for a 457 visa, let alone the $6,865 required to apply for a partner visa.[8] The Migration Council contends that raising the nomination fee would make employers think harder about using migrants on temporary work visas ahead of Australians by increasing the price difference between the two options.[9]

Another concern is that 457 visas reduce the incentive for business (and government) to invest in training: firms may find it easier to buy skills 'off-the-shelf', as it were—by recruiting temporary migrants—rather than put time, money and effort into developing the capacities of domestic workers. Again, there are checks in the system designed to work against this possibility. In order to qualify as sponsors of temporary migrants on 457 visas, employers must furnish evidence of meeting one of two training benchmarks—either recent payments equivalent to at least two per cent of payroll to an industry training fund operating in the same sector, or recent expenditure equivalent to at least one per cent of the payroll on training current Australian employees.[10] Both unions and employers question whether these benchmarks achieve the intended outcome (of getting more Australians trained and into jobs).

In 2014, an independent review of the 457-visa program commissioned by the federal government recommended replacing the benchmarks with an annual training contribution. Employers would pay a levy for each 457-visa holder on their books: the suggested starting rate was $400–$800 per migrant worker, depending on the size of the business, which would have raised in the order of $42 million in 2015. The extra revenue raised by the levy would be spent on training for disadvantaged Australians to enter the workforce, and on addressing critical skills shortages through the vocational education system.[11] The government accepted this recommendation, but is yet to act on it. In March 2016, after a year-long inquiry into temporary work visa programs, the Senate Education and Employment References Committee recommended a much higher training levy of $4,000 per 457-visa holder (although Coalition senators dissented from the recommendation).[12] A training levy would also act as a price signal to encourage firms to hire or train locals first.

Whether the current training benchmarks, or whatever replaces them, are sufficient to give primacy to local recruitment and training is debatable, however, not least because a significant number of people outside the labour market—such as the long-term unemployed, early school leavers, women returning to work after spending years raising children and production-line workers who have been made redundant by restructuring—often need intensive assistance to move into any job, let alone a skilled position. Training is what's known as a 'collective action problem'—it is in the interests of industry as a whole for all employers to train staff, but each individual employer fears their own investment may be wasted because of the possibility that a rival may save on the cost of training and poach their newly skilled workers. In the absence of effective industry-wide training, temporary migration schemes become a more attractive alternative.

This is a point made strongly by the global migration law firm Fragomen, which argues that Australia's skills shortages 'are a consequence of the significant reduction in university and vocational education funding by Australian governments, particularly in STEM [Science, Technology, Engineering and Mathematics] subjects and trades, over the last 20 years'. In other words, it is 'the lack of sufficient training and skills development opportunities for Australians' that drives business demand for temporary skilled migration, 'not the other way around'.[13]

The extensive use of 457 visas in the hospitality industry is illustrative of the problem. In the three years to 30 June 2015, more than 14,000 temporary 457 visas were issued to 'cooks' and 'cafe or restaurant managers', making these the first- and third-most frequently nominated occupations in the program during this period. In 2015 there were three times more cooks than general practitioners working in Australia on 457 visas.[14] It did not appear that these cooks were predominantly employed in mining camps or outback towns, where it might be hard to recruit locals, since about two-thirds of them were living in Victoria and New South Wales.

It is reasonable to question why we are importing so many cooks from overseas rather than training them locally. It takes one year of study to get a Certificate III in commercial cookery, and applicants do not need to have completed year 12 to qualify for the course. Cooking would appear to be an ideal employment pathway for Australians who are out of a job, especially as restaurant owners say that they have trouble filling positions in their kitchens. Yet according to the federal government's career handbook, *Australian Jobs 2015*, cooks suffer an above-average rate of unemployment, and almost half of them only work part time. So what is going on here? Is there a skills shortage in commercial cooking or not?

Part of the problem appears to be that Australia's vocational education system does a dismal job of producing qualified cooks, with the completion rate for certificates in the food trades languishing at around 30 per cent, a far worse result than in any other sector and well below the poor average for trades as a whole.[15] Research suggests that one reason the attrition rate is so high is that the life of a trainee cook is one of 'poor wages, unsociable hours and unpaid overtime'.[16] Even after qualifying, cooks often work broken shifts in a high-pressure environment for relatively low pay, and many end up leaving the industry. As a result, employers will probably continue to face challenges in recruiting domestically trained cooks until wages rise and conditions improve (and diners pay more in restaurants). This is unlikely to happen as long as employers can recruit offshore staff willing to accept prevailing pay and conditions, and so minimise their own training costs and keep wages down.

At $58,300, the average nominated base salary for 457-visa holders in the accommodation and food services industry is by far the lowest of any sector using temporary migrant labour—the next lowest is agriculture, forestry and fishing ($68,200).[17] Under the rules of the 457 scheme, any foreign cook employed on a 457 visa in Australia should be paid above the visa's minimum salary threshold of $53,900, but this is quite a high salary for cooks in Australia, where full-time median weekly earnings are less than $48,000. Which raises a question: why are restaurants employing foreign cooks on above-average pay, instead of increasing the wages they offer to attract Australian cooks? The answer may be that they are not: researchers Bob Birrell and Ernest Healy suspect that many employers of foreign cooks 'are almost certainly violating the rules by paying less than the minimum amount and/or perhaps requiring extra hours beyond the award level'.[18] To many Australians, an annual salary of less than $50,000 for working split shifts in a commercial kitchen is not very appealing; it may be much more attractive to a migrant from Nepal, Sri Lanka or the Philippines, where wages for the same work would be much lower. Given the contingent nature of their temporary visas, many foreign cooks succumb to pressure to work for much less than this, particularly if other pressure is being applied.

In a study of Indian 457-visa holders in Australia, Selvaraj Velayutham found that cultural prejudices rendered cooks in small Indian restaurants particularly vulnerable to exploitation by 'co-ethnics'.[19] He spoke to a number of cooks who were working more than 12 hours a day, seven days a week, for little or no pay. Employers had often used personal connections to recruit these workers from their home villages. As a result, hierarchies of caste and class were perpetuated in the Australian workplace. Indian employers justified exploitative treatment of their migrant workers on the basis that they were used to such conditions. The reference point for pay rates were wages in India or in other countries where large numbers of Indian migrant workers are employed, such as Singapore or the Gulf States.

It appears beyond dispute that the vocational-education system could and should do a better job of equipping locals to meet the needs of the hospitality industry. Whether the rise of the 457-visa system has contributed to the failings of trades training is a different question. Even the Productivity Commission, which supposedly offers the final expert word on all matters economic, cannot form a view on whether immigration has a negative effect on education and training. It says that it is a 'potential issue', but there is little in the way of recent research in the area and further evidence is required.[20]

Overall, there is no simple equation between adding a foreign worker and taking an Australian job. If an employer uses a 457 visa to fill a crucial position because no local candidate has the right skills, and the temporary migrant enables that enterprise to expand its operations, there will be a net increase in jobs in the economy. If a restaurant thrives by employing a foreign cook, this may create jobs for Australian waiting staff or butchers or vegetable growers or delivery drivers. Temporary workers also generate local employment through their own spending on goods and services. Migrants on 457 visas can also be part of the training solution rather than part of the training problem by passing on the skills they bring to Australia. In survey data analysed by the Migration Council Australia, more than three-quarters of 457 workers reported that they helped to train or develop other workers in the course of their job and more than two-thirds of employers said they used 457-visa holders to train Australian staff.[21]

The biggest concern with Australia's contemporary system of two-step, demand-driven skilled migration may not be that foreign workers take Australian jobs or reduce investment in local training, but that the 457 visa shifts the balance of power in the workplace in favour of employers and renders migrant workers more vulnerable to exploitation. It does this by reducing migrants' mobility in the labour market. It is not that 457 workers are irrevocably tied to one employer for the duration of their visa—they can seek an alternative position—but 457-visa holders are far less free than Australian workers to change jobs.

The first barrier to mobility for temporary migrants who want to change workplaces is that they must find an alternative employer willing and qualified to sponsor them for a 457 visa. It is risky to leave one sponsor without having lined up an alternative in advance—partly because visa holders are not eligible for any kind of government assistance, like unemployment benefits or job-placement services—and, more importantly, because under 'visa condition 8107', if a temporary migrant is unemployed and without a sponsor for more than 90 days, then their 457 visa lapses and they must leave Australia.[22] (Prior to 1 July 2013, the time frame for finding an alternative sponsor was just 28 days.)

A second barrier to mobility is that if a 457-visa holder switches employers, then the clock resets to zero on the qualifying period for permanent residence. The route from 457 visa to permanent residence is uncertain, even though it is now a core element of Australia's skilled-migration program. In most cases, it requires employer sponsorship. In the seven years to 30 June 2015 more than a quarter of all permanent skilled migrants travelled along this pathway. In 2014–15 that equated to almost 38,000 people being sponsored for permanent residence by their employers.[23]

In most cases, a temporary migrant on a 457 visa must work for an employer full time for two years before the employer can sponsor the foreign worker for permanent residence.[24] In reality the amount of time a temporary migrant is tied to a particular boss is even longer, because the applicant must continue working for the same employer while the application for residency is processed, which takes between five and eight months.[25] This can tie a worker to an employer despite underpayment, poor conditions or abuse.

The situation is different under labour agreements, like the deal George Lekakis struck for Fronditha. Labour agreements bring in overseas workers on 457 visas at lower skill levels, and the government assumes that these temporary migrants will leave Australia when the labour agreement expires. In fact, the immigration department specifically advises employers to 'avoid promising overseas workers that they will be sponsored for permanent residence' under a labour agreement.[26] The immigration minister will only consider exceptions in limited circumstances: an employer must show that there is a continuing long-term shortage of suitably skilled Australian workers and address structural issues like low pay that can lead to an over-reliance on migrant workers.[27] Even in these special cases—as with Fronditha Care—temporary migrant workers on 457 visas issued under a labour agreement can only be sponsored for permanent residence after working in Australia for 'at least three and a half years'.[28]

The contingent nature of a temporary 457 visa significantly reduces migrant workers' bargaining power and makes it less likely that they will leave a job, particularly if they aspire to become permanent residents (as more than two-thirds of 457-visa holders say they do).[29] This suits employers very well, because if migrants were granted permanent residence on arrival, then there is a fair chance that they would not stay long in jobs that were lower paid, more demanding, more remote or more dangerous than positions in other parts of the economy. Like Australian citizens and permanent residents, they would seek to move to higher-wage jobs with better conditions or in better locations. The best and brightest migrant workers would probably leave first. The rules of the 457 scheme mitigate against this to command greater loyalty from temporary migrants.

From an employer's perspective, requiring temporary migrants to work full time in the same enterprise for two or more years before seeking permanent residence makes a lot of sense. A firm that goes to the effort and expense of recruiting and inducting a migrant worker to meet a specific business need would be understandably frustrated if, soon after arrival, that worker decided to move on to greener pastures or was poached by a rival company. Fronditha's George Lekakis acknowledges this. 'You want to keep the staff you select,' he says.

From a migrant worker's perspective, however, the two-year threshold is a leash that ties them to a particular job, regardless of the pay and conditions they are expected to work under.

Before his appointment as CEO of Fronditha, George Lekakis chaired the Victorian Multicultural Commission for nine years. He's also held leadership positions with the Ethnic Communities' Council of Victoria and the Federation of Ethnic Communities' Councils of Australia. Despite his long career as an advocate for ethnic, religious and multicultural communities, Lekakis is also pragmatic. He says temporary migrants should only be able to transition to permanent residence if the economy needs them. He sees a parallel between today's temporary-migration arrangements and the postwar resettlement program, when displaced Europeans were sent to work on projects like the Snowy Hydro for at least two years in return for assisted passage to

Australia. 'It is the same modus operandi,' he says. 'They were wanted for jobs and wherever it might have been, off they went.'

There is a key difference, however. In the postwar era, there was a clear limit on the amount of time a migrant was expected to work in a particular job before gaining full freedom of movement in the labour market. There is no time threshold after which an employer is required to sponsor a temporary migrant to become permanent. If an employer prefers a temporary-migrant workforce, or remains undecided about a worker after two, three or four years, or if future staffing needs remain uncertain, then the firm can rehire the migrant on another temporary 457 visa. This enables employers to 'try before they buy', as it were. An enterprise can hire a temporary migrant 'on spec': if the worker does not live up to expectations because of skill deficits or attitude problems, or if the firm's labour needs change after a year or two, then it is easy to let that temporary migrant go again. In this respect, as researchers Chris Wright and Andreea Constantin write, temporary migrants can be regarded as 'disposable labour'—workers who are easier to control and dispense with.[30]

This does not necessarily mean that most employers have a callous, calculating or even conscious intention to treat 457 workers as disposable, but as long as migrants' visas are linked to their employment, disposability is a function of their temporary and contingent status. This may lead employers to perceive temporary migrants as diligent and loyal and to attribute these characteristics to some putative cultural trait, when in reality the migrant workers' reliance on the employer for visa sponsorship may be the dominant factor in shaping behaviour in the workplace. 'We tend to get great loyalty, particularly from our Filipino chefs,' a resource-industry executive told researchers from Edith Cowan University in a report funded by the Australian Mines and Metals Association. 'They commit to what they signed up for and they sign up for four years.' Another mining employer complained about Australian fitters 'jumping ship' for an extra 50 cents an hour: 'I mean, we'll train them up then they'll stay just for a month or two.' By contrast, 457-visa holders were perceived as more loyal, with a stronger work ethic and as less likely to seek a wage rise.[31]

In 2012, the immigration department commissioned a survey of 1,600 employers that were current or previous sponsors of migrant workers on 457 visas. In analysing the results, Wright and Constantin noted that only a tiny proportion of respondents claimed that they would try to address a vacancy in their firms by offering the job at a higher wage, even though this is generally considered to be the best way to probe whether a skills shortage actually exists. The researchers conclude that some claims of a skills shortage may have less to do with a lack of available qualifications in the labour market than with an employer's desire to attract workers with particular attitudes, including a willingness 'to undertake their duties in a compliant manner'.[32] Employers cited the two most important benefits of the 457 scheme as being that temporary migrants filled skilled vacancies and were highly skilled. It is notable, however, that the next highest ranked benefits were that temporary migrants have 'increased loyalty' and are 'harder working/have a better attitude'.[33]

If the link between sponsorship and visa status engenders loyalty to the firm and encourages diligent and compliant attitudes in overseas workers, then this lowers risk and increases flexibility for employers. The flip side of this picture is heightened risk and reduced flexibility for temporary migrants. In the parlance of industry, temporary migrant workers are the 'shock absorbers' for periods of 'labour-market readjustment'.[34] The logical extension of this metaphor is that when business conditions hit a pothole, it's migrant workers who feel the sharpest jolt and help ensure the rest of us enjoy a smoother ride.

The transfer of risk from employer to temporary migrant is evident in Fronditha Care's labour agreement. The organisation makes no promises to Greek-speaking migrants like Evgenia who invest upwards of $6,500 to undertake a Certificate III in aged care (plus any investment in learning English), beyond offering to consider them for an unpaid placement at the end of their training that might lead to casual work and then perhaps to a contract for a 457 visa. 'The students are taking all the risk,' acknowledges George Lekakis.

This transferal of risk does not give employers carte blanche. The law requires equal treatment for migrant and Australian workers, and there is some policing of the 457-visa scheme to ensure compliance, although monitoring is far from comprehensive. If an employer does the wrong thing by a temporary migrant then this can have its own costs—there is a risk of a valued worker quitting to seek another job or to leave Australia. The more highly skilled and in demand a migrant worker is, the stronger that worker's bargaining position in any negotiation.

But while migrants on 457 visas can be found in a diverse range of roles, the link between employment and visa status is common to all. There is a systemic difference between the position of temporary migrants in the labour market and the position of Australian residents and citizens. As Melbourne University legal scholar Joo-Cheong Tham puts it, the power of a sponsor to terminate employment can trigger 'a chain of events' that might lead to a migrant on a 457 visa being removed from Australia. This 'induces a lack of mobility' for these workers in the labour market, and if employers sense that workers lack the freedom to change jobs they may 'choose to engage in more exploitative practices'.[35] So while, legally, temporary migrants are supposed to enjoy the same wages, conditions and workplace rights as Australians, in reality they can experience differential treatment and may be more vulnerable to coercion and abuse.

A quick trawl through the newsfeed of the Fair Work Ombudsman throws up plenty of examples. A Sydney cafe that underpaid a pastry chef by $22,000 (the Indian chef was reluctant to raise concerns about her wages because she relied on her employer's support for her visa to remain in Australia); five experienced Chinese tradesmen on 457 visas who earned less than three dollars per hour for working 11 hours per day, seven days per week for a WA construction company (some of the workers had paid the firm $2,500 to secure their jobs in Australia); three nursing assistants from the Philippines who were recruited by a labour-hire firm and then not only underpaid, but also charged fees for training that was never provided (the health-care recruiting company was fined $48,000); the manufacturing business near Orange in Central New South Wales that made unlawful deductions from a 457 worker's pay and short-changed his hourly rate and leave entitlements (the Ombudsman ordered $15,600 in backpay).

This list could be much longer. In its first six years of operation, the Fair Work Ombudsman received close to 1,600 complaints from 457-visa holders and recovered almost $2 million in unpaid wages and entitlements.[36] Still, given that there were more than 600,000 temporary 457 visas issued during this period, that statistic could be read as suggesting that the exploitation of migrant workers is rare. This is the interpretation of employer organisations like the Business Council of Australia and the Australian Industry Group, which assert that concerns about widespread abuse in the 457 scheme are unfounded and that close to 99 per cent of employers do the right thing. The sometimes spectacular examples of exploitation by the Fair Work Ombudsman are, they argue, the exceptions that prove the rule and show the system is working: these are the one per cent of shonky operators, the few bad eggs in the vast ranks of law-abiding and well-intentioned employers, and they are getting caught by the workplace watchdog.[37]

There are other ways of cutting the data, though. Since 1 July 2013, the Fair Work Ombudsman, which has a dedicated overseas workers team, has had a specific responsibility under the Migration Act to monitor whether temporary migrant workers on 457 visas are paid properly and employed in the positions for which they were nominated. In the first two years after being given this mandate, the Fair Work Ombudsman identified potential breaches at about a quarter of the workplaces it assessed (466 referrals from 1,731 appraisals).[38] That is a high strike rate but it does not necessarily mean that one in four employers deliberately flout the rules, since it makes sense for the Fair Work Ombudsman to target workplaces or industries where it already has concerns (and some breaches may be inadvertent). Nevertheless, this data suggests that the treatment of 457 workers is less benign than employer groups would like us to believe.

In 2014 an independent inquiry into the 457 scheme commissioned by the federal government found that serious abuses were more likely in small businesses and in particular parts of the economy, notably the construction, food, hospitality, retail and service sectors.[39]

At its core the issue is structural: the right of 457-visa holders to live and work in Australia depends on their continued employment by a valid sponsor and in general this renders them less free, and therefore at greater risk of exploitation, than Australian workers. Industrial relations commissioner Barbara Deegan identified this structural issue in her 2009 review of the 457 program:

Despite the views of some employers and employer organisations, Subclass 457 visa holders are different from other employees in Australian workplaces. They are the only group of employees whose ability to remain in Australia is largely dependent upon their employment, and to a large extent, their employer. It is for these reasons that visa holders of this type are vulnerable and are open to exploitation.[40]

Based on the cases it sees, the community legal centre JobWatch says visa dependency makes 457 workers more vulnerable than Australians to underpayment, unfair dismissal, pressure to do unreasonable work, discrimination, harassment and demands by employers for payment in return for visa sponsorship.[41]

The link between employer sponsorship and permanent residence creates a particular choke point at which workers can be pressured into acceding to unacceptable demands. Again, Deegan identified this in her 2009 review, noting that an employer's ability to give or withhold sponsorship is very powerful and makes temporary migrants with 'aspirations towards permanent residency' particularly 'vulnerable to exploitation as a consequence of their temporary status'.[42] They may put up with 'substandard living conditions, illegal or unfair deductions from wages, and other similar forms of exploitation' in order not to jeopardise potential employer sponsorship. The situation is 'exacerbated where the visa holder is unable to meet the requirements for permanent residency via an independent application,'[43] which may be the case for an increasing number of migrants: if employer nomination on a 457 visa continues to emerge as the dominant pathway to permanent settlement, this will put pressure on the decreasing number of places available for independent migration without employer endorsement.

As researcher Salimah Valiani comments in the Canadian

context, the sponsorship that enables a migrant worker to get and keep a temporary visa gives employers 'yet more power in the already unequal employer-employee relationship'.[44] The additional role of sponsorship in making the transition to residency means that temporary migrant workers who want to remain permanently 'are thus rendered yet more dependent and exploitable by employers well aware of their employees' precarious legal and economic status'.[45]

The implications of these power dynamics extend beyond the potential exploitation of migrant workers to the broader labour market. Indian restaurant owners say they recruit Indian cooks offshore because it is impossible to find them locally. But as Selvaraj Velayutham notes, 'this is a somewhat circular argument, as the import of 457-visa labour has driven down wages and conditions such that few locals (including Indian permanent residents) are willing to do this work'.[46] Stephen Clibborn from the business school at the University of Sydney identifies the same issue: the exploitation and underpayment of vulnerable temporary migrant workers can create a race to the bottom on wages and conditions, particularly in sectors like hospitality and retail. 'Other vulnerable groups of workers, including Australia's youth, must then accept lower wages to gain employment,' he warns.[47]

The broader implications of the exploitation of temporary migrant workers for the labour market do not begin and end with Australia's main dedicated migrant labour scheme; the 457-visa program is, after all, quite small, with 457-visa holders accounting for only about one per cent of the total workforce. There are many more de facto migrant workers—most of them international students and backpackers—and their wages and conditions are far less likely to be regulated and monitored than those of 457-visa holders. As a result, these de facto labour migrants can end up in precarious and abusive situations.

9 | De Facto Labour Migration
Backpackers and Students

Katrina, who works part time in my local butcher, says she will never eat an Australian strawberry again. Katrina is from the United Kingdom, and she qualified for a second 12-month working-holiday visa by completing 88 days of 'specified work' (in agriculture, forestry, fishing, mining or construction) in a regional area. In Katrina's case this involved travelling a short distance out of Melbourne to the berry farms of the Yarra Valley. She says picking strawberries was very hard and she was supervised by 'some real nut jobs', who were constantly yelling and swearing at the workers. Backpackers were paid piece rates—that is, the amount of money they earned was determined by the weight of berries they could pick. Since there were too many pickers and not enough berries, Katrina ended up working very long days to earn a paltry $7 per hour—about a third of the minimum hourly wage of $21.61 that should be paid for horticultural work like fruit and vegetable picking or pruning.[1] (A written and signed agreement setting out the pay rate per piece is needed for piece work to be lawful. If there is no written agreement in place, workers are entitled to the minimum hourly award wage.[2])

Katrina put up with the conditions in order to get her second visa, and says she has met many other travellers who have had similar or worse experiences doing the same thing. In 2014–15, more than 40,000 young travellers secured a second working-holiday visa by working in a regional area. The Fair Work Ombudsman recognises that the need to get an employer's sign-off on the 88 days of specified work increases working holidaymakers' vulnerability in the labour market. The risk is heightened when backpackers are seeking work in remote locations.[3] It is not uncommon, for example, for hostels in rural towns to promise to organise jobs for travellers to qualify for a second working-holiday visa if they pay for their accommodation upfront. The son of a German friend was caught out in this way: Janik booked into a backpacker hostel in Ayr in north Queensland, paying rent in advance on the understanding that there would be work available, only to find himself hanging around for days twiddling his thumbs with 35 other young travellers who had been given the same assurances. Another German backpacker, Max, reported similar experiences at a different Queensland hostel: 'We arrived at the hostel and there were work boots everywhere and people returning from days on farms—we thought—this is great, there must be lots of work for everyone. We happily handed over a month's deposit and then basically sat back and waited. It was well over a week before we even got one day's work and then there was nothing for another week.'[4] On the basis of focus-group research with backpackers, Elsa Underhill from Deakin University concluded that 'false job vacancy information is endemic'.⁵ Half her respondents reported being misled in this way. Some had made an expensive trip to the Northern Territory on the promise of mango-picking work, only to discover on arrival that the entire harvest had failed.⁶

In late 2015, the Oasis Backpacker Hostel in Mildura was specifically recruiting working holidaymakers seeking a second-year visa via an online backpacker job board.⁷ The hostel's listing promised farm work 'available ASAP...lots of jobs starting, need people urgently to fill jobs'. The Oasis' Facebook page had a similar message: 'a very busy time ahead' with 'loads of work', it beckoned, but warned that the hostel was 'only taking confirmed bookings' because there were so few beds left.⁸ On the hotel-booking website TripAdvisor, the Mildura Oasis is ranked 'terrible' on the basis of eight reviews (in English, French and Italian) that all complain—among other things—about promises of work that were not fulfilled. 'Don't stay here!' writes 'Gizmo' from the United Kingdom. 'They give you enough days work to pay next weeks rent and that's all they care about!' Philippe S says it's a trap: 'Don't go! they say they are offering jobs for backpackers but its a lie, they just want you to book the hostel!'⁹ Similarly savage reviews crop up on other sites.¹⁰

The Oasis is not the only Mildura hostel to attract this kind of criticism. One backpacker reported having to wait until 11.30 at night to find out whether or not he and his girlfriend would get work the next day, and then being expected to start at 4.30 in the morning.¹¹ The Fair Work Ombudsman has warned specifically about one particular 'dodgy' hostel owner and labour-hire contractor, who holds out a promise of jobs and then 'charges up to $150 a week for backpackers to stay in sub-standard houses and caravans, with allegations of up to

32 people being accommodated in one home and 12 more sleeping in the garage'.[12]

When work does eventuate, it can turn out to be highly exploitative and underpaid. Mary posted the story of her 'Mildura nightmare' on another website for backpackers seeking rural jobs.[13] Mary and her boyfriend went to Mildura in the winter of 2014 to take up an offer of work citrus picking. Mary had seen the job ad online, and when she called to inquire, was told she would earn about $22 per hour (which corresponds to the award rate). A notorious local contractor called Don, who calls himself 'The Don' and 'the King of Mildura', picked the couple up from the airport and took them straight to an ATM so that they could hand him $900 in cash. Don insisted that they sign a document saying that the payment was a job-search fee, when in reality it was for two weeks' rent in advance in his 'backpackers' (at $150 per week each, plus a $150 bond).

Mary and her boyfriend thought that they had booked a private room for a couple, but they discovered on arrival that they were sleeping in bunk beds in an unheated shed along with four other travellers. 'Don's backpackers' was not a hostel, as such, but a four-bedroom house, plus shed and caravans, crammed with more than 30 people sharing only two showers. The work Mary had been promised turned out not to be fruit picking, but vine pulling—ripping dead grapevines off trellises. It is not easy work: the vines wrap themselves around the wires as they grow so it takes considerable force to pull them free and there is a constant risk of getting whipped on the face and body.[14] At the end of her first day, Mary discovered that her pay rate was 15 cents per pulled vine. She says the most she and her boyfriend could earn in a day was $30 each, leaving them just $60 per week income after paying 'The Don' for their accommodation.

While anecdotal stories like Mary's might not be considered reliable evidence, other backpackers make similar complaints about Don; one national TV current affairs program has wondered whether he might be Australia's worst boss.[15]

In mid-2015, Queensland's anti-discrimination commissioner Kevin Cocks reported that his staff had spent 18 months looking into the treatment of migrant workers in the rich farmlands of the Lockyer Valley, west of Brisbane, where they found unscrupulous contractors and landlords taking advantage of backpackers who needed to complete their 88 days of rural work to get a second working-holiday visa:

> The Commission has received reports that people have been working for as little as $3 per hour, or not receiving any pay at all…In other cases we have heard many stories of female workers being asked for sexual favours in exchange for a contractor signing off on their work form for their visa extension. Farmworkers have been injured on-site and contractors tell them to get themselves to a hospital. Many workers are working without any WorkCover because they have not completed the paperwork. Contractors rent accommodation to their workers, and often overcrowding is rampant with excessively high rents charged.[16]

Peter Hockings, executive officer of Bundaberg Fruit and Vegetable Growers, told ABC TV's *Four Corners* that he's heard numerous reports of working holidaymakers being offered three options by employers in return for signing off on their second-year visa application: 'They either continue working for nothing or they pay a significant lump sum—a cash lump sum—or provide sexual favours.'[17]

In 2015, along with that *Four Corners* exposé, the mistreatment of working holidaymakers in Australian agriculture received close attention from a Senate committee,[18] prompted parliamentary investigations in the states of South Australia, Victoria and Queensland,[19] and encouraged the federal government to set up a ministerial working group and the multi-agency Taskforce Cadena to tackle visa fraud and the exploitation of foreign workers.[20] It was also the subject of a long-term inquiry by the Fair Work Ombudsman, which reported that it had received about 2,000 requests for help from working holidaymakers over the previous two years.[21]

This deeper probing of Australia's agribusiness supply chains exposed abuses that were far more widespread, systematic and entrenched than the small-scale activities of backyard operators like 'The Don' of Mildura might suggest. The Ombudsman found, for example, that one of the two big players in the Australian chicken-processing industry routinely exploited working holidaymakers as part of its business model.[22] The Baiada Group produces the Lilydale and Steggles brands of chicken and its annual revenues exceed $1 billion. If you've ever bought a chook at a major supermarket, or eaten any kind of fast food with chicken in it, then chances are you've contributed to Baiada Group's income. Its main rival is Inghams Enterprises, and between them the two firms produce close to three-quarters of the chicken meat consumed in Australia. But while Inghams has around 9,000 direct employees, Baiada engages most of its labour via a complex chain of subcontractors. Despite being a huge, successful enterprise, the Baiada Group could not or would not provide any 'significant or meaningful documentation as to the nature and terms of its contracting arrangements' to Fair Work Inspectors.[23] It also denied inspectors access to its factories, preventing them from observing conditions or talking to workers.²⁴

When the inspectors attempted to follow the money through Baiada's supply chain, they found workers 'too scared to talk' and encountered 'inadequate, inaccurate and/or fabricated records'.²⁵ While there were usually three or four different tiers in the labour-supply chain, often there were no written contracts between the different entities, with payments apparently based on trust and verbal agreement. When the Fair Work Ombudsman attempted to call the subcontractors to give evidence, most simply shut up shop and went into liquidation.²⁶ Organiser George Robertson from the National Union of Workers points out that many labour-hire firms are not large companies: 'A lot of these operators are just people, usually men, with a phone and a bank account, who are providing labour to these producers,' he told the Senate inquiry into temporary migrant workers. 'In my experience, when I ask a worker, "Who do you work for?" they do not even know the name of the labour-hire company; they just know the name of a person who employs them.' He says workers rarely fill out employment documents and their pay usually comes cash in hand.²⁷

One of the principal labour suppliers to Baiada was a company called Mushland Pty Ltd. When Fair Work Inspectors started seeking information from Mushland, 'the phones of both the company director and accountant were disconnected and the Baiada Group was unable to provide any further contact details for the parties'.²⁸ When Fair Work Inspectors attempted to serve a notice on another subcontractor, they found the company's registered address was home to an automotive workshop that had been at same site for 25 years. No one there had ever heard of the labour-hire company inspectors were looking for. Attempts to find two other subcontractors led inspectors to clothing manufacturers that also had no connection to the poultry industry.[29]

Most of the subcontracted workers in the chicken-processing facilities investigated by the Fair Work Ombudsman were 'backpackers' from Taiwan and Hong Kong—that is, temporary migrants on working-holiday visas. Hong Kong joined the working-holidaymaker scheme in 2001 and Taiwan joined in 2004. In the next few years only a few thousand visas were issued to passport holders from these two territories. Around 2008–2009, however, things began to change. The growth in the number of visas granted was spectacular; the number rose sixfold in five years to peak at more than 47,000 visas in 2012–13. Prior to this there had also been a sudden sharp increase in the number of South Koreans coming to Australia on working-holiday visas, with the number of visas issued to South Koreans peaking at close to 40,000 in 2008–2009.[30] Numbers have dropped again for all three countries over the past two years but still remain relatively high. (It is interesting to note that while the working-holidaymaker program is reciprocal, the traffic tends to be one-way: in 2013, 15,704 Taiwanese were granted Australian working-holidaymaker visas, but only 31 Australians were granted the equivalent visa for Taiwan.[31])

The onset of the Global Financial Crisis may have driven more young people to seek work abroad and so contributed to the sudden increase in the number of working-holiday visas issued to travellers from Taiwan and Hong Kong between 2008 and 2012. But no other country experienced anything like the same growth in the number of visas issued to working holidaymakers over the same time period. Nor can the global crisis explain the earlier sharp rise in visa applications from South Korea, which predated the GFC. An alternative reason could be the emergence of organised labour-hire schemes to recruit workers from northeast Asia to fill jobs in the meat-processing industry and other sectors of the economy that employ casual labour.

Matt Journeaux, assistant secretary of the Queensland branch of the Australasian Meat Industry Employees Union (AMIEU), has 30 years' experience in abattoirs and processing plants. He told the 2015 Senate inquiry into temporary migrant workers that in 2010 he began noticing significant numbers of South Korean and Taiwanese working holidaymakers taking up unskilled jobs in the meat industry. In most, if not all, cases a third-party labour-hire company employed the workers.[32] Journeaux says that in some plants, four out of five workers are now on temporary visas and the union has discovered that inappropriate deductions are often made from their wages. Migrants have been required to pay a $500 'membership fee' to the labour-hire company, put up $300 for a training course, hand over $800 to get a second visa and been charged for the legally required vaccination against Q-fever or for tools of trade that should be provided for free by the employer.[33] Many have already paid hefty fees to labour brokers in Taiwan and Hong Kong to secure work in Australia in the first place. The AMIEU provided the Senate inquiry with a Taiwanese labour-hire contract for a job in a South Australian meatworks that required the worker to pay upfront fees of around $2,700.[34]

In 2012, the AMIEU began organising South Korean visa holders working in a smallgoods factory in Wacol near Ipswich. They found that the Koreans were being underpaid by up to $3.50 per hour and were missing out entirely on overtime and shift penalties. Superannuation contributions were being deducted from their wages, even though they had not been signed up to a super fund. Around 140 Korean workers joined the union, which managed to secure them hundreds of thousands of dollars in back pay. After this, according to union organiser Warren Earle, Koreans at the site were replaced with workers from Taiwan. Over the ensuing six to 12 months, Earle says, the workers' communication with the union stopped: 'I have translated documents into Cantonese and Mandarin to try and inform them, because I suspect something,' he told the Senate committee. 'Our members are telling me, through the friendships that they form with these workers, that the Taiwanese workers are now being told that if they go to the union they will not have a job. It's as simple as that.'[35]

Temporary migrants subcontracted to Baiada told both *Four Corners* and the Fair Work Ombudsman that they were often required to work up to 18 hours per day, six days a week, without any overtime or penalty payments. The AMIEU has provided the Senate committee with copies of a 'voluntary overtime application form', drawn up by 'Agribusiness Pty Ltd, a division of the AWX Group' in which workers purportedly 'volunteer' to work additional hours and public holidays 'at the current ordinary rate of pay'. Workers reported earning $12–15 per hour: they were told their pay was based on the number of kilograms of chicken processed and packed, but there was no independent record of these amounts. (There is, in any case, no provision for such piece-work payments under the relevant industrial award.) Sections of a chicken-processing plant are refrigerated to sub-zero temperatures to reduce the risk of microbial growth in the meat. Chun Yat Wong from Hong Kong described to the meatworkers' union how his fingers would be 'frozen to pain'. When he asked for a padded jacket like those worn by other workers he was told they were out of stock.[36] Fair Work Inspectors found one residential house in New South Wales with beds set up for 21 migrants, with rent deducted from their pay by the labour-hire company. The recruiters told workers they had to rent from the contractor or they would not get work (which is illegal). Assuming each worker was paying $100 a week in rent (and it could have been more), then the annual income from the property would have exceeded $100,000.

After conducting an exhaustive examination of the chicken-processing industry in the United States, the international development agency Oxfam concluded that cheap chicken has a human cost—the workers on the poultry-processing line. It found that workers earn low wages of diminishing value, suffer elevated rates of injury and illness, and often experience a climate of fear in the workplace.[37] It seems the situation in Australia may be similar, at least in processing plants supplying Baiada's chicken.

As Katrina's berry-picking experience and Mary's vine-pulling nightmare show, it is not just the price of chicken that is kept low through exploitative labour conditions and low wages. Major supermarket chains claim in their advertising that they are supporting 'Aussie jobs' by sourcing products from local suppliers: in many cases, however, foreign workers, who are paid much less than the legal wage, are the ones in those Australian jobs. Peter Hockings from Bundaberg Fruit and Vegetable Growers told *Four Corners* that there was a culture of exploitation in his industry, with contractors having 'a very strong stranglehold on the labour market'. Second-generation sugarcane grower Keith Pitt, the Nationals MP representing Bundaberg in the federal parliament, agrees. 'There is slave labour in this country,' he told *Four Corners*. 'I think you'd find that there's…a whole heap of crooks making an awful lot of money out of the exploitation of people who really don't know any different.'

Given the fly-by-night nature of labour-hire contractors it is very hard to pin down responsibility. The AMIEU's Matt Journeaux says when he raises workers' pay and conditions with a company like Baiada, it 'points the finger at the labour-hire company and says: "We don't employ them—it's them; it's not us."' At the retail end of the supply chain, the major supermarkets pride themselves on having ethical standards and policies. Woolworths, for example, insists that all their suppliers sign a written undertaking to abide by all Australian laws, regulations and community standards. What this amounts to in practice is a kind of get-out-of-jail-free card: when suppliers break workplace laws, the supermarket can deny any responsibility and wave its signed agreement with the supplier as if that indemnified the retailer against any wrongdoing.

Woolworths' ethical-sourcing policy includes an audit program for countries that are regarded as risky, but 'ethical sourcing auditing does not apply in Australia'. That is because Australia is graded as low risk on the basis of 'a strong rule of law, an independent judiciary, a good human rights track record and very good and independent enforcement agencies'.[38] Armineh Mardirossian, Woolworths' group manager for corporate responsibility, community and sustainability, told the Senate committee that the retailer does not use any labour-hire companies. While acknowledging that labour hire is part of the supermarket's supply chain, she said since Woolworths does not have contractual relationships with the growers or the labour-hire firms, 'it is therefore not possible for us to audit them, because they have no obligation to show us any documentation or to even allow us access to their systems'. The Fresh Food People are off the hook: it will always be someone else's responsibility to ensure that labour-hire firms, growers or others in the supply chain 'meet the requirements of the workplace laws'.[39]

Jobs in the meat industry and horticulture are advertised on Facebook pages and backpacker websites. Foreign-language job ads often breach Australian anti-discrimination laws by specifying that male or female workers are sought, or by asking applicants to provide details of their nationality, height or weight. Union organiser George Robertson told the Senate Committee that online recruiters are 'pretty blatant' in offering positions below award wages. In some cases, the position is advertised as 'not a white job'—meaning it is 'black labour', that is, off the books, cash-in-hand, no tax, no super, though perhaps with the promise of a certain level of income, such as 'the weekly rate at least will get to 900 Australian dollar'.[40]

It is not only working holidaymakers in the meat and horticulture industries who are employed as 'black labour'. When a joint investigation by Fairfax media and Monash University analysed 1,071 Chinese-language job advertisements on websites like yeeyi.com and backpackers.com.tw, it found that 80 per cent of the positions were offering pay rates below the relevant award or the minimum wage (of $17.29 per hour). It found jobs across the economy—'in food courts, cafes, factories, building sites, farms, hairdressers and retail'—advertised as paying between $10 and $13 an hour.[41]

It is not only working holidaymakers who fill these positions; in fact, most of these jobs will be taken up by international students. As of June 2015, there were around 375,000 international students in Australia with work rights,[42] yet there is relatively little research on their participation in the labour market. Some students don't need to work because they come from affluent backgrounds or have generous scholarships, but the available data suggests around two-thirds do work at some stage during their stay.[43] On this basis, Adelaide University legal scholar Alex Reilly estimates that there may be more than 200,000 international students employed in Australia at any one time. Assuming this figure is correct, he calculates that international students 'account for between one per cent and two per cent of the total Australian workforce of 11.4 million people, and approximately six per cent of the part-time workforce of 3.4 million people'.[44] In one qualitative study published in 2009, a third of the students interviewed identified paid employment as their main source of income. Of the students who revealed their hourly wages, a third were being paid $10 an hour or less.[45] In a more recent survey, Stephen Clibborn from the business school at the University of Sydney found that of 243 international students working part time, 60 per cent reported being paid less than the minimum wage.[46]

Often the rorts and rip-offs will involve small businesses like restaurants, shops and cafes offering workers cash-in-hand payments, but as with the backpacker scams in meat processing and fruit and vegetable harvesting, there is also evidence of systematic exploitation and abuse. The most prominent example so far exposed is the widespread underpayment of international students by 7-Eleven franchises. A joint investigative report by Fairfax Media and the ABC revealed that the viability of 24-hour trading in many convenience stores appears to be predicated on paying staff well below the minimum wage—frequently as little as $10 per hour. The 620 Australian stores in the 7-Eleven chain generate more than $3 billion in annual revenue. As *Four Corners* reported, abuses within the empire could not be 'explained away simply as the fault of a few rogue franchisees', but were done 'with the complicit knowledge of head office'.[47]

The report was prompted largely by the curiosity of Gold Coast resident Michael Fraser, who got chatting with the international student behind the counter in his neighbourhood 7-Eleven and discovered he was paid just $12 an hour for his 'never-ending shift'. Michael Fraser made asking 7-Eleven workers about their wages into his personal research project: 'I've been to sixty stores in three states and spoken to hundreds of people,' he told *Four Corners*. 'Every single person has been underpaid.'

There were various ways of covering up this illegality. Some international students worked double the number of hours that were documented, so that while the books showed they were receiving the correct wage, in reality they were only getting half. Others had the correct wages paid into their bank accounts on the condition that they then handed back a share of their earnings in cash. A worker at a 7-Eleven store in Regentville near Penrith to the west of Sydney detailed this experience in an online message to a help site set up by the Shop, Distributive and Allied Employees' Association (the union representing workers in retail and fast food industries): 'I receive $470/weekly for three night shifts and then my boss ring me and said that widraw 170$ and give me back. Means he is paying me $100 per night...He is still doing this and I have no proof for that coz I leave 170$ every Wednesday night in the 7 eleven office. And then he come in the Thursday morning and pick cash. If I will not pay him back then He will not give me work.'[48]

Other international students say that they were required to undertake days of voluntary 'training' before getting any paid shifts: 'i went to 7 eleven for a job at braddon [in Canberra]. They told me you have to get training for 2 weeks after that we will give you some shifts. i got training for more than 8 days but neither they gave me job nor even a single cent.'

Australia Post was also caught up in a scandal involving

international students being paid much less than the minimum wage to deliver parcels. As with the meat-processing industry, the exploitation was facilitated by a system of subcontracting. Between 2008 and 2015, Australia Post outsourced some of its delivery services to two firms: Oz Trade and RecSol. These companies then subcontracted the work to other businesses, MRSS and Magna Services. Every six months, Australia Post required Oz Trade and RecSol to confirm 'their compliance with employment laws and that their subcontractors were working within any visa conditions', but this was the extent of its monitoring.[49] Like Woolworths, Australia Post felt that it had met its ethical and legal obligations. ABC TV's *7.30* program spoke to international students who reported that they were paid between $9 and $15 an hour, with no superannuation or other entitlements. The postal workers union said it had been warning Australia Post for years about the underpayment of international students working as couriers, but an independent inquiry conducted by a law firm and a former Victorian police commissioner found that Australia Post had no way of monitoring how much its contractors paid their staff.[50]

Oz Trade and RecSol were owned by Baljit 'Bobby' Singh; MRSS and Magna Services were owned, respectively, by his associates Mukesh Sharma and Rakesh Kumar. Between them, the three men also owned two private colleges, St Stephen Institute of Technology and Symbiosis Institute of Technical Education. The Australian Federal Police allege that these institutions did not offer any meaningful education or training, but were instead used as shopfronts to organise visas for Indian students. The students were then employed via the contractors' labour-hire companies to deliver parcels. According to the federal police, on top of the $9 million in fees charged to international students, the colleges also raked in about $2 million in government funding as registered training organisations. The matter is now before the courts.

Industrial cleaning is another area where exploitation of international students is rife. There are around 25,000 cleaning businesses in Australia employing around 100,000 people. The Fair Work Ombudsman says that almost half of these cleaners were born overseas and that 10 per cent are students,[51] but the union United Voice says the share of students is much higher in industrial sectors of the industry: it estimates, for example, that around half the cleaners employed in Melbourne's central business district are international students and that underpayment occurs in at least one in four city office buildings.[52]

In 2012–13, a Fair Work audit of 578 cleaning businesses found that around one in four were not paying employees correctly and that many other firms had failed to keep proper records. Industrial cleaning is a high-pressure business, with workers often required to complete certain tasks, like cleaning a workstation, within a set period. In order to keep up, international students report working through scheduled breaks or working unpaid overtime at the end of their shifts.[53]

Again, complex subcontracting arrangements facilitate the evasion of proper pay and entitlements. As the Fair Work Ombudsman comments, 'the cleaning-services industry is characterised by layers of subcontracting, tight margins and a competitive tendering processes', which can result in 'the undercutting of minimum wages to present the lowest cost tender'.[54] It says this kind of multi-tier contracting makes breaches of workplace laws and obligations more likely: 'With each tier presumably taking a proportion of the contract value, the amount of money flowing to the actual workers reduces with each subcontracting arrangement—exacerbating the potential for workers to receive less than the statutory minimum payable to employees.'[55]

Sometimes the individual cleaner is treated as a contractor, and forced to supply an ABN and submit an invoice for their labour. This is amounts to sham contracting—a way of avoiding the payment of both tax and workplace entitlements like superannuation, penalty rates and holiday pay. (Sham contracting is also prevalent in the construction industry.) United Voice calculates that over the course of a year's work, a subcontracted cleaner is short-changed $10,000 to $15,000 in unpaid wages and entitlements.[56]

The Redfern Legal Centre in inner Sydney runs a free weekly clinic for international students. Solicitor Sean Stimson says sham-contracting arrangements in the cleaning industry are one of the most common problems that the centre deals with. He says students can end up in serious difficulties if they suffer a workplace injury (because independent contractors are not covered by workers compensation) or get caught out for failing to pay tax (which has not been deducted from their pay).

Underpayment in the hospitality industry is another frequent issue, but Sean Stimson says that international students are often reluctant to come forward with formal complaints because they fear that they could lose their visa for working more than the allowable 40 hours per fortnight. The restriction on working hours is a choke point that shifts the balance of industrial power towards employers: it can be used to put international students under duress in the same way that sponsorship for permanent residence can be used as leverage against workers on 457 visas, and the need to get the boss to sign off on 88 days of 'specified work' for a second visa renders working holidaymakers vulnerable to exploitation.

The reality is that many international students need to work more than 20 hours per week to cover their study fees and living costs. Once they have breached their visa rules by working extra hours, their employer has them over a barrel and can continue to demand that they work extra hours or accept underpayment. One of the 7-Eleven workers interviewed by *Four Corners* was pressured in exactly this way. When Mohamed Rashid Ullat Thodi challenged his pay and conditions, his employers at a Geelong convenience store warned him off making a formal complaint: 'They wouldn't say that they will be in trouble,' he told the program, 'they will say, "You're in trouble. You'll get deported because you're working more than twenty hours. You're breaching visa, visa conditions."'

'Most employers know that international students don't know their rights,' says Stimson. 'Many students take whatever work they can get.' When they are underpaid or overworked they feel that they 'just have to put up with it as part of the equation'.

Stimson says there is a degree of desperation in relation to accommodation, too. After employment matters, housing issues are the second biggest problem that international students bring to the legal centre. 'You find students living six to eight to a room and each paying one hundred and twenty to one hundred and fifty dollars per week in rent,' says the Redfern lawyer. 'As an Australian I take huge offence to the fact that this is what we are doing.'

In 2014, when fire engulfed the LaCrosse high-rise residential tower in central Melbourne, the evacuation revealed two-bedroom apartments housing up to 15 international students, with curtains dividing living areas in an attempt to create some privacy. Some students were sleeping on mattresses on open-air balconies, while others were taking turns to share beds in 'shifts'. Spaces that were meant to be used to store firefighting equipment were often filled with tenants' belongings.[57]

Shop owners, restaurant managers, cleaning contractors and farmers who pay under-award wages and roster staff on excessively long shifts can undercut rival businesses that do the right thing. This puts honest employers under commercial pressure to cut corners on workplace laws, too. And, as we have seen, it is not only small business that stands to gain: the downward pressure on wages cuts supply-chain costs, delivering cheaper prices to consumers and boosting the profits of national and global firms like Woolworths, Australia Post and 7-Eleven.

Of course, domestic students—and other young Australians—are also vulnerable in the labour market, though they can at least access government benefits and free public health care, and are more likely to be able to call on the support of nearby family members in times of trouble. Many international students and working holidaymakers lack both English language skills and local knowledge. As a result of these disadvantages, they tend to crowd into a narrower range of jobs than their domestic peers. In this highly competitive environment many feel that they have to put up with underpayment and abuse.[58]

There is also an argument, however, that the presence of large numbers of international students and working holidaymakers increases the risks faced by young Australians trying to get a job. Stephen Clibborn from the University of Sydney warns that if we allow temporary migrants to be underpaid, then employers will expect to pay lower wages to local staff, too.[59] The Australian Council of Trade Unions points out that around 240,000 working-holiday visas were granted to young travellers in 2013–14, a year in which almost 290,000 young Australians (aged 15 to 24) were out of work.[60] The implication is blunt: if there were fewer working backpackers, more young Australians would have a job.

Bob Birrell and Ernest Healy from Monash University support this view. They argue that 'job-hungry' migrants are out-competing young Australians for 'entry-level jobs'.[61] They calculate that migration is growing Australia's labour force at a faster rate than new jobs are generated, resulting in increasing unemployment for at least two groups of young Australians—those seeking relatively low-skilled jobs and recent graduates. Birrell and Healy's analysis has been heavily criticised: migration expert Henry Sherrell says that in bringing together two different data sets 'the authors are comparing apples with oranges.'[62] Economist Judith Sloane agrees: she says their use of the data makes no sense, and the assumptions they make to reach their conclusion 'are heroic, to say the least'.[63]

Critiquing Birrell and Healy's methodology does not, however, answer the question: are working holidaymakers and international students making life in the labour market more challenging for young Australians? The question is straightforward; the answer is not.

The simple assumption that migrants 'take jobs' is based on what economists call 'the lump of labour fallacy'—the idea that the number of jobs in the economy is fixed. The reality, of course, is that immigrants also create jobs through their spending on local goods and services. What is more, if immigrants 'complement' rather than 'displace' existing workers, then they potentially enable an enterprise to expand its operations and so generate additional employment.

Most international studies conclude that the overall impact of immigration on the existing workforce—in terms of both wages and employment—is small (and sometimes so small as to be statistically insignificant).[64] Some studies find a small positive effect, others a small negative effect. The impact may be influenced by cyclical factors: labour migration during a downturn will affect the employment of locals more than during a boom. Skilled and unskilled migration can have different effects and influence particular segments of the labour market in varying ways. There is strong evidence, for example, that skilled migration to Australia boosts the employment and income of low-skilled local workers, while holding down wage increases for higher-skilled workers.[65]

In Australia, the Productivity Commission 'found no discernible effect from immigration on wages, employment and participation in aggregate'. Looking beyond the big picture, however, the commission cautions that 'immigration may lead to higher unemployment and/or slower wage growth for specific groups' and that the risk of foreign workers displacing locals is 'more likely at the lower end of the skill spectrum and in the youth labour market'.[66] It blames weak economic conditions for high youth unemployment since 2008 and adds that while there is 'some tentative evidence to suggest that there may be some relationship between immigration and youth employment outcomes, it is not conclusive'.[67] The commission's overall assessment is that 'the labour-market implications of the work rights of the substantial and uncapped pool of international students, graduates and working holidaymakers are poorly understood'. More research is required.[68]

There are additional factors to consider here: almost half the farmers who answered a National Farmers' Federation business survey in 2014 said that a shortage of labour was the greatest impediment to their business. The NFF calculates that in 2008 some 22,000 fruit-picking positions went unfilled, costing horticultural farms an average of $100,000 each in wasted produce.[69] Working holidaymakers are estimated to constitute between 50 and 85 per cent of the seasonal workforce in horticulture. An evaluation of the working-holiday scheme based on a large-scale survey of travellers and employers in 2008 concluded that the overall impact of working holidaymakers on employment is positive: it calculated that for every 100 working holidaymakers who come to Australia, there is a net gain of five full-time jobs.[70]

Ninety per cent of the employers surveyed said that they tried to recruit Australians for the jobs filled by backpackers, but found local workers very difficult to find, because they were not available, didn't have the right skills, had better employment options elsewhere or weren't interested. More than 80 per cent of employers said working holidaymakers were 'important' or 'very important' to their businesses.[71] Even taking into account the fact that it may be in employers' interests to exaggerate their need for working holidaymakers (since an increased labour supply holds down wages), these results suggest that working holidaymakers are filling real gaps in the labour market.

Because backpackers stay in Australia longer than other international travellers, they also spend substantially more money during their visit, making them an important source of revenue for Australia's tourism industry. The 2008 survey estimated that the average working holidaymaker spent $13,218 and earned $4,756 during an Australian stay. Calculated across the whole program, that represented a net outlay of $1.14 billion in 2007–2008.[72] Since the scheme has grown substantially since then, with upwards of 80,000 additional visas issued each year, the value of the program today is probably even greater. Added to this are less tangible benefits of the working-holiday scheme, such as the fact that our reciprocal arrangements with other countries also enable tens of thousands of young Australians to benefit from the experience of living and working overseas.

The value of international education is more thoroughly documented than the income from the working-holiday scheme: in 2014, international education services supported nearly 130,000 jobs in Australia[73] and contributed around $17 billion to the Australian economy, making it Australia's fourth-largest 'export' (after iron ore, coal and natural gas).[74] Around half of this income came from tuition fees; the rest was generated by students' spending on goods and services. Along with their visiting family and friends, international students also make a significant contribution to the tourism industry. Australia has a six per cent share of the international student market. It is the third-most popular English-speaking destination after the United States and the United Kingdom, and has one of the highest concentrations of international students as a proportion of enrolments: about 20 per cent of the students at Australian universities come from overseas (as do five per cent of the students in vocational education and training).[75] It is hard to imagine how Australia's tertiary institutions would survive without this massive injection of international funds.

Since many students eventually become permanent residents, Australia gets a double benefit: it is getting locally acquired skills and qualifications, as well as socialisation into Australian life at no cost to government. Pay-as-you-go migration, indeed.

What can we conclude from all this? It is apparent from the data that while the working-holiday scheme is officially described as a cultural exchange program, and that the primary purpose of an international-student visa is supposed to be study, both these forms of migration now also operate as de facto temporary labour schemes. The hundreds of thousands of backpackers and overseas students present in Australia form a highly flexible low-wage labour force that is vulnerable to underpayment and abuse. This may well make young Australian workers more vulnerable, too.

Although it is hard to document empirically, it seems that working holidaymakers and international students are at greater risk of exploitation than migrants arriving under Australia's main dedicated temporary labour migration scheme, the 457-visa program. While 457 workers are more vulnerable to employer pressure than their Australian counterparts, and can be put under particular duress if they are seeking to make the transition to permanent residence, the employment of 457-visa holders is regulated and monitored far more closely than the employment of international students and backpackers.

So is a significant level of workplace abuse of backpackers and overseas students the necessary price to pay for Australian citizens and permanent residents to enjoy a comfortable life? Is this the inevitable cost of getting our fruit picked, bolstering the tourism industry, keeping our universities afloat, enjoying cheap takeaway chicken, having access to 24-hour convenience stores and reducing business costs by holding down the wages paid to office cleaners? Are young foreigners the eggs that have to get broken to make our successful economic omelette? If we wish to live up to our claims to be a liberal democracy—to be the country of 'a fair go'—then this is not an ethically acceptable bargain.

10 | An Unsettled World
How Australia Compares in the Global Trend to Temporariness

About 30 years ago, I sat in a small bar in Frankfurt's Westend, drinking beer with my friend Jörg. I had been living in Germany—West Germany, as it was then—for two years, studying German and politics at the Goethe University of Frankfurt, protesting against nuclear power and working as a builder's labourer in summer and as a snow-clearer in winter.

I was drinking with Jörg because I needed his advice: he was my closest friend in Frankfurt and, as the one German who was familiar with my life in Australia, the only friend who could help me to decide whether to return to Adelaide for the final year of my undergraduate arts degree, or stay on and complete my studies in Frankfurt. Although I did not conceive of myself as a temporary migrant at the time, I knew I had reached a crunch point—the decision felt like a choice between returning to Australia for good and committing myself to a future life and career in Germany. (Staying in Germany was a long-term proposition that would have ultimately led to a masters- or doctorate-level qualification after five or more years of study.) It was a wrenching decision, because after two years in Frankfurt I had put down roots, and not just in terms of close personal relationships. In some aspects of my life, I felt at home in Germany in ways that I had never felt at home in Australia.

For those of us who sit high enough up the slope of global inequality, temporary migration can be a life-changing adventure, as were my two years in Germany. My nephew currently has a temporary-entry visa for the United States so that he can work for a tech start-up in California; my niece is studying at a university in New York. I hope my son will have the chance to study and work overseas in future. If he does, he will join a diaspora of around one million Australians who live in other countries. We generally refer to these people as expatriates, which emphasises their enduring link with Australia, the country they have left, rather than as migrants, which would put the focus on their perhaps contingent relationship to the country they currently live in. The expat experience can be both exciting and difficult; an Australian living as a *metic*—a long-term temporary migrant in a foreign land—will generally be denied rights enjoyed by the host country's citizens, whether it be political voice or access to government services, yet may well decide that the opportunities outweigh the costs. Temporary migrants in Australia may feel the same way about being a *metic* here. We can acknowledge the agency of temporary migrants, and the deliberate trade-offs they choose to make, yet still critique temporary migration and the way it is organised, in Australia or anywhere else.

While temporary migration has only been around in Australia in its current form for a couple of decades, as a global phenomenon it is more deeply entrenched and has a longer and darker history. In fact, compared to most temporary-migration schemes around the world, Australia's arrangements could be seen as relatively progressive and 'migrant friendly'. Temporary migrant workers on 457 visas can, for example, bring family members with them to Australia. In many other countries, temporary migrant workers must travel alone, and may remain separated from partners and children for years at a time. The accompanying spouse of a 457-visa holder also has unrestricted work rights in Australia; under the roughly equivalent H-1B visa in the United States, spouses cannot work.

The 457-visa program offers a fairly accessible route to permanent residence and eventual citizenship. On my reading of the data, upwards of 40 per cent of the temporary skilled workers who have been issued a 457 visa over the past decade ended up becoming permanent Australian residents.[1] In many countries—like Singapore or the Gulf States or Japan—a temporary migrant has no prospect of legal membership in the host nation and will always be a 'guest worker' with limited rights and entitlements. Other states offer a very constricted pathway to residence that few will be eligible to take. In Australia, once employer sponsorship is secured, the transition from 457 visa to permanent residence is also relatively quick—processing times are from five to eight months. In the United States, by contrast, the transition from an H-1B temporary visa to 'lawful residence' can take more than a decade (depending on several factors, including which country a migrant comes from, since the United States sets country-based quotas).

At law, temporary migrants working in Australia enjoy the same pay and workplace rights and conditions as their Australian colleagues, and have potential avenues of redress when things go wrong, even if it is difficult to uphold such equality or address grievances in practice. In many countries, employment laws allow temporary migrants to receive a fraction of the local wage and provide few if any formal workplace rights.

Migrant workers in Australia on 457 visas can change jobs, even though there are practical obstacles to labour mobility. Compare this situation to Singapore, where workers are tied to their employers: if they lose their job for any reason, then they also lose their work permit and are sent home. Alex Au from the Singapore not-for-profit TWC2 (Transient Workers Count Too) describes this arrangement as 'horribly close to something that we thought we abolished 200 years ago, namely slavery'.[2]

The more extreme *kefala* sponsorship system that operates to differing degrees in the Gulf States of the Arabian Peninsula bonds foreign workers even more tightly to their employers, often trapping migrants in abusive situations as they struggle to pay back large debts they incurred in order to get recruited in the first place. Migrant workers cannot leave Saudi Arabia and Qatar without an 'exit permit' that authorities will only issue with the employer's consent. This and other practices, such as withholding passports or wages, enables employers to treat migrants as forced labour.[3] There are an estimated 11 million migrant workers in the Gulf region, mostly from Asia and Africa[4]—around one-fifth of these migrants are female domestic workers. Isolated in private homes, these women are at risk of being 'trapped in servitude' for years at a time, working extreme hours and enduring physical abuse, including sexual assault and beatings with sticks or cables.[5] According to a report by the International Trade Union Confederation, up to 10 Indonesian domestic workers seek refuge from their embassy in Qatar every day.[6] As the *Economist* put it in a headline, when it comes to migrant workers in the Middle East, 'Forget About Rights'.[7]

Not just there, but in Europe, too. In 2014, an investigative report by Germany's most highly regarded weekly newspaper, *Die Zeit*, revealed Romanian migrants were labouring in meatworks by day, and sleeping in the woods by night.[8] In a bucolic and picturesque corner of Lower Saxony, locals refer to these workers as *Waldmenschen*, or forest people. They are the fringes of a ghost army of eastern European migrant workers who kill, gut, cut and pack millions of chickens, pigs and cows annually for rock-bottom wages. It is an industry driven by the bottom line, because—as *Die Zeit* journalist Anne Kunze puts it—'we want to eat ever more meat, and we want to get it ever more cheaply'.[9] As in Australia, migrant meatworkers in Germany are employed via subcontractors; in the article, a union leader describes the system as 'mafia like'. Workers often pay brokers a fee upfront to secure the job and are then forced to pay inflated prices to stay in unhygienic and overcrowded housing supplied by their employer (or, if they fall out with the overseer, they may end up sleeping in the forest).

The system is an unintended consequence of Germany's attempts to protect itself from an influx of cheap labour as the European Union progressively expanded to the east. Although workers from the new member states had to wait seven years to enjoy full mobility within the EU labour market, free trade in services commenced immediately. As a result, within a few months, shelf companies had been set up Poland, Hungary and Romania offering contracts for 'labour services' to Germany's biggest meat processors. What is more, since the workers were hired locally, they were employed in accordance with local pay and conditions. The result is Romanian migrants slaughtering German pigs for Romanian wages, but paying German prices for food and lodging. According to *Die Zeit*, by 2014 around 40,000 foreign contract workers were slaughtering and processing 80 per cent of Germany's meat production and the trade in labour services was still expanding. In her award-winning investigation, journalist Anne Kunze sums up the system in one sentence: 'Human trafficking in low-wage workers, protected by the laws of the European Union'.[10]

The German experience with free trade in services is an example of what trade unions here fear could happen under the bilateral free-trade agreements that Australia has already struck with China and South Korea and continues to seek with other countries including India and Indonesia. Bob Kinnaird, former research director with the construction union CFMEU, argues that under such agreements, Australia is permanently surrendering its 'sovereign right to make laws concerning temporary migration, with no public debate'.[11] Because Australia had already unilaterally removed most of its trade barriers, says Kinnaird, negotiators had little to offer developing countries apart from relaxed entry rules for low- and semi-skilled migrant workers. Kinnaird predicts that the result will be 'greatly increased legal rights for employers to use temporary foreign labour, and to use these workers as industrial-relations weapons against Australian workers and unions'.[12]

When controversy flared over the migrant-labour provisions in Australia's free-trade agreement with China, the Labor Party refused to ratify the deal in the Senate until extra safeguards were put in place. The measures, which will also apply to other trade agreements, include a requirement for employers to test the local labour market before bringing in migrant workers under 'investment facilitation agreements'. Labor also asked for the minimum wage paid to migrant workers to be increased and indexed to the cost of living, and called for tighter regulation of licensing to ensure that the trade skills and qualifications of migrant workers are up to Australian standards.

Adelaide University labour-law expert Joanna Howe welcomed Labor's 'pragmatic and moderate' proposals, but says problems remain. She points out that there is still no need to test for domestic skills shortages before an employer brings in workers as 'contractual service suppliers' or 'installers and servicers'.[13] She warns, too, that while Chinese workers are entitled to Australian wages and conditions, 'it is highly unlikely' that the authorities will uncover breaches of Australian employment law 'due to the inadequacies of existing regulatory enforcement arrangements'.[14]

So while Australia's temporary-migration arrangements may be better than those of many other countries, that does not make them good enough. What is more, the logic of a globalised market will see continual pressure for further expansion of both dedicated and de facto temporary labour migration, along with decreased regulation and relaxed entry standards. As the global migration law firm Fragomen says, 'Australian businesses now compete in a world economy that operates as a single economic space'.[15] As the competitive pressures on Australian firms increase, so will demands for government to give business a freer hand in recruiting foreign labour.

The signs are already apparent. Business organisations consistently lobby to get rid of labour-market testing and hold down the minimum salary threshold in the 457-visa program. There is a push for greater latitude in offering pay below the threshold salary in certain circumstances.[16] There are regular calls from employer groups for lower skill levels on the 457-visa program. The peak hospitality-industry body, Restaurant and Catering Australia, for example, argues that there is no need for foreign cooks on 457 visas to have 'functional' English (level five on the IELTS language test) because 'many of the kitchens, especially in the ethnic cuisine, don't use English at all'.[17] The association points out that Canada only requires cooks on temporary visas to have 'a basic level' of language proficiency. It wants the Australian language requirement to be lowered to 'basic competence'—level 4 on the IELTS test—where English ability is limited to familiar situations and a person may have frequent problems in understanding and expression.[18] (It should be pointed out that the level of English required of migrant workers is intended to ensure that migrant workers can participate in Australian life, not just do their jobs.)

There is also continuing pressure to open up new visa categories for lower-skilled workers. Tourism operators in Western Australia are seeking a way to bring in Chinese-language speaking hospitality staff,[19] for example, and the Productivity Commission's 2014 inquiry into child care prompted calls for the government to open up a visa for foreign nannies to help families look after young children or ageing relatives in the home.[20] (Canada, which most resembles Australia in terms of temporary-migration regimes, already has a visa for live-in care-givers.)

In response to the White Paper on Developing Northern Australia, rules have been relaxed around the previously highly regulated Seasonal Worker Programme for migrants from Pacific Island nations and East Timor. A requirement that sponsoring employers must guarantee workers a minimum of 14 weeks' work has been scrapped, as has the annual ceiling on the number of workers that can be recruited. Like the 457 scheme, the size of the Seasonal

Worker Programme is now 'determined by employers' unmet demand for labour'.[21]

Originally restricted to employment in horticulture, the Seasonal Worker Programme has been expanded to aquaculture, cane and cotton farming, and proposals to extend it to other agricultural sectors are under active consideration. A trial of seasonal workers in the 'accommodation industry', which opened up jobs for waiters, kitchen hands, gardeners and cleaners, has been converted into a permanent program. It is initially limited to Western Australia, the Northern Territory, tropical north Queensland and South Australia's Kangaroo Island, but other locations are likely to be added over time. A trial of other seasonal jobs in tourism is underway in Northern Australia.[22]

With the enthusiastic backing of state and federal governments, Australia's educational institutions—public and private, secondary and tertiary—are constantly looking to maintain and expand their market. Currently around 80 per cent of Australia's international students come from the Asia-Pacific region, but the aim is to increase enrolments from other parts of the world, particularly Latin America, but also the Middle East and Africa.[23] There is also a push to exploit the 'go younger' trend in international education, with parents, particularly in China, sending their children to study in Australian high schools as a first step to tertiary study here.

In 2015, then education minister Christopher Pyne suggested that the value of international education to the Australian economy could double in a decade.[24] This rosy outlook presumably implies a doubling of international enrolments. If that were achieved, then in 2025 there would be around 750,000 international students living in Australia with the right to work 40 hours per fortnight during term time (and any number of hours during semester breaks). In addition, there would presumably be tens of thousands—perhaps even hundreds of thousands—of student graduates with unrestricted work rights on the post-study 485 visa.

The 485 visa was revamped in 2013 to make Australian higher education more attractive and help reverse a fall in enrolments by offering at least two years of post-study work rights to prospective international students. Both private training institutions and publicly funded TAFE colleges are lobbying to have these work rights extended to international students who complete vocational courses. There seems little doubt that granting post-study work rights would boost international enrolments in the sector, since it is expected that around four out of every five vocational students would apply for such a visa if it were available.[25] (Past experience with colleges being used as shopfront visa factories suggest there is good reason to tread with caution here.)

The number of working holidaymakers in Australia is also likely to continue to grow, particularly since there is now an annual quota of 5,000 work and holiday visas available to Chinese citizens. When the first tranche of 1,500 visas was made available in China in September 2015, all the places were snapped up within minutes. One applicant told China's *Global Times* that she paid an agency more than 7,000 Yuan—or A$1,500—to secure a place in the program.[26] This suggests that China could be the next frontier for fly-by-night labour-hire companies seeking a supply of temporary migrants who can be subcontracted to abattoirs or building sites.

China's visa allocation is the most generous in the work and holiday scheme, which has an annual cap on numbers for all participating countries (with the exception of the United States). Slovenia and the Slovak Republic joined the program from 1 January 2016, with 200 places each. Australia has signed but not yet activated similar agreements with Israel (500 places), Greece (500 places), Vietnam (200 places) and Papua New Guinea (100 places).[27] The annual caps, the lack of a second visa option and other requirements, like functional English and at least two years of undergraduate university study (again with the exception of applicants from the United States), make the work and holiday program (subclass 462) much more restrictive than the longer established and uncapped working-holidaymaker scheme (visa subclass 417), which is open to 19 states and territories. The number of working backpackers is likely to continue to grow, however, given that Australia is negotiating work and holiday agreements with a further 20 governments around the world.[28]

My point in laying out these examples is that temporary migration to Australia has gained its own momentum and become, to an extent, self-perpetuating. Significant sections of the Australian economy are now oriented towards finding employees or generating revenue via temporary migrants who come to Australia for extended periods of work, study and travel. Powerful players stand to benefit from a continued increase in the number of temporary visas issued each year and have—to varying degrees—an interest in opening up new temporary-migration categories, or in reducing regulation and easing restrictions on existing visa classes. At the same time, the federal government appears locked into a punitive and unconscionable deterrence regime that will condemn thousands of 'temporary' refugees to the anguish of an indefinitely unsettled life in Australia, Papua New Guinea or Nauru.

As Henry Sherrell put it when he was with the Migration Council Australia, 'migration'—which increasingly means temporary migration—will be 'one of the defining areas of public policy of the twenty-first century'.[29] Australia is too far down the road of temporary migration to turn back, but that does not mean we have to keep travelling at the same tempo and cannot chart a more considered course. It is not good enough for policy to be shaped by ad hoc responses to specific issues and self-interested lobbying efforts. We need to develop a more robust and cohesive approach, based on democratic principles, sound ethics and a clear sense of what it is that we want to achieve.

11 | Flexibility and Indifference
The Ethics of Temporary Migration

The writing of Judah Waten is not widely read these days, but in the 1950s Waten was an important voice in Australian migrant literature. His best-known book, *Alien Son*, is a collection of connected short stories that fictionalise the experiences of recent Jewish immigrants coming to terms with life in Australia in the lead-up to World War I. In part, the author was mining his own personal history: Waten was born in Odessa in 1911 and his family migrated to Australia via Palestine when he was an infant to escape the anti-Jewish pogroms of Czarist Russia. The son of the title narrates the stories: increasingly acculturated into Australian life and increasingly alien to his parents, he chronicles the very different ways in which 'Father' and 'Mother' respond to the challenges of a new country.

Mother initiated the move to Australia; to Father, 'the idea of leaving his native land seemed so fantastic that he refused to regard it seriously'.[1] Yet from the moment he arrived, Father 'put away all thoughts of his homeland and he began to regard the new country as his permanent home'.[2] Mother has the opposite reaction—before she is a day off the ship, she wants to go back:

> The impressions she gained on that first day remained with her all her life. It seemed to her there was an irritatingly superior air about the people she met, the customs officials, the cab men, the agent of the new house. Their faces expressed something ironical and sympathetic, something friendly and at the same time condescending. She imagined everyone on the wharf, in the street, looked at her in the same way and she never forgave them for treating her as if she was in need of their good-natured tolerance.[3]

While Father only looks forward, Mother can only look back. She is unable to settle and lives forever 'on one leg like a bird'. Their younger friend Mr Sussman sits between these two poles: he wavers about whether to stay in Australia or to return to his ageing parents in the old country. Father's counsel is emphatic: 'Make up your mind quickly. Take my advice Sussman, don't live in two worlds! My wife does. But it's no good.'

Waten's depiction of Mother is a powerful literary reminder that the condition of being 'unsettled' is tragic and painful. The mid-twentieth-century French philosopher Simone Weil argued that a sense of rootedness—of connection with place, people, culture and milieu—is a fundamental need of the human soul. She regarded as criminal anything that uprooted human beings. Criminal, too, is anything that prevents people from putting down roots.[4] As the character of Mother shows, a permanent legal right to stay does not guarantee that migrants will form an enduring connection with a new land, but extended periods of temporariness and uncertainty are very likely to work against it. The character of Father points to another human tendency: we may start to put down roots in a place without knowing it—perhaps even beyond our own volition—just as a plant pulled from the ground will seek to attach itself to any new patch of earth on which it is discarded.

In another episode in *Alien Son*, the wavering Sussman enlists for service in the war. 'Why do you have to give your life for the Russian Czar and his cousin the English King?' Mother chastises him. 'What have they done for you? Leave them to fight their other cousin, the Kaiser, and may they all break their heads.'[5] Sussman's customary eloquence deserts him. Finally he bursts out miserably: 'I must go like the others. Am I any different from them?'[6] The foreigner Sussman—mistakenly, in Mother's view—feels bonds of commitment to his fellow Australians. He must go to war like the others. Father accuses Sussman of joining up to run away, both from potential romantic involvement and from making a definite decision about his future in Australia. He tells Sussman that he'll have to come back to Australia after the war is over in any case:

> 'Maybe,' said Mr Sussman.
> And before he could say another word, Father interposed with, 'What maybe is there about it? You won't belong over there any more.'
> Then Father added, 'We belong to this new earth. It has sucked us in whether we know it or not.'[7]

As emotional, sensible, associative, communicative, learning animals, human beings do not have fixed desires and intentions—or fixed selves. We may plan to sojourn in another country for just a few months or years for the experience or the pay or the education or some combination of those things, but as time passes we may then find ourselves becoming embedded in this foreign place, perhaps even against our will, as we are changed by it. As political philosopher Joseph Carens puts it, we are 'embodied creatures', affected and formed over time by the place we live in and the people we live among:

> ...connections grow: to spouses and partners, sons and daughters, friends and neighbours and coworkers, people we love and people we hate. Experiences accumulate: birthdays and braces, tones of voice and senses of humor, public parks and corner stores, the shape of the streets and the way the sun shines through the leaves, the smell of flowers and the sound of local accents, the look of the stars and the taste of the air—all that gives life its purpose and texture.[8]

To me it is like standing at the water's edge on a gentle incoming tide: as the waves wash up and back around our legs, our feet sink slowly into the sand. We get sucked in, whether we intend to or not.

There is a vast political gulf between the writer Judah Waten, a committed communist, and the federal Liberal MP and Treasurer Scott Morrison, but both recognise that the human need for roots drives our propensity to become attached to place and people. In his time as opposition spokesman on immigration, Morrison made the following observation:

> When we arrive in this country, we become part of it—and it becomes a part of us—it becomes what [Sir Henry] Parkes described as 'the land of our adoption'. It changes

us—and in doing so it provides the basis for our connection with one another.⁹

Yet the thrust of contemporary migration policy—not just in Australia, but globally—is in the opposition direction: not towards settlement but temporariness, not towards belonging but contingency. This is sometimes presented in glowing terms as heralding a bright future: Michael Pezzullo, secretary of the Department of Immigration and Border Protection, says we are witnessing the 'revolution' of skilled workers choosing to live abroad on a temporary basis and not necessarily seeking to settle:

> These are mobile global citizens, who work in connection with the flows of global trade and investment. The traditional model of permanent migration simply can not respond quickly enough to changes in demand for skilled labour, and training of domestic labour in specialist skills takes time, and often falls short of the needs of industry in rapidly changing circumstances.¹⁰

Pezzullo predicts that government will increasingly use migration 'to tap into the global pool of human talent for a variety of purposes, of which permanent settlement is but one outcome, amongst others'. For the foreseeable future, he says, the total number of non-citizens in Australia on a temporary basis at any one time will be 'around 1.9 million, and growing—which is ten times the current annual permanent migration planning level'.¹¹ The predominant role of Pezzullo's department today is not permanent migration but 'border entry and control'.

Being a 'mobile global citizen' sounds appealing. It reminds me of the cigarette ads that were on TV when I was a kid: 'Peter

Stuyvesant—your international passport to smoking pleasure'. The Stuyvesant smoker flits gaily from Swiss ski slope to bronzed Brazilian beach, from sipping champagne on a Concorde one moment, to hitting the jackpot in a high-roller casino the next. Perhaps there is a global elite who fit this picture, who do not need to belong anywhere because, thanks to the size of their bank accounts and the colour of their passports, no door is ever closed to them—they are 'at home' in a bubble of luxury wherever they choose to touch down.

For most of us, the reality is more prosaic. Is the Filipino fitter earning good money on an outback Australian mine a 'mobile global citizen'? Or if the wages on offer in Zamboanga matched those in the Pilbara, would he choose to be a settled citizen of the Philippines, at home with his family? What about the Taiwanese 'backpacker' working in a Baiada chicken-processing plant on the outskirts of Newcastle? Is she 'working in connection with the flows of global trade and investment' or buffeted about by them? Is she a global citizen gathering international experiences or a foreigner who suffers a shitty job in Australia for less pay than a local because she has fewer choices?

As the late migration theorist Aristide Zolberg put it, temporary migrant workers are often 'wanted but not welcome'.[12] They meet pressing economic needs—which in the Australian context might mean picking fruit, staffing outback clinics or supplementing university funding—but their place in our society is carefully circumscribed and limited. For all his recognition of the ways in which migrants put down roots in Australia, Scott Morrison also wanted to prevent it from happening:

> We must be careful to manage the population impacts of… temporary migration, ensuring that we apply appropriate

constraints, most importantly that such entrants return home when their purpose and stay has been completed—whether it is to work, study or visit—without onward application entitlements.[13]

Policymakers are wont to present temporary migration as a neat and tidy affair, when it is anything but. Temporary migrants are expected to come to Australia, go about their business and then leave when their visa expires, on the assumption that temporariness is 'a neutral policy objective'.[14] Unfortunately for politicians, migration is an inherently messy process. As Canadian researchers Catherine Dauvergne and Sarah Marsden note, while 'workers [or students] may be invited, it is human beings who arrive'.[15] This is a contemporary reformulation of the famous observation made about European *Gastarbeiter* by Swiss playwright Max Frisch in 1965: '*Man hat Arbeitskräfte gerufen, und es kamen Menschen*'—we called for labour power and human beings came.[16]

The realities of international migration are never divorced from the injustices that mark our world—what Zolberg calls 'the profound inequality of worldwide political and economic conditions'—that tug or propel people across borders.[17] This is not to deny the agency of migrants themselves, but rather to emphasise it: temporary migrants are not pawns moved about to meet the needs of global capital; they are reasoning individuals who seek opportunities and evaluate their options in an imperfect world, and then make calculated if often highly constrained choices.

Nor is it to suggest that temporary migration is always bad or exploitative. The expansion of temporary-migration schemes in Australia and elsewhere opens up experiences and opportunities that would otherwise be denied to people. As the adage goes, the only thing worse than being exploited abroad is not being exploited at home—it may be better to be an underpaid and overworked cook in Australia than an unemployed and destitute cook in Nepal. The Filipino fitter working in the Pilbara may miss his children, but he can afford to provide them with better education, housing and health care. Chicken processing may be horrible, poorly paid work, but the Taiwanese backpacker may land a better job when she returns home, thanks to the English she learns while in Australia. Trained nurse Evgenia Skandalaki is not employed in her profession and has a lower-status job than the one she had in Greece, but she enjoys her work in aged care, likes living in Melbourne, is proud of her achievement in learning English and looks forward to becoming Australian at the end of her four-year contract.

It is not only individual migrants and their families who stand to gain, but the communities they come from, as remittances and skills flow back into their home economy. In enabling people to move from lower- to higher-wage countries—even temporarily—migration can have a powerful redistributive effect far in excess of anything achieved by foreign-aid flows. For theorist Martin Ruhs from the Centre on Migration, Policy and Society at the University of Oxford, this greater good makes it morally defensible to restrict the rights of temporary migrants, even in a democracy, in order for them to enjoy the benefit of working in a higher-wage country. He argues that migrant workers knowingly consent to such trade-offs. He notes that they will pay 'substantial recruitment fees and other costs' to secure a job in the Gulf States, even when they are aware of the draconian conditions that prevail there, 'in order to improve their incomes as well as raise the living standards of their families'.[18]

The experience of living and working in another country may be empowering in less tangible ways, too. Camilla Pivato, a qualified costume designer for stage and screen, came to Australia on a working-holiday visa and ended up packing fruit in a shed in Shepparton, a job she would never have considered at home in Italy (where, ironically enough, agricultural labour is the preserve of 'foreign workers'). Camilla not only enjoyed her Shepparton experience, she found it liberating: 'Australia has brought out things about myself that I thought wouldn't exist, such as the ability to adapt that I thought I didn't have any more.'[19] Camilla loved Australia so much she wanted to settle, and her employers agreed to sponsor her for an ongoing position on a 457 visa. Unfortunately, she was ripped off by a dodgy migration agent and inadvertently overstayed her visa. As a result, Camilla was kicked out of Australia and banned from returning for three years. After six months back in Italy, when I spoke to her by Skype, she was still devastated and heartbroken. 'It is hard to live anywhere else after Australia,' she told me. Camilla missed her job, her friends, even the smells of Shepparton. She felt stuck, her future on hold.[20] We can get sucked in, whether we intend to or not. We become a part of this country and it becomes a part of us.

So we should not kid ourselves that the temporary migration 'revolution' is all upside. Michael Pezzullo's assertion that permanent migration 'often falls short of the needs of industry in rapidly changing circumstances' could be reformulated as 'contemporary global capitalism requires workers that can be moved rapidly about the world to meet the needs of industry in rapidly changing circumstances'. This unmasks a view of migrants as units of production that must bend to economic need—it is to treat migrants as labour power, not as people.

Political economist Salimah Valiani sees the increased use of temporary migrant workers in Canada as 'part and parcel' of the type of labour-market restructuring that has led in recent decades to more casual jobs, reduced security of tenure and lighter workplace regulation. In other words, temporary migration is not just the ethically neutral outgrowth of an indifferent and unstoppable process of globalisation, but an expression of a particular set of economic and political arrangements that are shaped by—and benefit—some people more than others.

Sociologist Richard Sennett might characterise the contemporary shift to temporary migration as another manifestation of what he calls 'flexibility and indifference'. Sennett uses the term in writing about cities to discuss the shift from Fordist industrial systems where each worker had a tightly defined role—typified in the factory production line and the bureaucratic office—to 'delayered' organisations that put workers into teams to carry out specific tasks, and then reshuffle them for a new project when the task is complete. He says the mantra of the flexible workplace is 'no long term'. Career paths are replaced by jobs that can change abruptly and erratically. Such flexibility, argues Sennett, erases the time that is necessary to build trust and mutuality:

> The experience of being only temporarily in an organization prompts people to keep loose, not to get involved, because they are going to exit soon...This is not a world in which getting deeply involved with other people makes much sense in the long run.[21]

Sennett's point is that flexibility and indifference extend beyond the workplace into social relations generally, making them more superficial, short term and disengaged. As workers become more mobile, both geographically and within and between organisations, they are at greater risk of becoming detached from any particular place, or firm, or set of people. This contributes to an arrangement of power that promotes 'neither loyalty nor fraternity', but instead encourages withdrawal from civic participation and retreat into the private sphere.

I do not think it is too big a stretch to extend Sennett's analytical framework to encompass the rise of temporary migration. Take the example of IT workers in Selvaraj Velayutham's study of Indian 457-visa holders in Australia. They could be employed at the same firm for years, without developing meaningful relationships with local colleagues:

> It appeared that local employees of the client company were reluctant to 'invest time' in establishing friendships with these workers who were understood to be temporary and not 'real colleagues'. There was also some resentment towards them from local IT workers who had seen colleagues displaced or downsized by their corporation and replaced by contract labour. The very presence of 457 visa workers made permanent workers feel a sense of insecurity in terms of their own jobs.[22]

If we view temporary migration through Sennett's lens of flexibility and indifference, then we can see that it poses challenges not just for individual migrants, but also for democratic structures and institutions like citizenship and the universal franchise. What does it mean for an avowedly liberal, multicultural society like Australia if a significant proportion of the population is 'unsettled'—if they are 'wanted' for their temporary labour power or university fees, but not 'welcome' as engaged and active members of society? What does it mean for our democracy if a growing proportion of the population are twenty-first-century *metics*—paying taxes, abiding by laws, but having no say in the affairs of the nation and denied essential support in times of need? If government treats migration as a purely contractual arrangement then we will encourage migrants to treat their relationship to Australia in exactly the same way: to ask 'what is in it for me, what can I get out of this country?' rather than 'what is my connection to this country and what are my obligations?'

Malcolm Fraser made a similar point in a landmark speech on multiculturalism in 1981: 'I am talking here about basic human rights, not benevolence which the giver bestows or withdraws at will. No society can long retain the commitment and involvement of groups that are denied these rights.'[23] To focus on borders rather than belonging is to stab at the heart of the idea of the nation as an inclusive political community.

We must ask at this point whether temporary migration can ever be reconciled with liberal democracy. Is there a way of organising temporary migration that is compatible with the idea of an inclusive, pluralist society that upholds basic rights and fosters engagement and commitment? Or, as political theorist Michael Walzer argues, does temporary migration inevitably require such significant ethical compromises that we should oppose it altogether?

In his classic book *Spheres of Justice*, Walzer argues that temporary labour migration renders the nation equivalent to 'a family with live-in servants'. As he writes, this is 'not an attractive image, for a family with live-in servants is—inevitably, I think—a little tyranny'.[24] If we decide as a nation to import more workers, Walzer argues, then we should also enlarge our political community—migrants 'must be set on the road to citizenship'.[25] If we are unwilling to include migrants as full members of our society, then we should not admit them, but instead 'find ways within the limits of the domestic labour market to get socially necessary work done'.[26] For Walzer, these are our only two choices.

Bolting horses and stable doors come to mind in response to this argument, but to be fair to Walzer, he had in mind the 'exploited and oppressed' class of disenfranchised guest workers turning cogs and mopping floors in parts of Europe around 1970. Walzer's focus is on low-skilled temporary labour migration and he does not envisage a skilled temporary-migration scheme like Australia's 457 program, let alone the case of international students or backpackers who may migrate primarily for education and travel, but also work, and who may plan to return home after a definite period, but then have a change of heart.

Walzer's critique remains important, however, because it is an enduring expression of a communitarian philosophical position. The communitarian starting point is that questions of justice—decisions about how to share goods and services and to allocate rights and obligations—can only be made within a particular political community, which in our era means the nation state. A corollary of this view is that there must be ways of defining and limiting membership of this community—in other words, ways of including or excluding people from it. Membership cannot be completely open.

At its extreme, communitarianism morphs into an exclusivist nationalism—to the kind of argument that heterogeneous societies are doomed to fail because their members lack the shared cultural, historical, linguistic or racial background necessary to forge political agreements. The argument of a liberal communitarian like Walzer is far subtler. The logic of his position is that democratic justice of the kind that we aspire to in Australia *requires* borders because without the right to determine and police the boundaries of membership there can be no political community to make decisions: 'For it is only as members somewhere that men and women can hope to share in all the other social goods—security, wealth, honour, office and power—that communal life makes possible.'[27]

Ironies abound here: when I argue for fairer treatment of temporary migrants and refugees I am taking aim at the very institution, the nation state, that excludes them. Yet it is only through the decisions of such a democratically bounded political community that more inclusive policies can ever be realised.

One of the most fundamental freedoms accorded to citizens of a democratic community is the right to leave—it is a contradiction in terms to force someone to be a citizen of a democracy. Yet the freedom to leave is not matched by a corresponding right to arrive. Walzer defends this reality and says that immigration and emigration are 'morally asymmetrical'. He draws the analogy to membership of a club—a club 'can regulate admissions but cannot bar withdrawals'.[28] Zolberg finds the analogy faulty, since club membership is a matter of preference, whereas belonging to a political community is a human necessity. He points out the prospects for achieving a more democratic world—characterised by the types of national political communities that a liberal communitarian hopes to see flourish—rest to some degree on affluent western nations maintaining 'relatively open borders'.[29]

A liberal communitarian supports the right of citizens in a representative democracy like Australia to decide 'who will come to this country and the circumstances in which they come', but does not grant them carte blanche to do so in any way they choose. The democratic right to determine policy does not render every democratically determined policy right. If a majority voted for a return to the White Australia policy, that would not render racial discrimination compatible with liberal values. Nor does majority support provide a moral justification for the mandatory and indefinite detention of asylum seekers. As Joseph Carens points out, anyone who aspires to be a consistent liberal—that is, to attribute equal moral worth to all human beings—must also 'take seriously the moral claims of people who are outside a political community and want to get in'.[30]

Walzer and Carens have much to argue about: the former takes as his starting point the state's right to prevent an outsider from crossing its borders, the latter begins from the premise that the outsider has a prior right to cross. But they also share essential common ground: both agree that if a democratic country allows an outsider to live within the boundaries of the nation for an extended period, then at some point it must also offer them full membership of the political community. Walzer puts it this way:

> ...the principle of political justice is this: that the processes of self-determination through which a democratic state shapes its internal life, must be open, and equally open, to all those men and women who live within its territory, work in the local economy, and are subject to local law... Men and women are either subject to the state's authority, or they are not; and if they are subject, they must be given a say, and ultimately an equal say, in what that authority does.[31]

For his part, Carens argues that both 'the inner logic of democracy and a commitment to liberal principles require the full inclusion of the entire settled population'. It is a fundamental principle that everyone should be able to participate in shaping the laws by which they are to be governed and in selecting the representatives who will make those laws. 'Therefore, to meet the requirements of democratic legitimacy, every adult who lives in a democratic political community on an ongoing basis should be a citizen, or, at the least, should have the right to become a citizen if she chooses to do so.'[32]

This is qualitatively different from the predominant rights-based approach that seeks to enhance and enshrine certain protections for temporary migrants, such as equal pay and conditions at work. Expanding and upholding the rights of temporary migrants is important, but as researchers Catherine Dauvergne and Sarah Marsden argue, a rights-based approach can only go so far before running up against its inherent limitation—the underlying subordinate status of temporary migrants:

> Talking in rights terms inevitably calls up the 'right' of the state to exclude non-members as an aspect of sovereignty. This exclusion power undermines attempts to articulate rights claims for those with any type of temporary status, and reinforces a fundamental inequality between citizens and non-citizens.[33]

Martin Ruhs accepts this argument, but uses it to make the case for a putting a time limit on how long temporary migrants can stay in the host country. His utilitarian calculation is that it is legitimate for a democratic state to restrict some of the rights of migrants, in return for accepting more migrants overall. Ruhs sees swapping rights for visas as a necessary trade-off to promote the greater good of reducing global poverty through increased temporary migration from low- to high-wage countries.

Ruhs' hypothesis is that there is a negative relationship between openness and rights. In other words, the more expansive the rights and entitlements extended to migrants by a host country, the more restrictive will be its rules of admission. Countries that curtail rights, by contrast, will admit many more migrants, particularly low-skilled migrants on temporary visas. The Gulf States, Saudi Arabia and Singapore illustrate his point: each severely restricts rights for low-skilled migrants, but has large-scale foreign-labour programs. By contrast, the majority of temporary migrants who do low-skilled jobs in Australia enter the country on a visa primarily intended for a different purpose—holiday or study. The only formal migration program for low-skilled workers is the small and highly regulated (at least until recently) Seasonal Worker Programme for the Pacific Islands and East Timor.

Ruhs is not endorsing the brutal treatment of foreign workers in the Arabian Peninsula: he argues that migrants' fundamental civil and political rights should always be upheld, including freedom of thought and expression, freedom of religious belief and worship, and freedom of association. The crucial exception is the right to vote in national elections—a right that demarcates the boundaries of citizenship.[34]

Ruhs also accepts significant restrictions on certain social and economic rights of temporary migrants—such as access to government benefits and services, the right to family reunion and freedom of movement within the labour market.[35] His caveat is that all such restrictions must be temporary. He agrees with Carens that the passage of time 'increases the strength of migrants' moral claims to equality of rights'.[36] So for Ruhs, too, there must be a limit to temporariness—a point at which a migrant is either granted permanent residence or required to return home. In this sense, Ruhs is building on the liberal common ground shared by Carens and Walzer: the principle that people who live within the boundaries of a state and abide by its laws must be offered a path to full membership of the political community. Rather than Carens' bias towards inclusion, however, he leans towards Walzer's bias for exclusion, by proposing a time limit on temporary migration—to put it bluntly, you get kicked out before you can put down roots. He says rich countries will only let more migrants in if they can send them home again before they accrue the moral rights of membership.

If we applied Ruhs' thinking to Australia, then we would force temporary migrants to leave before their roots here reached too deep. In her 2008 review of the 457-visa system, industrial relations commissioner Barbara Deegan suggested such a policy: she recommended that no 457-visa holder be allowed to remain in Australia for more than a total of eight years. Deegan thought that if temporary migrants were unable to convert to permanent residency after that time, then they should not get another visa.[37] Deegan's recommendation was not adopted, but Canada has taken this approach. The cumulative duration or 'four in, four out' rule restricts any temporary foreign worker who arrived in Canada after 1 April 2011 to a maximum stay of four years.[38] When that time limit is passed, they must leave Canada and stay away for four more years before applying to come back. This four-year rule applies only to lower-skilled migrant workers, and critics say it entrenches 'unjust and unequal treatment based on class and labour qualifications'.[39] Canada's largest union organisation, the Canadian Labour Congress, says the rule removes any incentive for employers to adhere to standards on pay rates, benefits or working conditions, since they know workers are truly disposable.[40]

Australia's Seasonal Worker Programme for the Pacific Islands and East Timor also imposes time limits: seasonal workers can only stay in Australia for part of the year (usually a maximum of six months), though it is anticipated that they will come back again the following year. There is another consideration at work here: a primary purpose of the Seasonal Worker Programme is promoting development, so the idea is that workers take their savings home to invest in their own families and communities before returning for another stint of work the following season. The intent, too, is that seasonal workers still spend a significant chunk of each year with their families—that they keep their emotional roots in home soil. In this sense, the seasonal program is cyclical migration rather than long-term temporary migration.

To apply a fixed time limit for a specific visa category like the 457 visa is one thing, but as we have seen, temporary migrants move across different visa classes. If the aim is to stop temporary migrants staying too long, then restrictions would have to apply across the board. This would have profound repercussions. Let's say the time limit was five years. To enforce this, we would need to curtail post-study work rights for students and prevent them from switching to 457 visas. It would become problematic for backpackers to convert to student visas, because they would risk hitting the threshold before completing their course, especially if they wanted to undertake post-graduate study. Graduates would have to leave Australia and return to their home country before applying for permanent residency (as used to be the case). Such a restriction would face stiff resistance from the education lobby, because it would make Australian institutions far less attractive in the international market. We could extend the time limit to eight years, as suggested by Barbara Deegan, but, for me at least, this is too long. After eight years, roots are deep and our moral obligations have been engaged. Consider someone who comes to Australia aged 17 for the final two years of high school, completes four years of undergraduate study and then works for two more years on a 485 visa. Now aged 25, she has spent almost one-third of her young life in Australia. Her friends are here, she regards Australia as home and she feels Australian. If she cannot qualify for permanent residence, is it ethically acceptable to say, 'Sorry. Leave now. You have no place here'?

In my view, a hard and fast time limit that triggers a migrant's exclusion from Australia after four or eight years is likely to create more problems and ethical dilemmas than it solves.

Carens, Walzer and Ruhs all agree that it is ethically unacceptable to render migrants indefinitely temporary, because this risks creating a group of 'second-class residents' excluded from the political community of the nation and the benefits and rights of citizenship. Yet this is what can happen in Australia today. Many New Zealanders and recently arrived refugees face the prospect of living permanently in Australia on temporary visas; migrant workers can potentially have their temporary 457 visas repeatedly renewed; and after they graduate, international students can end up hopping precariously across temporary-visa categories over an extended period of time.

Consequently, the starting point for a consistent liberal response to temporary migration must be a pathway to permanent residence that is, after a certain period of time, unconditional—not one that depends on an employer's endorsement, or a particular qualification, or the ability to achieve a certain score on an English-language test, or a person's health status, or whether they arrived by plane with a visa rather than by boat and without one.

So we must set a threshold after which migrants are offered

membership. What should this time limit on temporariness be? Ruhs considers four years to be a 'reasonable' period, though he is considering when to send temporary migrants home rather than make them permanent. He offers little justification for choosing this number beyond gut feeling:

> Anything less than three years seems to me 'too short' to ensure that the policy generates the intended benefits for receiving countries as well as migrants and their countries of origin, while restrictions that last longer than five years seem to come close to 'long term' or 'permanent exclusion' from equal citizenship.[41]

Carens opts for a five- to seven-year threshold for a transition to full membership of the host society.[42] He also admits that he can offer no concrete justification for a particular number:

> Why five years rather than four or six? No one can pretend that the answer to this question entails any fundamental principle...But if one asks why five years rather than one or ten, it is easier to make the case that one is too short and ten too long, given common European understandings of the ways in which people settle into the societies where they live.[43]

There is no mathematical formula to help us out here. As Carens says, the argument that time has moral force—that the longer a migrant stays in a country, the stronger their claim to membership—does not provide clear demarcation points: 'The extremes will be clear; the middle will be fuzzy.'[44]

Yet opting for a particular number of years must be a reasoned decision rather than an arbitrary one. It will take into account other political considerations and established norms and standards. We have already set time thresholds in relation to a raft of other migration questions in Australia. A permanent resident, for example, must wait two years to become eligible for most social-security payments.[43] In order to apply for citizenship, a migrant must have been living in Australia on a valid visa for four years, including the last 12 months as a permanent resident.[46] In order to apply for a partner visa an unmarried couple must have been in a de facto relationship for at least 12 months.[47] To be eligible for Malcolm Turnbull's new pathway to permanent residency New Zealanders must have been living in Australia for at least five years. Crossing a 10-year threshold gives New Zealanders on special category visas limited access to government benefits[48] and, if they came to Australia as children, enables them to access the concessional loans scheme for tertiary study (rather than pay upfront fees).[49] A child born in Australia to parents who are not citizens or permanent residents gains an independent right to citizenship after living here for 10 years.[50]

If I apply gut feeling to the question, then 10 years seems too long a qualification period. It moves beyond Carens' fuzzy middle to an unacceptable extreme. Carens notes a European Union directive that recommends that 'third-country nationals (that is, people from outside the EU) be granted a right of permanent residence if they have been legally residing in a single EU state for five years'.[51] (Time spent in the country as a student is discounted by 50 per cent as long as the applicant has held another temporary resident status in addition to student status.[52]) In Canada, a temporary migration scheme for live-in caregivers leads to permanent residency after two years of full-time employment.[53]

The point of such examples is not to suggest that there is an objectively identifiable or average time period at which temporary migration should transition to permanent residence. Rather, it is to agree with Carens that 'some threshold must be established beyond which the right to stay is indefeasible'. Migrants who live in Australia for a significant period of time, who contribute to the economic life of the nation through their labour and their taxes, who possibly pay fees to study, are people who, for all intents and purposes, make Australia their home.

Conclusion
Crafting a Democratic Response to Temporary Migration

In Herman Melville's partly autobiographical 1849 novel *Redburn: His First Voyage*, the eponymous narrator reflects on the nature of borders. Witnessing the hardships of destitute Irish emigrants below decks on an Atlantic crossing, Redburn responds to contemporary debates about whether or not America should allow these multitudes of foreign poor to land on its shores with the thought that:

> ...if they can get here, they have God's right to come; though they bring all Ireland and her miseries with them. For the whole world is the patrimony of the whole world; there is no telling who does not own a stone in the Great Wall of China.'[1]

Redburn makes this point in passing, before going on to consider practical changes that might improve the situation on emigrant ships. 'Much good might be done', he suggests, if existing American laws 'restricting ships to a certain number of emigrants' were enforced; likewise, an English ordinance that supposedly required ships to stock 'a fixed supply of food for every emigrant embarking from Liverpool'. Redburn laments that captains are not compelled to supply steerage passengers 'with decent lodgings, and give them light and air', nor to place the galley 'in a dry place of shelter' so the emigrants can prepare their meals in foul weather.

Like Redburn, I am interested in practical politics and better outcomes. Since we cannot wipe away global inequalities or transform the international economic system, we must work within the world as we find it and not as we wish it would be. So the question is how we in Australia can best respond to the revolution that is temporary migration in terms of ethically informed but practical and achievable public policy. Can we draw on the more positive elements of our history as a settler society to craft a response that is better than our current arrangements and which at least attempts to be consistent with the (admittedly not uncontested) claim that Australia is a liberal democracy with a commitment to citizenship-based multiculturalism?

In order to do this, we must first return to the issue raised in the last chapter: fundamental principles of liberal democracy require us to set a threshold of years after which migrants are offered membership of the political community. In other words, we must answer the question, what is the time limit on temporariness?

I propose that anyone who has lived in Australia lawfully and with work rights for a continuous period of eight years (or, allowing for reasonable absences, for at least eight of the past 10 years) qualifies for permanent residence. The type of temporary visa, or combination of temporary visas, that person has held is irrelevant—they could be New Zealanders on special category visas, they might have spent time living in limbo as an asylum seeker on a bridging visa, they might be long-term students, or they might have changed status from backpacker to student to migrant worker. What counts is that, after eight years, they become Australian. (Exceptions would apply: for example, if a temporary migrant had been convicted of a serious crime and spent time in prison.)

Migrants who arrive as children would be treated more generously, by discounting the eight-year qualification period by six months for every year that a migrant lived in Australia between the ages of 14 and 18. So the qualification period for a New Zealander or international student who comes here at age 16 is seven years—they become eligible for permanent residence at age 23. A child who arrived at age 14 becomes eligible for permanent residence after six years at age 20. This is an attempt to give appropriate weight to the significance of the formative teenage years in shaping a person's sense of place and belonging—it is the period when we begin to separate from our parents and put down our own independent roots.

Under this proposal, children who arrive in Australia at age 12 or younger become eligible for permanent residency in their own right when they turn 18. There is no logical or ethical defence of current arrangements where children born in Australia to foreign parents are included in the life of the nation after ten years, whereas children who arrive when they are a few days, weeks, months or years old can remain permanently excluded, no matter how long they stay.

Refugees would be in a different category: in my scheme they would be granted permanent status from the moment that their claims for protection are recognised as legitimate. If this is a political step too far, then temporary protection visas should become permanent if there is still no prospect of a person returning safely to their homeland after two years (including any time spent on a bridging visa).

Setting an eight-year threshold would, of course, have unintended consequences: it would give temporary migrants a target to aim at and the incentive to find a means to stay in Australia for at least eight years. We would need some safeguards, such as measures to prevent people without legitimate claims from attempting to reach the eight-year threshold through protracted legal proceedings. An eight-year rule would motivate some migrants to hop from visa to visa in order to clock up the qualifying time for permanent residence. But if the value of temporary labour migration and international education to Australia's economy and society is so great that we create a system that enables migrants to do this (because we want to attract them to study at our universities or pick our fruit), then this is a consequence we have to countenance. The alternative, creating a subclass of migrants who are indefinitely temporary, is not acceptable. (It should go without saying that no migrant would be forced to become a permanent resident—the point is that, after eight years, the option should be available to them.)

This approach would almost certainly require an increase in the size of the annual permanent migration program. Australians concerned about population size might object at this point that the nation cannot sustain all those extra people, but such concerns are misplaced. Anyone who is living in Australia long term as a twenty-first-century *metic* is already counted as part of the population; enabling those temporary migrants to become permanent residents changes their status, but makes no difference to overall numbers. If we want to limit population size, then we will need to put an annual cap on temporary migration in the same way that we put an annual cap on permanent migration.

My proposal for an eight-year threshold acknowledges the reality of mobility in a globalised world, but aims to swing the policy pendulum away from a purely contractual approach to temporary migration, and back towards an assumption of migration-as-settlement as the basis for a citizenship-based multicultural society.

With a wider, clearer pathway to permanent residency, many other questions fall away, such as questions about if or when temporary migrants should qualify for government benefits for Medicare services or the National Disability Insurance Scheme. These would all come with residence. It would not, however, solve all dilemmas. A range of other more specific measures is needed to offer greater protection to temporary migrants, especially in the workplace.

Firstly, 457 visas: we should require any employer who wants to retain a 457-visa holder on staff for more than two years to sponsor that temporary migrant for permanent residence, rather than allowing sponsorship to be optional. Two years' full-time employment is long enough to demonstrate that the temporary migrant is filling an ongoing gap in the enterprise and the labour market. It is also long enough for the employer to assess the worker's suitability. If an employer does not want to sponsor the visa holder for permanent residence, then the firm should be prevented from recruiting another temporary worker for the same position or similar work. This would broaden the pathway from 457 visa to permanent residence, and make clear that 457-visa holders cannot be treated as disposable labour or as an alternative to local recruitment.

The current inadequate system of labour-market testing under the 457 scheme should be scrapped, too, because it is ineffective. Instead, the federal government should establish an independent expert commission to identify skills shortages that can potentially be filled by temporary (or permanent) migrant workers. This approach was recommended by a 2014 inquiry into the 457 program, based on the persuasive arguments of Adelaide University legal scholars Joanna Howe and Alex Reilly. While noting that labour-market testing as it currently operates is ineffective, they point out that leaving it up to employers to identify shortages is not an appropriate alternative, since employers' judgements will be swayed by self-interest. A better option is an independent authority with its own research capacity 'relying upon both hard economic data and engagement with stakeholders to develop a view as to whether a particular occupation is in shortage *and* whether this shortage is best addressed through migration' (as opposed to, say, training more locals).[2]

The federal government has already accepted the idea—subject to consultation—of a levy on employers for each 457-visa holder on a firm's books.[3] The amount of such a levy will be hotly contested, with suggestions ranging from $400 to $4,000.[4] It must be high enough to encourage employers to make a serious effort at local recruitment, without crippling businesses that cannot find the skilled staff they need in Australia. The extra revenue raised by such a levy would boost funding in the vocational education system, which is the most important pathway to secure employment for Australians from disadvantaged backgrounds.

Given that the 457 scheme is a major pathway to permanent residency, settlement services such as adult migrant English classes should be made available, if needed, to the family members of 457-visa holders. As the Migration Council Australia points out, offering settlement services on arrival would increase opportunities for social and economic integration, and would be consistent with the services provided to migrants in the family stream of the migration program and to the dependents of certain skilled migrants.[5]

Secondly, working holidaymakers: the working-holidaymaker scheme should be nudged back towards facilitating extended travel and cultural experiences, and away from being a de facto mechanism for recruiting low-wage migrant workers. The first step is to scrap the option of backpackers gaining a second working-holiday visa in return for three months' work in a rural industry. This creates a choke point that gives unconscionable power to employers in the workplace.

If we need more fruit-pickers and other seasonal workers in rural and remote Australian, then the Seasonal Worker Programme for the Pacific and East Timor is a more appropriate way to meet this demand for labour, as long as it remains closely regulated. Recent allegations of labour-hire companies ripping off Pacific Island workers in Queensland and Victoria are disturbing,[6] but it is nevertheless easier to monitor the employment conditions of teams of workers deployed under a centrally organised Seasonal Worker Programme than it is to keep track of what happens to tens of thousands of working holidaymakers independently entering the rural labour market. One of the original intentions behind the Seasonal Worker Programme was that it would help build people-to-people links between Australia and the Pacific, with church groups and service clubs (like Lions and Rotary) engaging seasonal workers in local activities, or even fundraising for development projects in the workers' home villages.[7] Embedding the program in the community in this way would reduce the likelihood of workplace abuses occurring and increase the likelihood of them being reported.

The Seasonal Worker Programme has the added benefit of generating employment and increasing family incomes in small nations that are highly dependent on Australian aid. Ideally, a seasonal-labour program would also include training opportunities so that workers could take home useful skills (such as courses in first aid or safe pesticide handling). The cyclical nature of the Seasonal Worker Programme is better for productivity than the working-holidaymaker scheme: as the same workers return year on year they become increasingly proficient in the skills appropriate to the workplace, whereas each new batch of backpackers always starts from scratch.[8]

Experience in New Zealand and Canada shows that cyclical seasonal-labour schemes can be viable and beneficial.[9] A regulated scheme with a development focus will, however, entail higher costs for employers than current arrangements, which is why the option of a second working-holiday visa should be removed. As long as it exists, the Seasonal Worker Programme will continue to be stymied, because employers will find it cheaper to hire backpackers.

Thirdly, international students: the 40-hours-per-fortnight work restriction should be scrapped. Again, it gives employers too much leverage over student workers. Tertiary students are adults: they can make up their own mind about how much to work alongside study. This change may need to be accompanied by more vigilant monitoring of students to ensure that they are meeting attendance requirements and completing work to an appropriate standard.

Universities and colleges should also devote far more resources to the welfare of international students, including the provision of free, independent legal advice to help students with problems in employment, housing and migration matters. In most cases, the level of support international students receive is dismal when compared to the revenue that they generate for education providers. Sean Stimson from Redfern Legal Centre argues that it is 'short-sighted' not to provide students with more support. He calculates that the upfront cost of funding a full-time solicitor to provide advice would be justified if it saved a university from losing just a few fee-paying students each year. It might also attract additional students. 'If we did better at this we would compete better in the international market,' he says. Better student support would lead to a better reputation for Australian education providers.

More generally, temporary migrants living in Australia and paying tax as workers or university fees as students should not have to pay fees for their children to go to government schools. Their children should also be completely covered, like Australian kids, by free vaccination programs. Victims of domestic violence should have access to crisis services including emergency accommodation and income support, regardless of their visa status; otherwise we are giving them little choice but to return to an abusive relationship.

There is also a need for a pathway to permanent residency for the foreign parents of Australian-citizen children. It is unconscionable, not to mention a ridiculous waste of time and resources, to force foreign parents to go through the long and ludicrous process of claiming to be refugees in order to finally be able to seek ministerial intervention to enable them to remain living in the same country as their children.

We need to scrutinise existing legislation and administrative systems to bring them into line with the reality of twenty-first-century mobility. In areas like superannuation, insurance, and workers compensation and rehabilitation there is often an assumption—usually embedded deep in the fine print—that people are Australian citizens or permanent residents. We need to make sure that the equal entitlements of temporary migrants are fully recognised and enshrined in law. It is unacceptable that, when a company goes bust, the government steps in to cover the unpaid wages and entitlements of Australian workers, but not those of temporary migrants.

Other changes have less to do with migration and visa rules than with labour law. Australia has some of the most lax arrangements for subcontracting and outsourcing workers in the developed world. As Tim Kennedy, national secretary of the National Union of Workers, puts it: 'If you sell alcohol in Victoria you need a licence, if you want to trade people you need nothing.'[10] Anyone with a mobile phone and a spreadsheet can set up a labour-hire business, and sham contracting is widespread. Tighter entry requirements and increased regulation would not only benefit foreign migrants, but many vulnerable Australian workers, too.

Authorities like the Fair Work Ombudsman need greater resources to monitor and police work practices—again, this would benefit Australian workers as well as migrants.

Having laid out some concrete policy suggestions, let me return to the two overarching questions I asked at the start of this book, and respond to them in reverse order. The second question that I posed was about what sort of country we want Australia to be. Do we hold to the positive conception—however historically simplistic—of Australia as a settler society where migrants become full members of the political community and make this country their home? Malcolm Fraser again offers pithy advice on what makes a successful multicultural society: 'To have one's heritage respected, to be treated with dignity on one's own terms, to contribute as full and equal participants in Australian society, these are issues of the most fundamental importance.'[11]

Do we aspire to Fraser's ideal, or are we content for the proportion of *metics*—of provisional not-quite-Australians—to continue to grow? In other words, is there a threshold we should not cross—a point at which the number of long-term temporary migrants tips the balance and changes the nature of Australian society and the assumptions underpinning Australian multiculturalism?

I think that there probably is a threshold we should not cross. As with setting time limits for a transition to permanent residence, there is no magic mathematical formula or objective test to work out what this threshold is. I would suggest a maximum of 10 per cent of the population. This figure is obviously open to challenge, but part of my intention in writing this book is to promote discussion.

The consequence of this argument is that we may need to consider whether temporary migration, like permanent migration, should be subjected to an annual cap. In other words, putting a limit on the number of international students we admit to study in Australia, on the number of temporary-skilled 457 and working-holidaymaker visas that we issue, and perhaps even on the number of New Zealanders who can live and work in Australia (though this might mean scrapping the Trans-Tasman Travel Arrangement).

Limiting long-term temporary migrants to 10 per cent of the population still leaves considerable room for temporary migration to grow. (By my estimates, at around one million people, temporary migrants currently make up just under five per cent of the population.)

Which returns me to my prior question: how long is it reasonable for a migrant to live in Australia without being accepted as an Australian? To keep someone on the outer, like the *metics* of ancient Greece? My answer in policy terms is a maximum of eight years. Again, the number is open to debate—it could be argued, for example, that less weight should be given to time spent on a student or working-holidaymaker visa compared to dedicated work visas like the 457 and 485 visas—but the question itself is not one we can ignore, at least if we want to be consistent with the claims of liberal democracy.

My thinking is influenced by Joseph Carens, who poses the question this way:

> What are the claims of non-citizens who are present on the territory of a state but who are not permanent residents? Does the normative map of democracy have room for them? Is it even acceptable any longer to admit people to democratic states without access to long-term residence and without granting them most of the rights of citizens?[12]

Carens' answer to this final question is no. I think we have to agree with him. Australia's normative map must make room for long-term temporary migrants and, after a certain threshold is crossed, offer them a pathway to citizenship. If we refuse to do this, then we will have to admit that our map is neither truly liberal nor democratic.

Postscript

By the time I completed this manuscript at the end of May 2016, Ilaria De Fusco, Adam Gaster and Belinda Pei (Chapter 4) had all been granted permanent residence. Sherene, her mother, Sima, and her brothers, Mohamad and Khalid, were still on bridging visas and waiting to see if they would be recognised as refugees and granted temporary protection visas by the Australian government. They were hopeful but anxious about what the pending closure of the Manus Island detention centre would mean for their husband and father, Ali, who was still there.

Acknowledgments

This book is built around personal stories. It was the experiences of temporary migrants—particularly when those experiences raised questions of justice and ethics—that sent me looking for data and theory to help me better understand the bigger picture. I am deeply grateful to all those people who trusted me enough to share their stories with me, and I hope that I have done them justice.

This book also draws on the work of many other scholars and journalists who write about temporary migration. I thank them for their insights and hope that I have cited their work accurately and appropriately. I am particularly indebted to Joo-Cheong Tham at Melbourne University Law School and Shanthi Robertson at the Institute for Culture and Society at the University of Western Sydney, whose work has helped to shape my thinking in significant ways. Henry Sherrell, formerly of the Migration Council Australia, read several draft chapters and has been a valuable source of advice, encouragement and productive criticism since the project's inception. I am also grateful to Paul Hamer at Victoria University in Wellington for his detailed feedback on draft chapters, particularly those dealing with New Zealand. Thanks to my friends and colleagues in the Global Research Flagship at the Institute for Social Research at Swinburne University, particularly Klaus Neumann and Sandy Gifford, and to all the other members of our informal refugee discussion group—the conversations over dinner have been important to me. Thanks also to Richie and Susie, for keeping an eye on the swell and getting me away from the computer and onto a surfboard when I most needed to clear my head.

Thank you to the team at Text Publishing. Michael Heyward was willing to back this book because he thought the issue was important. Alaina Gougoulis's editing was attentive, careful and sympathetic. It was a great pleasure to work with Alaina and the book was much improved by her corrections, comments and suggestions.

Some bits of this book were originally published in a different form in *Griffith Review* and in *Inside Story*. My friend Peter Browne, editor of *Inside Story*, read the entire manuscript and provided invaluable suggestions. Peter encouraged me to expand my journalism from radio into print more than 25 years ago and he has informed and improved my writing ever since. Finally, thanks to my partner, Julie Shiels. Julie not only read a draft of the entire book and helped me improve its shape and flow (and much else besides), but she made the whole thing happen in the first place. Julie kept reminding me that what I most wanted to do was write, and she helped me to create the space in my life that makes writing possible. Without her, nothing would have happened.

Endnotes

Introduction

1. Peter Dutton, Minister for Immigration and Border Protection, 'All Australians Encouraged to Reflect this Australia Day', media release, 26 January 2016, http://www.minister.border.gov.au/peterdutton/2016/Pages/All-Australians-encouraged-to-reflect-this-Australia-Day.aspx (accessed 8 April 2016)
2. Prior to 1984, any British subject could vote after living in Australia for just six months. In the early 1980s, Commonwealth and state parliaments amended electoral laws to make citizenship the basis of the franchise, but British people already on the roll had their voting rights grandfathered, since it was considered 'unfair' to disenfranchise them.

Chapter 1: The New Metics

1. Eric Richards, *Destination Australia: Migration to Australia Since 1901*, UNSW Press, Sydney, 2008, p. x
2. Klaus Neumann, *Across the Seas*, Black Inc. Publishing, Melbourne, 2015, p. 134
3. Neumann (2015), p. 104
4. Gwenda Tavan, *The Long, Slow Death of White Australia*, Scribe, Melbourne, 2005, pp. 50–51
5. Tavan (2005), p. 169
6. Nino Culotta (aka John O'Grady), *They're a Weird Mob*, Text Classics, 2012 (first published 1957), p. 251
7. Neumann (2015), p. 122
8. Malcolm Fraser, Prime Minister of Australia, 'Multiculturalism: Australia's Unique Achievement', Inaugural Address, Institute of Multicultural Affairs, Melbourne, 30 November 1981
9. John Hirst, 'Australia's Post-War Migration Was a Success, Let's Admit It', *The Conversation*, 25 June 2014, http://theconversation.com/australias-post-war-migration-was-a-success-lets-admit-it-28390 (accessed 7 January 2015)
10. Tavan (2005), pp. 104–5
11. Quoted in Tavan (2005), p. 139
12. Department of Immigration and Border Protection (DIBP), Fact sheet—Abolition of the White Australia Policy, http://www.border.gov.au/about/corporate/information/fact-sheets/08abolition (accessed 25 July 2015)

13 Shanthi Robertson, *Transnational Student-Migrants and the State: The Education-Migration Nexus*, Palgrave Macmillan, Melbourne, 2013 p. 68
14 Robertson (2013), p. 166
15 Graeme Hugo, 'Calling Australia Home', *Griffith Review*, no. 6 (November 2005)
16 John Howard, 'Joint Press Conference with the Prime Minister of New Zealand the Hon Helen Clark MP', Port Moresby, Papua New Guinea, 25 October 2005, http://pmtranscripts.dpmc.gov.au/preview.php?did=22004 (accessed 8 April 2016)
17 Michael Gordon, 'Costello Rules Out Importing Islanders', *Age*, 5 July 2006
18 Chris Bowen, Minister for Immigration and Citizenship, 'The Genius of Australian Multiculturalism', speech to the Sydney Institute, 17 February 2011 (accessed 25 February 2015 via PANDORA, National Library of Australia Web Archive, http://pandora.nla.gov.au/)
19 Joseph Carens, 'Live-in Domestics, Seasonal Workers, and Others Hard to Locate on the Map of Democracy', *Journal of Political Philosophy* 16, no. 4 (2008):419–445
20 Carens (2008), p. 419
21 Joseph Carens, *The Ethics of Immigration*, Oxford University Press, New York, 2013, p. 23
22 Carens (2013), p. 31
23 Carens (2008), p. 419
24 Carens (2008), p. 419
25 Carens (2013), p. 45
26 Carens (2013), p. 2
27 Michael Walzer, *Spheres of Justice: A Defense of Pluralism and Equality*, Basic Books, New York, 1983, p. 53
28 Siew-Ean Khoo, Graeme Hugo and Peter McDonald, 'Which Skilled Temporary Migrants Become Permanent Residents and Why?', *International Migration Review* 42, no. 1 (2008):193–226

Chapter 2: The Rise and Rise of Temporary Migration

1 Janet Phillips and Michael Klapdor, 'Migration to Australia since Federation: A Guide to the Statistics', Parliamentary Library background note, Parliament of Australia, updated 29 October 2010
2 Demetrios Papademetriou, 'Rethinking Emigration: Turning Challenges into Opportunities', Transatlantic Council Statement, Migration Policy Institute, November 2015, http://www.migrationpolicy.org/research/rethinking-emigration-turning-challenges-opportunities-transatlantic-council-statement (accessed 8 April 2016)

3   Michael Pezzullo, 'Immigration and Nation Building in Australia: Looking Back, Looking Forward', Australian National University Public Lecture, 21 April 2015, https://www.border.gov.au/about/news-media/speeches-presentations/2015/immigration-and-nation-building-in-australia (accessed 22 April 2015)
4   Phillips and Klapdor (2010)
5   Malcolm Fraser, Prime Minister of Australia, 'Multiculturalism: Australia's Unique Achievement', Inaugural Address, Institute of Multicultural Affairs, Melbourne, 30 November 1981
6   Department of Immigration and Border Protection (DIBP), New points test for general skilled migration visas, *Migration Blog*, 16 June 2011, http://migrationblog.border.gov.au/2011/06/16/new-points-test-for-general-skilled-migration-visas/ (accessed 14 July 2015)
7   Gareth Larsen, 'Family Migration to Australia', Parliamentary Library research paper, 23 December 2013
8   Janet Phillips, 'Australia's Humanitarian Program: A Quick Guide to the Statistics since 1947', Parliamentary Library research paper, 7 January 2015
9   Department of Immigration and Multicultural Affairs, 'Annual Report 1999–2000'
10   Graeme Hugo, 'Australia's Most Recent Immigrants 2001' (Table 2.25: 'Year of arrival by birthplace region by sex, 2001', p. 50), Australian Bureau of Statistics, 12 July 2004
11   Stephen Easton, 'Feathers Ruffled: How Hawks Took Over the Immigration Nest', *Mandarin*, 9 February 2015, http://www.themandarin.com.au/21226-feathers-ruffled-hawks-take-immigration-nest/ (accessed 15 April 2015)
12   Michael Pezzullo, Secretary, Department of Immigration and Border Protection, 'Reflections on Australia Day: Settlement of the Nation and Beyond', address to staff, https://www.border.gov.au/about/news-media/speeches-presentations/2015/reflections-on-australia-day (accessed 15 April 2015)
13   Department of Education and Training, Summary of the 2014 first half year higher education student statistics, http://www.education.gov.au/selected-higher-education-statistics-2014-student-data (accessed 14 July 2015)
14   Australian Education Network, International student university enrolment numbers, http://www.universityrankings.com.au/international-student-numbers.html (accessed 15 July 2015)
15   Matthew Drummond, '457 Visas Deliver Onshore Boost', *Australian Financial Review*, 16 March 2013
16   Australian Government, 'Business Temporary Entry: Future Directions', report

by the Committee of Inquiry into the Temporary Entry of Business People and Highly Skilled Specialists, Canberra, 1995

17 Brendan O'Connor, Minister for Immigration and Citizenship, 'Reforms Needed to Curb 457 Rise', media release, 4 April 2013 (accessed 3 April 2015 via PANDORA, National Library of Australia Web Archive, http://pandora.nla.gov.au/)

18 Bianca Hall, '457 Visas: More than 10,000 Are Rorting System, Says Minister', *Sydney Morning Herald*, 28 April 2013

19 Janet Phillips and Harriet Spinks, 'Skilled Migration: Temporary and Permanent Flows to Australia' (Table 3: Temporary migration: overseas student and business long stay (subclass 457) visa grants since 1996–97), Parliamentary Library background note, Parliament of Australia, updated 6 December 2012

20 DIBP, 'Temporary entrants and New Zealand citizens in Australia as at June 30 2015'

21 DIBP, 'Subclass 457 quarterly report, quarter ending at June 30 2015'

22 Elsa Koleth, 'Overseas Students: Immigration Policy Changes 1997–May 2010', Parliamentary Library background note, Parliament of Australia, 18 June 2010

23 DIBP, 'Temporary entrants and New Zealand citizens in Australia as at June 30 2015'

24 DIBP, Genuine temporary entrant, http://www.border.gov.au/Trav/Stud/More/Genuine-Temporary-Entrant (accessed 15 July 2015)

25 Minister for Immigration and Citizenship, 'Direction No 53—Assessing the Genuine Temporary Entrant Criterion for Student Visa Applications', effective 5 November 2011, http://www.border.gov.au/StudyinginAustralia/Documents/direction-53-assessing-gte.pdf (accessed 8 April 2016)

26 DIBP, Genuine temporary entrant

27 Minister for Immigration and Citizenship (2011)

28 DIBP, Student visa living costs and evidence of funds, http://www.border.gov.au/Trav/Stud/More/Student-Visa-Living-Costs-and-Evidence-of-Funds# (accessed 15 July 2015)

29 DIBP, Student visa assessment levels, http://www.border.gov.au/Trav/Stud/Stud (accessed 15 July 2015)

30 DIBP, Student visa living costs and evidence of funds

31 DIBP, 'Working Holiday Maker Visa Programme Report, 30 December 2015'

32 DIBP, 'Working Holiday Maker Visa Programme Report, 30 December 2015'

33 The Parliament of the Commonwealth of Australia, Joint Standing Committee on Migration, 'Working Holiday Makers: More Than Tourists', Canberra, August 1997

34 Amanda Vanstone, Minister for Immigration and Multicultural Affairs, 'Enhancements to Working Holiday Maker Program to Help Address Seasonal Labour Shortages', media release, 14 April 2005 (accessed 8 April 2015 via PANDORA, National Library of Australia Web Archive, http://pandora.nla.gov.au/)

35 Amanda Vanstone, Minister for Immigration and Multicultural Affairs, 'Working Holiday Visa Enhancements a Boost for Backpackers and Regional Employers', media release, 9 May 2006 (accessed 8 April 2016 via PANDORA, National Library of Australia Web Archive, http://pandora.nla.gov.au/); DIPB, Working Holiday visa (subclass 417): Specified work, https://www.border.gov.au/Trav/Visa-1/417- (accessed 9 April 2016)

36 Yan Tan et al., 'Evaluation of Australia's Working Holiday Maker (WHM) Program', National Institute of Labour Studies, Flinders University, 27 February 2009

37 The 2001 figure is drawn from Department of Immigration and Multicultural and Indigenous Affairs 'Annual Report 2000–1'. The figure for 2011 comes from Department of Immigration and Citizenship, 'Working Holiday Maker Visa Programme report, 30 June 2011'.

38 DIBP, 'Working Holiday Maker Visa Programme Report, 30 June 2015'

39 DIBP, 'Working Holiday Maker Visa Programme Report, 30 June 2015'

40 DIBP, 'Working Holiday Maker Visa Programme Report, 30 June 2015'

41 DIPB, Fact Sheet 49—Working Holiday Visa Programme, https://www.border.gov.au/about/corporate/information/fact-sheets/49whm (accessed 4 April 2015)

42 DIPB, Working Holiday visa (subclass 417): Visa applicants, https://www.border.gov.au/Trav/Visa-1/417- (accessed 9 April 2016)

43 Shanthi Robertson, 'Intertwined Mobilities of Education, Tourism, and Labour: The Consequences of 417 and 485 Visas in Australia', in *Unintended Consequences: The Unexpected, Unwanted and Sometimes Tragic Outcomes of Migration Law and Policy*, edited by Marianne Dickie, Dorota Gozdecka and Sudrishti Reich, ANU Press, Canberra, 2016

44 Sherry Huang, evidence to Senate Education and Employment References Committee Inquiry into Australia's Temporary Visa Programs, Melbourne, 18 May 2015, Hansard transcript, p. 16 (accessed 6 July 2015)

45 Kate McMillan and Paul Hamer, 'Kiwis in Australia Deserve Better', *New Zealand Herald*, 10 October 2013

46 DIBP, 'Immigration detention and community statistics summary, 30 December 2015'

47 Department of Employment, Department of Immigration and Border Protection, Department of Agriculture, Fair Work Ombudsman, submission to the Joint Standing Committee on Migration Inquiry into the Seasonal Worker Programme, July 2015

48 Department of Employment, Seasonal Worker Programme expansion—Q&A, 18 June 2015, https://docs.employment.gov.au/system/files/doc/other/expansion_of_the_seasonal_worker_programme_-_faqs.pdf (accessed 13 January 2015)

49 Department of Immigration and Citizenship, 'Population flows, Immigration aspects 2010–11 edition', 2011

50 Stephen Howells, 'Report of the 2010 Review of the Migration Amendment (Employer Sanctions) Act 2007', Commonwealth of Australia, 2011

51 The distinction between 'dedicated' and 'de facto' migrant labour programs comes from Joo-Cheong Tham, Iain Campbell and Martina Boese, 'Why Is Labour Protection for Temporary Migrant Workers So Fraught? A Perspective from Australia', in *Temporary Labour Migration in the Global Era: The Regulatory Changes,* edited by Joanna Howe and Rosemary Owens, Routledge, London, 2016

52 Includes both primary and secondary visa holders; WHM includes both working-holidaymaker visas and work and holiday visas. Chart data is assembled from the following publicly available immigration department publications: annual reports, student visa program trends, subclass 457 state/territory summary reports and working-holidaymaker visa program reports.

53 Figures are at 30 June for each year. Chart data is assembled from the following publicly available immigration department publications: immigration updates (2005–2010), and temporary entrants and NZ citizens in Australia quarterly reports (2011–2015).

54 Individuals are counted as contributing to net overseas migration if they remain in Australia for longer than 12 months within a 16-month period. See Department of Immigration and Border Protection, 'Net overseas migration statistics', http://www.border.gov.au/about/reports-publications/research-statistics/statistics/live-in-australia/net-overseas-migration (accessed 15 July 2015)

55 Data for the years 2001–2002 to 2012–13 are drawn from Australian Bureau of Statistics, 3412.0—Migration. Figures for 2013–14 and 2014–15 are an estimate based on DIBP, 'Regional net overseas migration 2004–05 to 2017–18'

56 Mark Cully, 'Migrant Labour Supply: Its Dimensions and Character', paper presented to the Australian Labour Market Research Workshop, University of Sydney, 15–16 February 2010. The figure varies between 4.2 per cent and 6.4 per

cent of the overall labour force and between 17.9 per cent and 22.3 per cent of the labour force in the 20- to 24-year-old age bracket, according to the assumptions made about how active these temporary long-stay migrants are in the workforce.

57 DIBP, 'The Outlook for Net Overseas Migration as at September 2015' (Table 4: Year ending forecasts of net NOM), p. 8

58 Migration Council Australia, 'More than Temporary: Australia's 457 Visa Program', May 2013

59 Siew-Ean Khoo, Graeme Hugo and Peter McDonald, 'Which Skilled Temporary Migrants Become Permanent Residents and Why?', *International Migration Review* 42, no. 1 (2008):193–226

60 Cindy Tilbrook, 'International Students: Perspectives and Graduate Outcomes', *AIEC 2007*, conference, Melbourne, 9–12 October 2007

61 Beverley Jackling, 'The Lure of Permanent Residency and the Aspirations and Expectations of International Students Studying Accounting in Australia', *People and Place* 15, no. 3 (2007):31–41

62 Fifty-one per cent of the primary grants of subclass 457 visas in 2013–14 (26,430 out of 51,940 visas) went to onshore applicants. In 2012–13, 49 per cent of 457 visas (33,440 out of 68,480) were granted to onshore applicants. DIBP, 'Subclass 457 State/Territory summary report 2012–13' and 'Subclass 457 State/Territory summary report 2013–14'. (Unfortunately, information about onshore visa grants is not included in the subsequent 2014–15 edition of this report.) The main categories of visa holders applying for 457 visas onshore were existing 457-visa holders, international students and graduates and working holidaymakers. There were a small number of tourists included.

63 DIBP, 'Student visa program quarterly report, quarter ending at 30 June 2014' (Table 7.01: Number of visas granted in 2014–15 to 30 June 2015 by visa category where the last visa held was a student visa—comparison with same period in previous year) p. 68

64 DIBP, 'Student visa program quarterly report, quarter ending at 30 June 2014' (Table 7.01)

65 DIBP, 'Student visa program quarterly report, quarter ending at 30 June 2014' (Table 7.01)

66 DIBP, 'Australia's Migration Trends 2012–13' (Table 7.4: Characteristics of temporary entrants in Australia as at June 30, 2011 to 2013), p. 108. Unfortunately, this information was not included in the subsequent 2013–14 edition of this annual publication.

67 Australian Bureau of Statistics, 6250.0—Characteristics of Recent Migrants, Australia, November 2013 (Table 3: Recent migrants and temporary residents, Selected characteristics—By labour force status), June 2014

Chapter 3: Mind the Gap!

1 Melbourne School of Population and Global Health, Indigenous Eye Health Unit, The Trachoma Story Kit, http://iehu.unimelb.edu.au/the_trachoma_story_kit/introduction (accessed 25 October 2013)
2 *Workers Rehabilitation and Compensation Act* (NT) pt V div 4 (2)
3 Department of Immigration and Border Protection (DIBP), 'Temporary Work (Skilled) (Subclass 457) Visa', https://www.border.gov.au/Forms/Documents/1154.pdf (accessed 17 April 2016)
4 DIBP, 'Temporary Work (Skilled) (Subclass 457) Visa'
5 At the time of writing, in the lead-up to the 2016 federal election, neither bill is proceeding, but there is no reason to suppose that the Coalition would not seek to introduce similar measures if returned to government.
6 Safety, Rehabilitation and Compensation Legislation Amendment Bill 2014, http://www.aph.gov.au/Parliamentary_Business/Bills_Legislation/Bills_Search_Results/Result?bId=r5200 (accessed 15 July 2015)
7 Safety, Rehabilitation and Compensation Amendment (Improving the Comcare Scheme) Bill 2015, http://www.aph.gov.au/Parliamentary_Business/Bills_LEGislation/Bills_Search_Results/Result?bId=r5434 (accessed 15 July 2015)
8 Australian Council of Trade Unions, submission to the Senate Standing Committee on Education and Employment Inquiry into the Safety, Rehabilitation and Compensation Amendment (Improving the Comcare Scheme) Bill 2015, April 2015
9 United Voice, Swan Cleaning Services update, 5 June 2013, http://www.unitedvoice.org.au/news/swan-cleaning-services-update (accessed 20 October 2013)
10 *Fair Entitlements Guarantee Act 2012* (Cth) pt 2 div 1 sub-div A para 10 (1) (g). Special category visa holders are New Zealanders.
11 Madeleine Heffernan and Clay Lucas, 'International Students Taken to the Cleaners', *Age*, 2 June 2013
12 Explanatory Memorandum, Family And Community Services Legislation Amendment (New Zealand Citizens) Bill 2001 (emphasis in the original). On arrival in Australia, New Zealanders are automatically issued with a special category visa (SCV) that entitles them to work and live indefinitely in the country.

New Zealanders resident in Australia prior to 2001 were exempt from the changes and are described as 'protected SCV holders'.

13 Hayden Donnell, 'New Zealand Pair Upset at Flood Cash "Racism"', *New Zealand Herald*, 21 January 2011

14 David Faulkner, 'The Unequal Treatment of New Zealanders in Australia', 2013, http://papers.ssrn.com/sol3/papers.cfm?abstract_id=2304476 (accessed 20 October 2013)

15 New Zealand High Commission Canberra, Australia, Floods assistance, http://www.nzembassy.com/australia/news/queensland-floods-assistance (accessed 14 May 2014)

16 Department of Human Services (DHS), Ex-gratia assistance for New Zealand non-protected special category visa holders—Queensland floods January 2013, http://www.humanservices.gov.au/spw/customer/forms/resources/em037-130212en.pdf (accessed 20 October 2013)

17 DHS, Ex-gratia assistance for New Zealand non-protected special category visa holders—New South Wales floods January 2013, http://www.humanservices.gov.au/spw/customer/forms/resources/em039-130215en.pdf (accessed 20 October 2013)

18 DHS, New South Wales bushfires—October 2013, http://www.humanservices.gov.au/customer/services/centrelink/dra-nsw-bushfires-october-2013 (accessed 25 March 2014)

19 DHS, Western Australia bushfires—January 2014, http://www.humanservices.gov.au/customer/enablers/centrelink/australian-government-disaster-recovery-payment/western-australia-bushfires-january-2014 (accessed 25 March 2014)

20 Oz Kiwi, Facebook post, 15 June 2013, https://www.facebook.com/OzKiwi2001/posts/472101999534536 (accessed 10 November 2014)

21 Superannuation Complaints Tribunal, Determination Number D13-14\90, File Number 11-1691, 25 November 2013

22 The Commonwealth Department of Health confirmed the eligibility criteria (email correspondence, 13 October 2013).

23 Department of Health, Victorian Government, Free Vaccine Victoria—criteria for eligibility, http://www.health.vic.gov.au/immunisation/free-vaccine.htm (accessed 13 October 2013)

24 Department of Health, Victorian Government, Vaccines—eligibility criteria for free vaccines, https://www2.health.vic.gov.au/public-health/immunisation/immunisation-schedule-vaccine-eligibility-criteria/vaccines-eligibility-criteria-for-free-vaccines (accessed 18 April 2016)

25 Department of Health, 'Update: No Jab, No Pay—Immunisation Catch-Up Arrangements', September 2015, http://www.immunise.health.gov.au/internet/immunise/publishing.nsf/Content/clinical-updates-and-news/$File/Update-No-Jab-No-Pay-Immunisation-Catch-Up-Arrangements%28D15-1126865%29.pdf (accessed 18 April 2016)

26 National Centre for Immunisation Research and Surveillance, 'Biennial Report: January 2010–November 2011', 2012, p. 52, http://www.ncirs.edu.au/publications/reports/NCIRS-biennial-report-2010-2011.pdf (accessed 15 May 2014)

27 National Health Performance Authority, 'Healthy Communities: Immunisation Rates for Children in 2012–13', 2014, p. vi, http://www.myhealthycommunities.gov.au/Content/publications/downloads/NHPA_HC_Report_Imm_Rates_March_2014.pdf (accessed 15 May 2014)

28 NHMRC Centre for Research Excellence in Population Health, 'Protecting Australia: Closing the Gap in Immunisation for Migrants and Refugees: Proceedings from a Stakeholder Workshop', 9 August 2013, p. 9, http://www.creimmunisation.com.au/sites/default/files/newsevents/events/CREMigrantRefugeeWorkshop_ProceedingsRecommendations.pdf (accessed 15 May 2014)

29 Department of Education, NSW Government, 'Temporary Residents Program', http://www.detinternational.nsw.edu.au/media-assets/trp/fees.pdf and 'Schedule of Visa Subclasses & Enrolment Conditions' (Document Version June 2015), http://www.detinternational.nsw.edu.au/media-assets/trp/visa-subclasses.pdf (both accessed 16 July 2015)

30 Education and Training Directorate, ACT Government, Fees and charges, http://www.det.act.gov.au/school_education/international_students/fees-and-charges (accessed 29 April 2016). If 457-visa holders in the ACT have a job that appears on the federal government's list of skilled occupations deemed to be in short supply in the Australian economy, they can apply for a fee waiver.

31 Department of Training and Workforce Development, WA Government, Dependants of 457 visa holders, http://www.eti.wa.edu.au/your-study-options/study-at-school/dependants-of-457-visa-holders (accessed 16 July 2015)

32 Department for Education and Child Development, Government of South Australia, Proposed public contribution fee for 457 visa holders, http://www.decd.sa.gov.au/aboutdept/a8_publish/modules/publish/content.asp?navgrp=Aboutdept&id=visacontribution&extra=?reFlag=1 (accessed 14 April 2016)

33 Joseph Carens, 'Live-in Domestics, Seasonal Workers, and Others Hard to Locate

on the Map of Democracy', *Journal of Political Philosophy* 16, no. 4 (2008), p. 429

34 Department of Education and Training, Government of Victoria, 2015 Victorian government schools international student tuition and other fees, http://www.study.vic.gov.au/shadomx/apps/fms/fmsdownload.cfm?file_uuid=23335506-E6D3-4F8E-8A7E-532321D1F04C&siteName=deecd (accessed 16 July 2015)

35 Department of Training and Workforce Development, WA Government, Dependants of other visa holders, http://www.eti.wa.edu.au/your-study-options/study-at-school/dependants-of-other-visa-holders#not-573-574 (accessed 16 July 2015)

36 Education Queensland International, Queensland Government, Program fees, https://www.eqi.com.au/programs/program-fees.html and Department of Training and Workforce Development, WA Government, Dependants of 573 or 574 visa holders, http://www.eti.wa.edu.au/your-study-options/study-at-school/dependants-of-573-574-visa-holders (accessed 16 July 2015)

37 Migration Council Australia, 'More than Temporary: Australia's 457 Visa Program', May 2013

38 Henry Sherrell, Migration Council Australia, 'Economic growth: What Is the Contribution of Migration?', presentation to the Migration Institute of Australia national conference *Migration 2015*, 29 October 2015

39 Jane Shields, 'Calls for Family Violence Services to be More Culturally Diverse', *Breakfast*, ABC Radio National, 15 August 2016, http://www.abc.net.au/radionational/programs/breakfast/calls-for-family-violence-services-to-be-more-culturally/6696672 (accessed 22 April 2016)

40 Judicial College of Victoria, '5.6.4.7—Visa dependency', *Family Violence Bench Book*, http://www.judicialcollege.vic.edu.au/eManuals/FVBBWeb/index.htm#34143.htm (accessed 15 July 2015)

41 Khanh Hoang, 'The ALRC's Commonwealth Laws and Family Violence Inquiry', Immigration Advice and Rights Centre Inc., 1 March 2012, http://www.iarc.asn.au/BlogRetrieve.aspx?PostID=274901&A=SearchResult&SearchID=51939340&ObjectID=274901&ObjectType=55#sthash.qnOBnM1Z.dpuf (accessed 15 July 2015)

42 Federation of Ethnic Communities' Council Australia, 'Submission: Independent Review of 457 Visa Programme', 5 May 2014, http://www.fecca.org.au/images/submissions/fecca%20submission%20to%20the%20independent%20review%20of%20the%20457%20visa%20program%20-%20family%20violence%20provisions.pdf (accessed 16 July 2015)

43 Pallavi Sinha, 'Time to act on domestic violence', *World News Australia*, SBS, 24 November 2014, http://www.sbs.com.au/news/article/2014/11/25/time-act-domestic-violence-0 (accessed 15 July 2015)

44 Australian Law Reform Commission (ALRC), 'Family Violence and Commonwealth Laws—Improving Legal Frameworks', 8 February 2012, p. 501

45 ALRC (2012), p. 502

46 Interview broadcast on ABC Radio National's *Law Report*, 'Foreign Parents, Australian Children', 7 July 2015, http://www.abc.net.au/radionational/programs/lawreport/foreign-parents-australian-children/6597136

47 Cameron Atfield, 'Australian Toddler "Deported by Proxy" to Solomon Islands: Family', *Sydney Morning Herald*, 29 March 2015

48 DIBP, Fees and charges for visas, http://www.border.gov.au/Trav/Visa/Fees (accessed 24 April 2016)

49 I have reported on Francesca Teua's case more comprehensively elsewhere. See Peter Mares, 'Australian Children, Foreign Parents and the Right to Stay', *Inside Story,* 2 March 2015, http://insidestory.org.au/australian-children-foreign-parents-and-the-right-to-stay; and Peter Mares, 'Foreign Parents, Australian Children', *Law Report,* ABC Radio National, 7 July 2015, http://www.abc.net.au/radionational/programs/lawreport/foreign-parents-australian-children/6597136

50 Department of Immigration and Citizenship (DIAC), 'Ministerial intervention statistics, July–December 2012-13', 2013, http://www.border.gov.au/ReportsandPublications/Documents/statistics/min-stats-australia-2012-13.pdf#search=public%20interest%20powers (accessed 16 July 2015)

51 DIAC (2013)

52 DIBP, Unique or exceptional circumstances, http://www.border.gov.au/Trav/Refu/Mini/circumstances (accessed 16 July 2015)

53 In the new wording around exceptional circumstances for ministerial intervention, the only reference to rights of children is oblique: 'Strong compassionate circumstances that if not recognised would result in serious, ongoing and irreversible harm and continuing hardship to an Australian citizen or an Australian family unit, where at least one member of the family is an Australian citizen or Australian permanent resident.' http://www.border.gov.au/Trav/Refu/Mini# (accessed 29 April 2016)

54 DIBP, Unique or exceptional circumstances, http://www.border.gov.au/Trav/Refu/Mini/circumstances (accessed 16 July 2015)

Chapter 4: Indefinitely Temporary

1. Department of Immigration and Border Protection (DIBP), Fact sheet—priority processing for migration visas, http://www.border.gov.au/about/corporate/information/fact-sheets/24apriority-skilled (accessed 17 July 2015)
2. DIBP, Regional Sponsored Migration Scheme visa (subclass 187), https://www.border.gov.au/Trav/Visa-1/187- (accessed 22 April 2016)
3. DIBP, Skilled migration visa processing times, https://www.border.gov.au/Lega/Lega/8#a (accessed 17 July 2015)
4. DIBP, Allocation dates for General Skilled Migration applications, https://www.border.gov.au/Trav/Work/Work/Allocation-dates-for-General-Skilled-Migration- (accessed 17 July 2015)
5. Peter Mares, 'Living at the Wrong End of the Queue', *Inside Story*, 7 April 2015, http://insidestory.org.au/living-at-the-wrong-end-of-the-queue
6. @SandiHLogal, Twitter, 24 April 2015
7. DIBP, Fees and charges for visas, http://www.border.gov.au/Trav/Visa/Fees (accessed 17 July 2015)
8. DIPB, Form 1006, Application for a Bridging visa B, http://www.border.gov.au/Forms/Documents/1006.pdf (accessed 17 July 2015)
9. DIBP, 1 July 2011—Points Test for certain skilled migration visas, http://www.border.gov.au/WorkinginAustralia/Documents/points-test.pdf (accessed 17 July 2015)
10. DIBP, SkillSelect—18 December round results, https://www.border.gov.au/Trav/Work/Skil/18-december-2015-round-results (accessed 29 January 2016)
11. DIBP, SkillSelect: occupational ceilings, https://www.border.gov.au/Trav/Work/Skil (accessed 17 July 2015)
12. Department of Immigration and Citizenship, 'Annual Report 2012–13', p. 41
13. Chris Evans, Minister for Immigration, 'Changes to Australia's Skilled Migration Program', speech, Australian National University, Canberra, 8 February 2010 (accessed 17 July 2015 via PANDORA, National Library of Australia Web Archive, http://pandora.nla.gov.au/)
14. Evans (2010)
15. Evans (2010)
16. DIBP, '2013–14 Migration Programme Report', 2014
17. DIBP, Contributory parent visa (subclass 143), http://www.border.gov.au/Trav/Visa-1/143-# (accessed 20 July 2015)
18. DIBP, Parent visa queue, https://www.border.gov.au/Trav/Brin/Fami/Capping-and-queuing/Parent-visa-queue (accessed 20 July 2015)

19 DIBP, Other family visa queue, https://www.border.gov.au/Trav/Brin/Fami/Capping-and-queuing/Other-family-visa-queue (accessed 18 July 2015)
20 The federal government attempted to repeal both the 'other family' and 'parent non-contributory' visa classes in 2014. DIBP, Changes to Other Family and Non-Contributory Parent visas, http://migrationblog.border.gov.au/2014/06/03/changes-to-other-family-and-non-contributory-parent-visas/ (accessed 22 April 2016)
21 Bridget Brennan, 'Chinese High School Student Numbers Increasing in Australia', *PM*, ABC Radio, 30 March 2015, http://www.abc.net.au/pm/content/2015/s4207613.htm (accessed 15 July 2015)
22 Victorian Government, 'Victoria's Future Industries: International Education Discussion Paper', July 2015
23 DIBP, 'Student visa and temporary graduate visa programme quarterly report, quarter ending at 30 June 2014'
24 *Migration Regulations 1994* (Cth) Migration Legislation Amendment Regulation 2013 (No. 1) sch 2. See also Peter Mares, 'We Know About the 457. What About the 485?', *Inside Story*, 28 March 2013, http://inside.org.au/we-know-about-the-457-what-about-the-485/
25 DIBP, Temporary graduate visa (subclass 485), https://www.border.gov.au/Trav/Visa-1/485- (accessed 18 April 2016)
26 Michael Knight, 'Strategic Review of the Student Visa Program 2011', report to the Australian Government, June 2011
27 Bernard Lane, 'Knight Delivers for Universities: But Training Misses Out', *Australian*, 23 September 2011
28 DIBP, 'Simplification of the Skilled Migration and Temporary Activity Visa Programmes, Proposal Paper', December 2014, p. 26. It is too soon to know if this estimate will be accurate. The revamped 485 visa (technically called the Temporary Graduate (Subclass 485) Post-Study Work stream visa) is only available to students who were granted their first student visa after November 2011, thus significant take-up of the visa only started to become apparent in 2015. Close to 10,000 visa applications were lodged in the six-month period to 31 December 2015, which was almost three times the number that were lodged in the corresponding period for the previous year. DIBP, 'Student visa and temporary graduate programme report, six monthly report ending at 31 December 2015'.
29 Daryl Passmore, 'Aussie Siblings Face Exile After Immigration Minister Peter Dutton's Department Leaves Family in Limbo', *Sunday Mail* (Qld), 13 December 2015

30 'Phil and Amy Fight to Stay in Oz', *The Project*, Channel Ten, 28 January 2016, http://tenplay.com.au/channel-ten/the-project/top-stories-january-2016/phil-and-amy-fight-to-stay-in-oz (accessed 15 February 2016)

Chapter 5: New Zealanders

1 Kate McMillan and Paul Hamer, 'Kiwis in Australia Deserve Better', *New Zealand Herald*, 10 October 2013
2 State Library of South Australia, Military Records, New Zealand (Maori Wars) 1845–1863, http://guides.slsa.sa.gov.au/content.php?pid=76180&sid=594745 (accessed 21 December 2015)
3 Graeme Hugo, 'Future Immigration Policy Development in Australia and New Zealand', *New Zealand Population Review* 30, no. 1&2 (2004):23–42; Lynda Sanderson, 'International Mobility of New Migrants to Australia', *International Migration Review* 43, no. 2 (Summer 2009):292–331
4 Australian Bureau of Statistics, 3412.0—Migration, Australia 2013–14
5 New Zealand Government, 'Migration Trends and Outlook 2014/15', Ministry of Business, Innovation and Employment, November 2015
6 Department of Immigration and Border Protection (DIBP), 'Australia's Migration Trends 2012–13' (Table 7.2), p. 106
7 DIBP, 'Australia's Migration Trends 2012–13', p. 5
8 Australian Government Productivity Commission and New Zealand Productivity Commission (PC), 'Strengthening Trans-Tasman Economic Relations: Supplementary Report D—People Movement', Canberra, 2012, p. 1
9 In New Zealand's case there were exceptions to this rule for people from its Pacific territories of Cook Islands, Nuie and Tokelau. Ann Beaglehole, 'Immigration regulation—Controlling Pacific Island immigration', Te Ara—the Encyclopedia of New Zealand, http://www.teara.govt.nz/en/immigration-regulation/page-6 (accessed 25 April 2016)
10 Paul Hamer, '"Unsophisticated and unsuited": Australian Barriers to Pacific Islander Immigration from New Zealand', *Political Science* 66, no. 2 (2014):93–118
11 Hamer (2014), p. 96
12 Quoted in Hamer (2014), p. 96
13 The case is cited in Hamer (2014), p. 98
14 Quoted in Hamer (2014), p. 98
15 Hamer (2014), p. 104
16 Department of Prime Minister and Cabinet, 'Australia–New Zealand Cooperation',

joint communiqué, 22 January 1973, http://pmtranscripts.dpmc.gov.au/release/transcript-2785 (accessed 27 November 2014)

17　Department of Foreign Affairs and Trade, The Trans-Tasman Travel Arrangement, https://www.dfat.gov.au/geo/new_zealand/trans-tasman-travel-arrangements.html (accessed 27 November 2014)

18　New Zealand High Commission, Canberra, Australians in New Zealand, http://www.nzembassy.com/australia/relationship-between-new-zealand-and-australia/australians-new-zealand (accessed 12 Nov 2014)

19　PC (2012), p. 2

20　Hugo (2004), p. 36

21　DIPB, Fact Sheet 17—New Zealanders in Australia, https://www.immi.gov.au/media/fact-sheets/17nz.htm (accessed 7 November 2014)

22　*Migration Act 1958* (Cth) pt 2 div 3, sub div A para 30 (2)

23　See, for example, 'It's a temporary visa in that it expires as soon as the New Zealand citizen leaves Australia, but it remains in place for as long as they remain in Australia.' Department of Education, FAQs—New Zealand special category visa holders, https://www.education.gov.au/faqs-new-zealand-special-category-visa-holders (accessed 1 February 2016)

24　See, for example, DIBP, 'Australia's Migration Trends 2012–13', p. 5

25　Oz Kiwi, Legislation defining the status of New Zealanders, blog post, 6 March 2016, http://www.ozkiwi2001.org/2016/03/06/legislation-defining-the-status-of-new-zealanders/ (accessed 18 April 2016)

26　David Smith et al., *Citizenship in Australia*, Department of Immigration and Citizenship, 2011

27　Australian Bureau of Statistics, 2011 Census, QuickStats Country of Birth, New Zealand, http://www.censusdata.abs.gov.au/census_services/getproduct/census/2011/quickstat/1201_0 (accessed 21 March 2016)

28　David Faulkner, 'The Unequal Treatment of New Zealanders in Australia', 2013, http://papers.ssrn.com/sol3/papers.cfm?abstract_id=2304476 (accessed 20 October 2013)

29　My own calculation based on data contained in the following publications: Department of Immigration and Citizenship, 'Trends in Migration: Australia 2010–11', 2012 and 'Australia's Migration Trends 2011–12', 2013; DIBP, 'Australia's migration trends 2012–13', 2014 and 'Australia's migration trends 2013–14', 2014.

30　Paul Hamer, '200,000 New Zealanders Live in Australia Without a Helping Hand', *Right Now*, 14 April 2016, http://rightnow.org.au/writing-cat/opinion/200000-new-

zealanders-live-in-australia-without-a-helping-hand/ (accessed 18 April 2016)
31 Letter from Senator Mitch Fifield, Assistant Minister for Social Services, to Senator Dean Smith, 19 March 2014, quoted in Parliamentary Joint Committee on Human Rights, Seventh Report of the 44th Parliament, June 2014
32 McMillan and Hamer (2013)
33 This was done through the *Family and Community Services Legislation Amendment (New Zealand Citizens) Act 2001.*
34 Tamara Walsh, 'New Zealanders in Crisis in Australia: The Absence of a Social Safety Net', *New Zealand Universities Law Review* 26 (2015):673–702
35 Australian Government, Study Assist: FAQs NZ, http://studyassist.gov.au/sites/studyassist/helpfulresources/pages/faqs-nz#CurrentArrangements (accessed 1 February 2016)
36 Faulkner (2013)
37 National Welfare Rights Network, 'Observations on Australia's Performance Regarding its Social Security Obligations Under Clauses 26 and 27 of the United Nations Convention on the Rights of the Child', December 2010, http://www.welfarerights.org.au/Policy%20papers%20%20submissions/NWRN%20CROC%20Report%202010.doc (accessed 13 Nov 2014)
38 Australian Institute of Health and Welfare, 'Specialist Homelessness Services 2012–13', p. 43, http://www.aihw.gov.au/WorkArea/DownloadAsset.aspx?id=60129545638 (accessed 11 August 2014)
39 Walsh (2015), p. 691
40 Of the population of the Gold Coast, 8.6 per cent are New Zealand-born, as are 7.9 per cent of the population of the City of Logan, which lies immediately north of the Gold Coast. The actual share of New Zealanders is likely to be higher, because not all New Zealand citizens are New Zealand-born. I.d (Informed Decisions), Community profile City of Gold Coast, http://profile.id.com.au/gold-coast/birthplace (accessed 13 November 2014) and Community Profile, City of Logan, http://profile.id.com.au/logan (accessed 27 November 2014)
41 Senate Legal and Constitutional Legislation Committee, 'Migration Amendment (Character and General Visa Cancellation) Bill 2014 [Provisions]', report, November 2014, pp. 13–14
42 January figure provided verbally by the New Zealand High Commission; other data from DIBP, Immigration detention statistics (monthly reports January to December 2015), https://www.border.gov.au/about/reports-publications/research-statistics/statistics/live-in-australia/immigration-detention (accessed 23 February 2016)

43 The number of Iranians built up because the government of Iran refused to accept forced returns of failed asylum seekers.
44 DIBP, 'Visa Cancellations under s.501 statistics for 2014/15 financial year', freedom of information release FA15/09/00665, 1 December 2015
45 Information provided by New Zealand government sources.
46 Brook Sabin, 'Christmas Island: The "Kiwi Alcatraz"', *3 News*, 18 October 2015, http://www.3news.co.nz/world/christmas-island-the-kiwi-alcatraz-2015101816#ixzz3qHOQLqbW (accessed 2 November 2015)
47 Kelvin Davis, Labour Corrections spokesperson, interview, *3 News*, 27 October 2015, http://www.3news.co.nz/nznews/davis-nz-should-refuse-to-back-australian-unbid-2015102710#ixzz3qHNgSNjJ (accessed 2 November 2015)
48 Sam Sachdeva, 'John Key Sparks Walk-out After Saying Labour Backs Rapists and Murderers', *Stuff.nz.co*, 10 November 2015, http://www.stuff.co.nz/national/politics/73884590/John-Key-sparks-walk-out-after-saying-Labour-backs-rapists-and-murderers (accessed 12 November 2015)
49 Senate Legal and Constitutional Affairs Legislation Committee, 'Migration Amendment (Character and General Visa Cancellation) Bill 2014 [Provisions]', report, November 2014, p. 13–14
50 NSW Council for Civil Liberties, submission to the Legal and Constitutional Affairs Committee of the Australian Senate concerning the Migration Amendment (Character and Visa Cancellation Bill) 2014, 28 October 2014
51 Michael Gordon, 'Peter Dutton Stands by Decision to Revoke Visa of Decorated Australian Soldier', *Sydney Morning Herald*, 11 November 2015. In March 2016, Ko agreed to return to New Zealand rather than face the prospect of indefinite detention in Perth, but said he intends to continue a legal challenge against his deportation from there. Elle Hunt, 'New Zealand Soldier Held Without Charge Says He Was Assaulted in Australian Jail', *Guardian* (Australian edition), 25 March 2015
52 Sudrishti Reich, Christine Giles and Andrew Bartlett, Australian National University College of Law: Migration Law Program, submission to the Senate Legal and Constitutional Affairs Committee inquiry into the Migration Amendment (Character and General Visa Cancellation) Bill 2014
53 See Tahu Kukutai and Shefali Pawar, 'A Socio-Demographic Profile of Māori Living in Australia', National Institute of Demographic and Economic Analysis, University of Waikato, working paper no. 3, June 2013, and Paul Hamer, 'Māori in Australia: an update from the 2011 Australian census and the 2011 New Zealand

general election', Victoria University of Wellington, working paper, October 2012
54 Hamer (2012)

Chapter 6: Fear in the Family

1. Naomi Woodley, 'Gillard Gives Historic Speech to NZ Parliament', *PM*, ABC Radio, 16 February 2011, http://www.abc.net.au/pm/content/2011/s3140734.htm?site=northwest (accessed 12 Nov 2014)
2. ABC News Online, 'Australia Doubles NZ Quake Help', 23 February 2011, http://www.abc.net.au/news/2011-02-22/australia-doubles-nz-quake-help/1953726 (accessed 12 November 2014)
3. Greg Ansley, 'Aussies Unlikely to Remove Bias Against Migrants Despite PM Declaring NZ is "Family"', *New Zealand Herald*, 3 October 2013
4. Malcolm Turnbull, Prime Minister of Australia, Joint press conference with New Zealand Prime Minister John Key, Auckland, 17 October 2015, https://www.pm.gov.au/media/2015-10-17/transcript-prime-minister-hon-malcolm-turnbull-mp-and-prime-minister-rt-hon-john (accessed 25 April 2016)
5. The Australian Workers' Union, Victorian Branch, 'More than 50% of Australian Shearers Are Out of Work. Why?', pamphlet, 1991, Archives New Zealand, reference no. ABHS W5533 22128, box 175
6. Clyde Holding, 'Proposal for Caucus Regarding New Zealand Immigration', 11 August 1992, Archives New Zealand, reference no. ABHS W5533 22128, box 175
7. Chris Peters, 'Hatred of Kiwis Alleged in Australian Community', *Evening Post*, 18 June 1986
8. Senator Robert Ray, Minister for Immigration, Local Government and Ethnic Affairs, 'Kiwis Are Young, Mobile and Working', News Release 115/88, 21 October 1988, Archives New Zealand, reference no. ABHS W553322128, box 174
9. New Zealand High Commission, Canberra, 'TTTA: Contribution of NZ residents to Australian Tax Revenues', Note for file 89/2/1, 20 May 1986, Archives New Zealand, Reference No. ABHS W5533 22128, box 175
10. Australian Bureau of Statistics, *New Zealanders in Australia*, 4102.0—Australian Social Trends, September 2010
11. Australian Government Productivity Commission and New Zealand Productivity Commission (PC), 'Strengthening Trans-Tasman Economic Relations: Supplementary Report D—People Movement', Canberra, 2012, p. 35
12. Natasha Bita, 'Kiwi Layabouts Are Flooding In', *NT News*, 28 December 2013. The New Zealand lobby group Oz Kiwi laid a formal complaint about the article. See

http://www.iwinaus.org/ayden-marsh-smith-in-response-to-the-kiwi-layabout-article/ (accessed 22 March 2016)

13 Natasha Bita, 'Immigration Back Door', *Australian*, 28 December 2013

14 'New Zealand Migration to Australia Soars 40 Per Cent', news.com.au, 28 December 2013, http://www.news.com.au/lifestyle/real-life/new-zealand-migration-to-australia-soars-40-per-cent/story-fnixwvgh-1226790754690 (accessed 12 November 2014)

15 'Kiwis Treated as Second Class Citizens', *A Current Affair,* Channel 9, 13 January 2014, http://aca.ninemsn.com.au/article/8783207/second-class-kiwis (accessed 12 November 2014)

16 Paul Hamer, '"Unsophisticated and unsuited": Australian Barriers to Pacific Islander Immigration from New Zealand', *Political Science* 66, no. 2 (2014):93–118

17 Bob Birrell and Virginia Rapson, 'New Zealanders in Australia: The End of an Era?', *People and Place* 9, no. 1 (2001):2-15

18 Hamer (2014), p. 93

19 Study quoted in PC (2012), p. 35

20 Study quoted in PC (2012), p. 35

21 Oskar Alley, 'Aussie Kiwis "Should Not Get a Bean"', *Dominion*, 11 December 2000, quoted in Alan Gamlen, 'Creating and destroying diaspora strategies', Oxford Diasporas Programme, International Migration Institute, University of Oxford, Working Paper 31, April 2011

22 Statistics New Zealand, '2013 Census QuickStats about Culture and Identity', April 2014, http://www.stats.govt.nz/Census/2013-census/profile-and-summary-reports/quickstats-culture-identity.aspx# (accessed 21 November 2014)

23 Statistics New Zealand (2014)

24 Statistics New Zealand, 'International Travel and Migration September 2015', 21 October 2015, http://www.stats.govt.nz/browse_for_stats/population/Migration/IntTravelAndMigration_HOTPSep15/Commentary.aspx (accessed 18 April 2016)

25 New Zealand Government, 'Migration Trends and Outlook 2014/15' (Figure 2.1: Annual permanent and long-term migration flows, 1984/85–2014/15, p. 5), Ministry of Business, Innovation and Employment, November 2015

26 Bernard Lagan, 'New Zealand Rejects Bid to Halt Back-door Migration', *Sydney Morning Herald*, 4 December 2000

27 Birrell and Rapson (2001), p. 3

28 Richard Bedford, Elsie Ho and Graeme Hugo, 'Trans Tasman Migration in Context: Recent Flows of New Zealanders Revisited', *People and Place* 11, no. 4

(2003):5–62
29 Priscilla Williams, New Zealand's Deputy High Commission, 'Summary of Discussion with Tony Harris, the acting head of Department of Immigration, Local Government and Ethnic Affairs', 21 July 1988, Archives New Zealand, reference no. ABHS W5533 22128, box 174
30 Letter from Australian High Commissioner to W. F. Birch MP, 29 May 1992, Archives New Zealand, reference no. ABHS W5533 22128, box 175
31 Janet Phillips and Harriet Spinks, 'Boat Arrivals Since 1976', Parliamentary Library research paper, Parliament of Australia, updated 23 July 2013
32 New Zealand High Commission, File Note, from Canberra to Wellington, 'Australia: TTTA and New Zealand visa policy', 1 June 1992, Archives New Zealand, Reference no. ABHS W5533 22128, box 175. Most of the 23,000 'illegals' referred to arrived in Australia by plane on valid visas and sought asylum after clearing immigration controls.
33 New Zealand High Commission, file note, 'Australia: TTTA and New Zealand visa policy', 1 June 1992
34 Hamer (2014), p. 109
35 Hamer (2014), p. 109
36 Bernard Orsman and Scott Inglis, 'Last-Chance Amnesty for Overstayers', *New Zealand Herald*, 20 September 2000
37 Phillip Williams, 'New Zealand Amnesty on Migrants', *AM*, ABC Radio, 22 September 2000, http://www.abc.net.au/am/stories/s185661.htm (accessed 27 November 2014)
38 New Zealand High Commission, file note, 30 August 1989, Archives New Zealand, reference no. ABHS W5533 22128, box 174
39 Telex message from Wellington to New Zealand High Commission in Canberra, 28 September 1988, Archives New Zealand, reference no. ABHS W5533 22128, box 174
40 Immigration New Zealand, Samoan quota scheme, http://www.immigration.govt.nz/migrant/stream/live/samoanquota/ (accessed 13 November 2014)
41 Immigration New Zealand, Pacific access category, http://www.immigration.govt.nz/migrant/stream/live/pacificaccess/ (accessed 13 November 2014)
42 Statistics New Zealand (2014)
43 Senator Andrew Bartlett, 'Family and Community Services Legislation Amendment (New Zealand Citizens) Bill 2001', second reading speech, Senate Hansard, 8 March 2001, pp. 22,802–22,804

44 Bartlett (2001), p. 22,804
45 Bartlett (2001), p. 22,803
46 Phil Goff, New Zealand Minister of Foreign Affairs and Trade, 'The Trans-Tasman Relationship: A New Zealand Perspective', *The Drawing Board: An Australian Review of Public Affairs* 2, no. 1 (2001):1–9. The article is adapted from an address given to the Otago Foreign Policy School at the University of Otago in Dunedin, New Zealand, on 29 June 2001.
47 Department of Social Services, 'Documents on the file "2010/06137 Business Development—Policy—Pathway to residency for New Zealanders who are non-protected special category visa (SCV) holders"', freedom of information release, http://www.dss.gov.au/sites/default/files/files/foi_disclosure_log/Documents/foi_10_11_053.pdf (accessed 14 November 2014)
48 David Drummond, Director of the Long Term Residents Section Department of Immigration, speaking in Melbourne on 2 August 2013, transcribed and posted on Facebook by Oz Kiwi, https://www.facebook.com/OzKiwi2001/posts/494801333931269 (accessed 14 November 2014)
49 Joe Hockey, Treasurer, 'Australia and New Zealand Government Response to the Joint Productivity Commissions' Report on Economic Integration', 9 May 2014, http://jbh.ministers.treasury.gov.au/files/2014/05/Aus-NZ-Joint-Response-Productivity-Report.pdf (accessed 14 Nov 2014)
50 Andrea Petrie, 'Kiwis Seek Support from PM's Wife', *Sydney Morning Herald*, 15 September 2013
51 John Key, Prime Minister of New Zealand, 'Joint Media Conference with John Key', 19 February 2016, http://www.malcolmturnbull.com.au/media/joint-media-conference-with-prime-minister-key-sydney (accessed 21 March 2016)
52 Department of Employment, *Australian Jobs 2015*, 28 April 2015, https://docs.employment.gov.au/documents/australian-jobs-2015-publication (accessed 21 March 2016)
53 Department of Immigration and Border Protection (DIBP), An additional pathway to permanent residence for 'non protected' Special Category Visa (SCV) holders, http://www.border.gov.au/Visasupport/Pages/an-additional-pathway.aspx (accessed 22 March 2016)
54 Tahu Kukutai and Shefali Pawar, 'A Socio-Demographic Profile of Māori Living in Australia', National Institute of Demographic and Economic Analysis, University of Waikato, working paper no. 3, June 2013
55 Kukutai and Pawar (2013)

56 Ruth Wynn Williams, 'New Path to Aussie Citizenship for Kiwis "A Bandaid"', *One News*, 20 February 2016, https://www.tvnz.co.nz/one-news/world/new-path-to-aussie-citizenship-for-kiwis-a-bandaid.html (accessed 22 February 2016)

57 DIBP, An additional pathway to permanent residence for 'non protected' Special Category Visa (SCV) holders

58 Malcolm Turnbull, Prime Minister of Australia, 'Joint Media Conference with John Key', 19 February 2016, http://www.malcolmturnbull.com.au/media/joint-media-conference-with-prime-minister-key-sydney (accessed 21 March 2016)

59 John Key (2016)

60 Radio New Zealand, 'New Australian Citizenship Rules "Not a Solution"', 20 February 2016, http://www.radionz.co.nz/news/political/296994/new-citizenship-rules-'not-a-solution' (accessed 22 March 2016)

61 DIBP, An additional pathway to permanent residence for 'non protected' Special Category Visa (SCV) holders

62 Department of Foreign Affairs and Trade, The Trans-Tasman Travel Arrangement, https://www.dfat.gov.au/geo/new_zealand/trans-tasman-travel-arrangements.html (accessed 27 November 2014)

63 Wayne Swan MP, House of Representatives, Hansard, 6 March 2001, p. 25,109

64 Bedford et al. (2013), p. 54

65 Richard Bedford, 'The Quiet Revolution: Transformations in Migration Policies, Flows and Outcomes, 1999–2004', *New Zealand Georgrapher* 60, no. 2 (2004):59-62

66 Birrell and Rapson (2001), p. 13

67 Australian Bureau of Statistics, 3412.0.55.002—Information Paper: Further Improvements to Net Overseas Migration Estimation (Table 2), December 2013

Chapter 7: Asylum Seekers and Refugees

1 Kevin Rudd, Prime Minister of Australia Transcript of joint press conference, Brisbane, 19 July 2013, http://parlinfo.aph.gov.au/parlInfo/download/media/pressrel/2611766/upload_binary/2611766.pdf;fileType=application%2Fpdf#search=%22media/pressrel/2611766%22 (accessed 3 November 2015)

2 Australian Government, 'Report of the Expert Panel on Asylum Seekers', August 2012, p. 14

3 Rudd (2013)

4 Department of Immigration and Border Protection (DIBP), 'Immigration detention and community statistics summary, 31 March 2015'

5 I wrote about Syed's story in more detail in 'Refuge Without Work', *Griffith Review*

45 (August 2014), https://griffithreview.com/articles/refuge-without-work/
6 Australian Council of Social Service, 'Poverty in Australia 2012', http://www.acoss.org.au/wp-content/uploads/2015/06/Poverty_Report_2013_FINAL.pdf (accessed 1 December 2015)
7 Chris Bowen, Minister for Immigration, 'No Advantage for Onshore Boat Arrivals', media release, 21 November 2012, (accessed 30 April 2014 via PANDORA, National Library of Australia Web Archive, http://pandora.nla.gov.au/)
8 Senator Chris Evans, Minister for Immigration and Citizenship, 'Budget 2008–09: Rudd Government Scraps Temporary Protection Visas', media release, 13 May 2008, http://parlinfo.aph.gov.au/parlInfo/search/display/display.w3p;query=Id%3A%22media%2Fpressrel%2F4JGQ6%22 (accessed 30 Nov 2015)
9 Janet Phillips, 'Boat Arrivals in Australia: A Quick Guide to the Statistics', Parliamentary Library research paper, Parliament of Australia, 23 January 2014
10 Mary Ann Kenny et al., 'Temporary Protection Visas', Curtin University, November 2013, http://basp.org.au/wp-content/uploads/2013/11/TPV-November-2013-2.pdf (accessed 30 November 2015)
11 Refugee and Immigration Legal Service, submission on the Migration and Maritime Powers Legislation Amendment (Resolving the Asylum Legacy Caseload) Bill 2014, Senate Legal and Constitutional Affairs Committee, 31 October 2014
12 Chris Sidoti, foreword to Fethi Mansouri and Melek Bagdas, 'Politics of Social Exclusion: Refugees on Temporary Protection Visas in Victoria', Centre for Citizenship and Human Rights, Deakin University, 2002
13 Elibritt Karlsen, 'Permanent Residency for Save Haven Enterprise Visa Holders?', *Flagpost*, Australian Parliamentary Library, 28 November 2014, http://www.aph.gov.au/About_Parliament/Parliamentary_Departments/Parliamentary_Library/FlagPost/2014/November/Safe_haven_Enterprise_visa (accessed 13 December 2015)
14 Australian Senate, Answer to Question Taken on Notice, Budget Estimates Hearing, Immigration and Multicultural Affairs Portfolio, 26 May 2005, www.aph.gov.au/%7E/media/Estimates/Live/legcon_ctte/estimates/bud_0506/dimia/a1-25.ashx (accessed 17 April 2016)
15 Law Council of Australia, submission on the Migration and Maritime Powers Legislation Amendment (Resolving the Asylum Legacy Caseload) Bill 2014, Senate Legal and Constitutional Affairs Committee, 5 November 2014
16 UNHCR, submission on the Migration and Maritime Powers Legislation Amendment (Resolving the Asylum Legacy Caseload) Bill 2014, Senate Legal and

Constitutional Affairs Committee, 31 October 2014
17 Law Council of Australia (2014)
18 Nicole Hasham, 'Turnbull Government Accused of Ineptitude as Refugee Visa Scheme Stumbles', *Age*, 28 March 2016
19 Eric Tlozek, 'Refugee Tries to Return to Detention on Manus Island after Resettlement in Lae', ABC News Online, 31 March 2016, http://www.abc.net.au/news/2016-03-31/refugee-returned-to-manus-island-after-being-resettled/7286358 (accessed 26 April 2016)
20 Eric Tlozek, 'Resettlement Delay Putting Manus Island Asylum Seekers at Risk, Causing Social Problems, Officials Say', ABC News Online, 1 October 2015, http://www.abc.net.au/news/2015-10-01/Papua New Guinea-resettlement-delay-putting-manus-refugees-at-risk/6820310 (accessed 30 November 2015)
21 Abraham Avediba, 'Job Market Opens to Refugees', *Post Courier*, 8 December 2015
22 Joy Kisselpar, '52 Refugees to Settle in PNG', PNG Loop, 11 December 2015, http://www.looppng.com/content/52-refugees-settle-png (accessed 15 December 2015)
23 Kisselpar (2015)
24 Michael Gordon, 'Punitive, Immoral and Now Illegal: The Verdict on Manus Island', *Age*, 26 April 2016
25 Rimbink Pato, PNG Minister for Foreign Affairs and Immigration, 'Government Approves the National Refugee Policy', media release, 20 October 2015, http://www.immigration.gov.pg/images/Media_Release_-_Government_Approves_the_National_Refugee_Policy.pdf (accessed 30 November 2015)
26 Government of Papua New Guinea, 'National Refugee Policy', June 2015, http://www.immigration.gov.pg/images/PNG_National_Refugee_Policy_FINAL_ENDORSED_BY_CABINET.pdf (accessed 30 November 2015)
27 Nicole Hasham, 'Manus Island Detention Centre to Close, PNG Prime Minister Says Following Court Bombshell', *Sydney Morning Herald*, 28 April 2016
28 Francis Keaney and Louise Yaxley, 'Manus Island Detention: PNG Responsible for Asylum Seekers, Peter Dutton Says', ABC News Online, 29 April 2016, http://www.abc.net.au/news/2016-04-28/png-responsible-for-manus-island-asylum-seeker-dutton-says/7369032 (accessed 1 May 2016)
29 'Julie Bishop on Australia's Syrian Refugee Intake', *Breakfast*, ABC Radio National, 10 September 2015, http://www.abc.net.au/radionational/programs/breakfast/julie-bishop-on-australias-syrian-refugee-intake/6763908 (accessed 11 September 2015)

Chapter 8: The Pros and Cons of Temporary Migrant Labour

1. Gareth Larsen, 'The Subclass 457 Visa: A Quick Guide', Parliamentary Library research paper, Parliament of Australia, 11 November 2013
2. Larsen (2013)
3. University of NSW Human Rights Clinic, 'Temporary Migrant Workers in Australia', issues paper, 15 October 2105
4. Michaelia Cash, Assistant Minister for Immigration and Border Protection, Speech to the Migration Institute of Australia conference, Canberra, 5 November 2014, http://www.konnecting.com/news/403/157/Assistant-Immigration-Minister-Michaelia-Cash-speaks-at-MIA-Confernce (accessed 16 December 2015)
5. Australian Government Productivity Commission (PC), 'Migrant Intake into Australia', draft report, November 2015, p. 23
6. Robert Gregory, 'The Two-Step Australian Immigration Policy and Its Impact on Immigrant Employment Outcomes', Institute for the Study of Labour (IZA), discussion paper no. 8061, 2014
7. Annabel Hepworth, 'Skilled Migration: Business Groups Reignite Push for 457 Visa Reform', *Australian*, 14 January 2016
8. Department of Immigration and Border Protection, Fees and charges for visas, https://www.border.gov.au/Trav/Visa/Fees (accessed 5 January 2016)
9. Migration Council Australia, submission to the inquiry of the Senate Education and Employment References Committee into the impact of Australia's temporary work visa programs on the Australian labour market and on temporary work visa holders, May 2015
10. Department of Immigration and Border Protection, Temporary work (skilled) visa (subclass 457), https://www.border.gov.au/Trav/Visa-1/457- (accessed 5 January 2016)
11. John Azarias, Jenny Lambert, Peter McDonald and Kate Malyon, 'Robust New Foundations: A Streamlined, Transparent and Responsive System for the 457 Programme', report of an independent review into integrity in the Subclass 457 programme, September 2014
12. Senate Education and Employment References Committee, 'A National Disgrace: The Exploitation of Temporary Work Visa Holders' (recommendation 15), March 2016
13. Fragomen Worldwide, submission to the Senate Education and Employment References Committee Inquiry into the Impact of Australia's Temporary Work Visa Program on the Australian Labour Market and on Temporary Work Visa

Holders, 1 May 2015
14 DIBP, 'Subclass 457 quarterly report, quarter ending 30 December 2015'
15 National Centre for Vocational Education Research, 'Completion and Attrition Rates for Apprentices and Trainees 2014', Commonwealth of Australia, 2015
16 Roger Harris et al., 'Factors That Contribute to Retention and Completion Rates for Apprentices and Trainees', National Centre for Vocational Education Research, research report, 2001
17 DIBP, 'Subclass 457 quarterly report, quarter ending 30 December 2015'
18 Bob Birrell and Ernest Healy, 'Immigration and Unemployment in 2014', research report, Centre for Population and Urban Research, Monash University, August 2014
19 Selvaraj Velayutham, 'Precarious Experiences of Indians in Australia on 457 Temporary Work Visas', *Economic and Labour Relations Review* 24, no. 3 (2013):340–361
20 PC (2015), p. 171
21 Migration Council Australia, 'More Than Temporary: Australia's 457 Visa Program', May 2013
22 DIBP, 'Temporary Work (Skilled) (Subclass 457) Visa', https://www.border.gov.au/Forms/Documents/1154.pdf (accessed 17 April 2016)
23 Data calculated from DIBP publications, 'Subclass 457 quarterly report, quarter ending at 30 June 2015' and '2014–15 Migration Program Report'.
24 A 457-visa holder can be sponsored for permanent residency under the Temporary Residence Transition stream of the Employer Nomination Scheme (visa subclass 186) or the Regional Sponsored Migration Scheme (visa subclass 187).
25 DIBP, Skilled migration visa processing times, https://www.border.gov.au/Lega/Lega/8 (accessed 20 December 2015)
26 DIBP, 'Labour Agreements: Information about Requesting a Labour Agreement', December 2015, https://www.border.gov.au/WorkinginAustralia/Documents/requesting-labour-agreement.pdf (accessed 21 December 2015)
27 DIBP, 'Labour Agreements' (2015)
28 DIBP, 'Labour Agreements' (2015)
29 Migration Council Australia (2013), p. 4
30 Chris Wright and Andreea Constantin, 'An analysis of employers' use of temporary skilled visas in Australia', submission to the Senate Education and Employment References Committee Inquiry into the Impact of Australia's Temporary Work Visa Program on the Australian Labour Market and on Temporary Work Visa

Holders, 1 May 2015. In using the term 'disposable labour' they are drawing on the work of Michael Piore in *Birds of Passage: Migrant Labor and Industrial Societies*, Cambridge University Press, New York, 1979.

31 Susanne Bahn, Ghialy Yap and Llandis Barratt-Pug, '457 Workers in the Western Australian Resources Industry', research report, Edith Cowan University and Australian Mines and Metals Association, November 2012, http://www.amma.org.au/wp-content/uploads/2012/11/20121107ECU_Research_Report.pdf (accessed 29 December 2015)

32 Wright and Constantin (2015)

33 Wright and Constantin (2015)

34 Bahn et al. (2012)

35 Joo-Cheong Tham, submission to the inquiry of the Senate Education and Employment References Committee into the impact of Australia's temporary work visa programs on the Australian labour market and on temporary work visa holders, 29 April 2015

36 My calculation using data contained in Department of Employment, Department of Immigration and Border Protection, Department of Education and Training, Department of Industry and Science, Department of Social Services, Fair Work Ombudsman, and Safe Work Australia, joint submission to the Senate Education and Employment References Committee Inquiry into the Impact of Australia's Temporary Work Visa Program on the Australian Labour Market and on Temporary Work Visa Holders, (Attachment D.2 Fair Work Ombudsman—Subclass 457 Compliance and Enforcement Data, 1 July 2009 to 31 December 2014), 15 July 2015 and Fair Work Ombudsman, *Annual Report 2014–15*.

37 See the Business Council of Australia and Australian Industry Group submissions to the Senate Education and Employment References Committee Inquiry into the Impact of Australia's Temporary Work Visa Program on the Australian Labour Market and on Temporary Work Visa Holders.

38 My calculation based on data in Fair Work Ombudsman, 'Annual Report 2013–14' and 'Annual Report 2014–15'.

39 Azarias et al. (2014)

40 Barbara Deegan, 'Visa Subclass 457 Integrity Review Final Report', Department of Immigration and Citizenship, October 2008, p. 69

41 Jobwatch, submission to the inquiry of the Senate Education and Employment References Committee into the impact of Australia's temporary work visa programs on the Australian labour market and on temporary work visa holders, May 2015

42 Deegan (2008), p. 23
43 Deegan (2008), p. 49
44 Salima Valiani, 'The Shifting Landscape of Contemporary Canadian Immigration Policy: The Rise of Temporary Migration and Employer-Driven Immigration', in *Producing and Negotiating Non-Citizenship: Precarious Legal Status in Canada*, edited by Luin Goldring and Patricia Landolt, University of Toronto Press, Toronto, 2013, p. 60
45 Valiani (2013), p. 62
46 Velayutham (2013), p. 352
47 Stephen Clibborn, 'Silence on Wage Fraud Won't Wash in Election Campaign', *Sydney Morning Herald*, 20 April 2016

Chapter 9: De Facto Labour Migration

1 Fair Work Ombudsman, Piece rates and commission payments, https://www.fairwork.gov.au/pay/minimum-wages/piece-rates-and-commission-payments (accessed 2 January 2016)
2 Fair Work Ombudsman, Harvest trail campaign, https://www.fairwork.gov.au/how-we-will-help/helping-the-community/campaigns/national-campaigns/harvest-trail-campaign (accessed 2 January 2016)
3 Fair Work Ombudsman, 'Fair Work Ombudsman to Review Entitlements of Overseas Visa-Holders on Working Holidays', media release, 4 August 2014, https://www.fairwork.gov.au/about-us/news-and-media-releases/2014-media-releases/august-2014/20140804-working-holiday-entitlements-review (accessed 29 December 2015)
4 Hannah Shakir, 'Farm Work in Australia: Tips, Advice and Stories', *BBM*, 2 September 2012, http://www.bbmlive.com/farm-work-in-australia/ (accessed 29 December 2015)
5 Elsa Underhill and Malcolm Rimmer, 'Layered Vulnerability: Temporary Migrants in Australian Horticulture', journal article submitted as a submission to the Senate Education and Employment References Committee Inquiry into the Impact of Australia's Temporary Work Visa Program on the Australian Labour Market and on Temporary Work Visa Holders, 2015
6 Underhill and Rimmer (2015)
7 Backpacker Job Board, Farms jobs for second year visa, http://www.backpackerjobboard.com.au/job/20640/farm-jobs-for-second-year-visa-at-mildura-oasis-backpackers/ (accessed 29 December 2015)

8 Facebook, https://www.facebook.com/OasisBackpackersMildura/ (accessed 29 December 2015)
9 TripAdvisor, Mildura Oasis Backpacker Hostel, https://www.tripadvisor.com.au/Hotel_Review-g255355-d1234488-Reviews-Mildura_Oasis_Backpacker_Hostel-Mildura_Victoria.html (accessed 29 December 2015)
10 See, for example, Hostelz.com, Mildura Oasis Backpacker Hostel, https://www.hostelz.com/hostel/122494-Mildura-Oasis-Backpacker-Hostel (accessed 29 December 2015)
11 Charlotte King and Deb Banks, 'The Peaks and Pitfalls of Fruit-Picking', ABC Mildura-Swan Hill, 18 August 2014, http://www.abc.net.au/local/stories/2014/08/18/4069296.htm (accessed 29 December 2015)
12 Fair Work Ombudsman, 'Growers, Hostels, Labour-Hire Contractors, Cautioned Over Backpacker, Seasonal Worker Entitlements', media release, 5 January 2015, https://www.fairwork.gov.au/about-us/news-and-media-releases/2015-media-releases/january-2015/20150105-dont-get-ripped-off-this-harvest-season (accessed 27 April 2016)
13 My Mildura nightmare, Fruitpickingjobs.com, http://www.fruitpickingjobs.com.au/my-mildura-nightmare/ (accessed 29 December 2015)
14 See Ben Campero, 'Working in Mildura is SHIT', YouTube, https://www.youtube.com/watch?v=-9JJmFdO0MA (accessed 29 December 2015)
15 See, for example, 'Australia's Worst Boss?', *A Current Affair*, Channel 9, 25 January 2012, http://www.pomsinoz.com/forum/chewing-fat/193263-backpackers-if-youre-heading-mildura.html (accessed 29 December 2015); 'Recruiter Rage', *A Current Affair*, Channel 9, 19 November 2012, https://www.youtube.com/watch?v=3XezfzT_iOk (accessed 29 December 2015); Fruitpickingjobs.com, Suspect operator targets backpackers in Mildura (no date), http://www.fruitpickingjobs.com.au/suspect-operator-targets-backpackers-in-mildura/ (accessed 29 December 2015); King and Banks (2014); Mildura—der Horror auf Erden (Mildura—horror on earth), blog post, 16 March 2014, http://yvo-downunder.myblog.de/yvo-downunder/art/8059177 (accessed 30 December 2015)
16 Kevin Cocks, 'Commissioner's Foreword', *Balancing the Act*, Anti-Discrimination Commission Queensland newsletter, issue 37, Winter 2015, http://www.adcq.qld.gov.au/__data/assets/pdf_file/0003/7707/Issue-37-Winter-2015.pdf (access 29 December 2015)
17 Caro Meldrum-Hanna and Ali Russell, 'Slaving Away', *Four Corners*, ABC TV, 4 May 2015, http://www.abc.net.au/4corners/stories/2015/05/04/4227055.htm (acc-

essed 30 December 2015).

18 Senate Education and Employment References Committee, The impact of Australia's temporary work visa programs on the Australian labour market and on the temporary work visa holders, http://www.aph.gov.au/Parliamentary_Business/Committees/Senate/Education_and_Employment/temporary_work_visa (accessed 30 December 2015)

19 ABC News Online, 'SA Announces Parliamentary Inquiry into Labour Hire Industry Following Four Corners Report', 6 May 2015, http://www.abc.net.au/news/2015-05-06/parliamentary-inquiry-into-labour-hire-industry/6449714 (accessed 30 December 2015); Government of Victoria, Inquiry into the labour hire industry and insecure work, http://economicdevelopment.vic.gov.au/about-us/strategies-and-initiatives/inquiry-into-the-labour-hire-industry-and-insecure-work (accessed 30 December 2016); Kallee Buchanan, 'Queensland Government Launches Farm Worker Inquiry', *ABC Rural*, ABC, 4 December 2015, http://www.abc.net.au/news/2015-12-04/qld-launches-farm-worker-inquiry/7001810 (accessed 30 December 2015)

20 Senator Michaelia Cash, Minister for Employment, 'Ministerial Working Group to Help Protect Vulnerable Foreign Workers', media release, 15 October 2015, https://ministers.employment.gov.au/cash/ministerial-working-group-help-protect-vulnerable-foreign-workers (accessed 30 December 2015)

21 Fair Work Ombudsman, 'Fair Work Ombudsman to Review Entitlements of Overseas Visa-Holders on Working Holidays', media release, 4 August 2014, https://www.fairwork.gov.au/about-us/news-and-media-releases/2014-media-releases/august-2014/20140804-working-holiday-entitlements-review (accessed 29 December 2015)

22 Fair Work Ombudsman (FWO), 'A Report on the Fair Work Ombudsman's Inquiry into the Labour Procurement Arrangements of the Baiada Group in New South Wales', June 2015

23 FWO (2015), p. 2

24 FWO (2015), p. 2

25 FWO (2015), p. 3

26 FWO (2015), p. 18

27 Senate Education and Employment References Committee, The impact of Australia's temporary work visa programs on the Australian labour market and on the temporary work visa holders, Hansard transcript of Melbourne hearing, 18 May 2015, p. 16

28 FWO (2015), p. 18
29 FWO (2015), p. 23
30 My calculations using data contained in Department of Immigration and Border Protection (DIBP), Working Holiday Maker visa program reports to June 30 for years 2011–2015 and Department of Immigration and Citizenship, 'Working Holiday and Work & Holiday Visa Grants 2005–06 to 2009–10 Program Years', 2010.
31 Senate Education and Employment References Committee, 'A National Disgrace: The Exploitation of Temporary Work Visa Holders', March 2016, p. 105
32 Senate Education and Employment References Committee, The impact of Australia's temporary work visa programs on the Australian labour market and on the temporary work visa holders, Hansard transcript of Brisbane hearings, 12 June 2015, p. 10
33 Senate Education and Employment References Committee, The impact of Australia's temporary work visa programs on the Australian labour market and on the temporary work visa holders, Hansard transcript of Brisbane hearings, 12 June 2015, p. 11–13
34 Australian Meat Industries Employees Union, 'Chinese contract issued in Taiwan by Taiwanese labour hire company with links to Australian labour hire company Scottwell International', tabled document 12, Senate Education and Employment References Committee, The impact of Australia's temporary work visa programs on the Australian labour market and on the temporary work visa holders, Sydney public hearing, 26 June 2015
35 Senate Education and Employment References Committee, The impact of Australia's temporary work visa programs on the Australian labour market and on the temporary work visa holders, Hansard transcript of Brisbane hearings, 12 June 2015, p. 15
36 Australian Meat Industries Employees Union, 'Opening statements for Mr Chun Yat Wong (Sky) and Ms Chiung-Yun Chang (Amy)', tabled document 1, Senate Education and Employment References Committee, The impact of Australia's temporary work visa programs on the Australian labour market and on the temporary work visa holders, Sydney public hearing, 26 June 2015
37 Oxfam America, 'Lives on the Line: The Human Cost of Cheap Chicken', 26 October 2015, http://www.oxfamamerica.org/explore/research-publications/lives-on-the-line/ (accessed 30 December 2015)
38 Senate Education and Employment References Committee, The impact of Australia's temporary work visa programs on the Australian labour market and

on the temporary work visa holders, Hansard transcript of Melbourne hearing, 18 May 2015, p. 4
39 Senate Education and Employment References Committee, The impact of Australia's temporary work visa programs on the Australian labour market and on the temporary work visa holders, Hansard transcript of Melbourne hearing, 18 May 2015, pp. 11–12
40 Job ad quoted in FWO (2015), p. 15
41 Ben Schneiders and Royce Millar, '"Black Jobs": Rampant Exploitation of Foreign Workers in Australia Revealed', *Sydney Morning Herald*, 1 October 2015
42 DIBP, 'Temporary entrants and New Zealand citizens in Australia as at June 30 2015'
43 Chris Nyland et al., 'International Student-Workers in Australia: A New Vulnerable Workforce', *Journal of Education and Work* 22, no. 1 (2009):1-14
44 Alexander Reilly, 'Protecting Vulnerable Migrant Workers: The Case of International Students', *Australian Journal of Labour Law*, no. 25 (2012):181-208
45 Nyland et al. (2009)
46 Paul Karp, 'More Than 60% of International Students in Sydney Underpaid—Survey', *Guardian* (Australian edition), 17 February 2016
47 Adele Ferguson and Klaus Toft, '7-Eleven: The Price of Convenience', *Four Corners*, ABC TV, 31 August 2015, http://www.abc.net.au/4corners/stories/2015/08/30/4301164.htm (accessed 12 January 2016)
48 Shop, Distributive and Allied Employees Association, 'Redacted sample of comments made by 7-Eleven employees when they registered on the SDA's www.24sevenhelpline.com.au', tabled document 1, Senate Education and Employment References Committee, The impact of Australia's temporary work visa programs on the Australian labour market and on the temporary work visa holders, Melbourne public hearing, 24 September 2015
49 Allens Linklaters, 'Review of Australia Post's Arrangements with Oz Trade and RecSol', 24 November 2015, https://auspost.newsroom.com.au/Content/Home/02-Home/Article/Release-of-report-into-contractor-compliance/-2/-2/6073 (accessed 4 January 2016)
50 Madeleine Morris, 'Police Raid Contractors' Homes in Australia Post Fraud Investigation, Foreign Student Scam; Three Charged', *7.30*, ABC TV, 5 August 2015, http://www.abc.net.au/news/2015-08-05/contractors-raided-in-australia-post-investigation/6673556 (accessed 4 January 2016); Allens Linklaters (2015)
51 Fair Work Ombudsman, 'National Cleaning Industry Follow-up Campaign

2012–13'
52 United Voice, 'A Dirty Business: The Exploitation of International Students in Melbourne's Office Cleaning Industry', 2013
53 Victorian TAFE International and United Voice, 'Taken to the Cleaners: Experiences of International Students Working in the Australian Retail Cleaning Industry', November 2012
54 Fair Work Ombudsman, 'National Cleaning Industry Follow-up Campaign 2012–13', February 2015
55 Fair Work Ombudsman, 'Sham contracting and the misclassification of workers in the cleaning services, hair and beauty and call centre industries', November 2011
56 United Voice (2013)
57 Chris Vedelago and Cameron Houston, 'No Stop to Slums in the Sky', *Age*, 3 May 2015; Aisha Dow, 'Slum Squeeze: Overseas Students Taking Turns to Sleep in Overcrowded Melbourne High Rises', *Age*, 21 May 2015
58 Nyland et al. (2009)
59 David Taylor, 'Nearly All Foreign Students in Sydney Underpaid, Research Shows', *PM*, ABC Radio, 21 April 2016, http://www.abc.net.au/pm/content/2016/s4447728.htm (accessed 28 April 2016)
60 Australian Council of Trade Unions, submission to the inquiry of the Senate Education and Employment References Committee into the impact of Australia's temporary work visa programs on the Australian labour market and on temporary work visa holders, 1 May 2015
61 Bob Birrell and Ernest Heally, 'Immigration and Unemployment in 2014', Centre for Population and Urban Research, Monash University, research report, August 2014
62 Henry Sherrell, Immigration and unemployment in 2014: did they take our jobs?, blog post, *Value for Money*, 10 August 2014 (accessed 21 August 2014). This blog has since been shut down.
63 Judith Sloan, 'Migrants No Threat to Jobs', *Australian*, 26 August 2014
64 Australian Government Productivity Commission (PC), 'Migrant Intake into Australia', draft report November 2015, p. 164
65 PC (2015), p. 166
66 PC (2015), p. 10
67 PC (2015), p. 10
68 PC (2015), pp. 21–22
69 Quoted in PC (2015), p. 305

70 Yan Tan and Laurence Lester, 'Labour Market and Economic Impacts of International Working Holiday Temporary Migrants to Australia', *Population, Space and Place*, 18 (2012):359–83
71 Tan and Lester (2012), p. 375
72 Tan and Lester (2012), p. 369
73 Australian Government, 'Draft National Strategy for International Education', April 2015
74 Department of Education and Training, Export income to Australia from international education activity in 2014, research snapshot, June 2015, https://internationaleducation.gov.au/research/Research-Snapshots/Documents/Export%20Income%20CY2014.pdf (accessed 7 January 2015)
75 Australian Government Productivity Commission, 'International Education Service', research paper, April 2015

Chapter 10: An Unsettled World

1 This is my own approximation based on dividing the number of 457-visa holders granted permanent residency between 2002–2003 and 2014–15 (404,755) by the total number of 457 visas issued in the period 2000–2001 and 2012–13 (974,248). The reason for opting for a two-year lag between the two numbers is that it roughly accounts for the two-year period of continuous employment required before an employer can sponsor a 457-visa holder for a permanent visa. Pre-2007 data is drawn from immigration department annual reports; post-2007 data is drawn from the annual Subclass 457 State and Territory summary reports.
2 Claudia Taranto, 'Migrant workers Stuck in Singapore's Legal Limbo When Work Permits Are Cancelled', *Earshot*, ABC Radio National, 15 June 2015, http://www.abc.net.au/radionational/programs/earshot/migrant-workers-trapped-in-limbo-when-work-permits-are-cancelled/6542834 (accessed 31 January 2016)
3 Human Rights Watch, 'Gulf Countries: Increase Migrant Worker Protection', media release, 23 November 2014, https://www.hrw.org/news/2014/11/23/gulf-countries-increase-migrant-worker-protection (accessed 31 January 2016)
4 Manolo Abella, 'Outlook on Migration in Asia in 2015', *Migration Policy Practice* IV, no. 5 (December 2014–January 2015):13–15
5 International Trade Union Confederation (ITUC), 'Facilitating Exploitation: A review of Labour Laws for Migrant Domestic Workers in Gulf Cooperation Council Countries', November 2014
6 ITUC (2014), p. 4

7 'The Middle East's Migrant Workers: Forget About Rights', *Economist*, 10 August 2013
8 Anne Kunze, 'Die Schlachtordnung', *Die Zeit*, 11 December 2014 (translations are my own)
9 Kunze (2014)
10 Kunze (2014)
11 Bob Kinnaird, The high price of Labor's capitulation on ChAFTA, blog post, *Pearls and Irritations*, 11 November 2015, http://johnmenadue.com/blog/?p=4960 (accessed 29 January 2016)
12 Kinnaird (2015)
13 Joanna Howe, 'Labor's Worker Safeguards Will Break the ChAFTA Deadlock But Could Have Gone Further', *Conversation*, 15 October 2015, https://theconversation.com/labors-worker-safeguards-will-break-the-chafta-deadlock-but-could-have-gone-further-49060 (accessed 13 January 2016)
14 Joanna Howe, 'The Impact of the China–Australia Free Trade Agreement on Australian Job Opportunities, Wages and Conditions', report commissioned by the Electrical Trades Union, University of Adelaide, September 2015
15 Fragomen Worldwide, submission to the Senate Education and Employment References Committee Inquiry into the Impact of Australia's Temporary Work Visa Program on the Australian Labour Market and on Temporary Work Visa Holders, 1 May 2015
16 See, for example, Annabel Hepworth, 'Skilled Migration: Business Groups Reignite Push for 457 Visa Reform', *Australian*, 14 January 2016
17 Michael Sweet, '457 Visa Changes on the Way?', *Neos Kosmos*, 15 April 2014
18 Restaurant and Catering Australia, 'Visa Subclass 457: Submission to the Independent Integrity Review', April 2014
19 Claire Nichols, 'WA Looks to Chinese Tourism for Much-Needed Economic Boost', *Breakfast*, ABC Radio National, 1 February 2016, http://www.abc.net.au/radionational/programs/breakfast/wa-looks-to-chinese-tourism-for-much-needed/7128740 (accessed 3 February 2016)
20 Matt Wade, 'Call for Asian Nannies to Reduce Childcare Costs', *Sydney Morning Herald*, 29 March 2014
21 Department of Employment, Seasonal Worker Programme expansion—Q&A, 18 June 2015, https://docs.employment.gov.au/system/files/doc/other/expansion_of_the_seasonal_worker_programme_-_faqs.pdf (accessed 13 January 2015)
22 Department of Employment (2015)

23 Australian Government, 'Draft National Strategy for International Education', April 2015
24 Christopher Pyne, Minister for Education and Training, 'Harnessing the Knowledge Boom: Putting International Education at the Heart of Australia's Future Prosperity', media release, 1 April 2015, https://ministers.education.gov.au/pyne/harnessing-knowledge-boom-putting-international-education-heart-australias-future-prosperity (accessed 14 January 2016)
25 The Centre for International Economics, 'Economic Impact of Streamlined Visa Processing and Post Study Work Rights: The Vocational Education and Training Sector', report for NSW Department of Trade and Investment, Regional Infrastructure and Services, August 2014
26 'New Australia Work and Holiday visas snapped up', *Global Times*, 14 October 2015 http://china.org.cn/travel/2015-10/14/content_36811188.htm (accessed 14 January 2016)
27 Department of Immigration and Border Protection (DIBP), 'Working Holiday Maker visa programme report, 30 June 2015'
28 DIBP, 'Working Holiday Maker visa programme report, 30 June 2015'
29 Henry Sherrell, You get what you deserve: big business and immigration policy, blog post, *Value for Money*, https://henrysherrell.wordpress.com/2015/08/04/you-get-what-you-deserve-big-business-and-immigration-policy/ (accessed 4 August 2015). This blog has since been shut down.

Chapter 11: Flexibility and Indifference

1 Judah Waten, *Alien Son*, Lloyd O'Neil Pty Ltd, 1952, p. 177
2 Waten (1952), p. 178
3 Waten (1952), pp. 178–9
4 Simone Weil, 'Draft for a Statement of Human Obligations' (1952) in *Simone Weil—Selected Essays: 1934–1943*, Oxford University Press, New York, 1962
5 Waten (1952), p. 76
6 Waten (1952), p. 76
7 Waten (1952), p. 78
8 Joseph Carens, *Immigrants and the Right to Stay*, Boston Review Books, MIT, Boston, 2010, p. 17
9 Scott Morrison, 'Doing Far More to Build Our Nation', address to the Affinity Intercultural Foundation, Sydney, 17 July 2013, http://www.affinity.org.au/wp-content/uploads/2013/07/Morrison-Doing-far-more-to-build-our-nation-170713.

pdf (accessed 18 April 2016)
10 Michael Pezzullo, Secretary Department of Immigration and Border Protection, 'Immigration and Nation Building in Australia: Looking Back, Looking Forward', public lecture, Australian National University, 21 April 2015, http://www.immi.gov.au/About/Pages/speeches-pres/immigration-nation-building-australia.aspx (accessed 22 April 2015)
11 Along with long-term temporary migrants, Pezzullo's figure of 1.9 million includes about half a million people in Australia at any one time on short-term visitor visas.
12 Aristide Zolberg, 'Why Not the Whole World? Ethical Dilemmas of Immigration Policy', *American Behavioral Scientist* 56, no. 9 (2012):1204–1222
13 Scott Morrison, 'Our Nation', address to the 2011 Federation of Ethnic Community Councils of Australia Conference, Adelaide, 18 November 2011, http://australianpolitics.com/2011/11/18/morrison-promises-to-protect-the-borders-of-our-values.html (accessed 18 April 2016)
14 Catherine Dauvergne and Sarah Marsden, 'The Ideology of Temporary Labour Migration in the Post-Global Era', *Citizenship Studies* 18 no. 2 (2014):224-242
15 Dauvergne and Marsden (2014), p. 225
16 Max Frisch, *Überfremdung* in *Öffentlichkeit als Partner*, Suhrkamp, Berlin, 1967, p. 209 (translations are my own)
17 Zolberg (2012), p. 1213
18 Martin Ruhs, *The Price of Rights: Regulating International Labour Migration*, Princeton University Press, Princeton, 2013, p. 128
19 Camilla Pivato speaking in the trailer for the film *88 Giorni* (*88 Days*), https://vimeo.com/131071052 (accessed 28 January 2016)
20 Peter Mares, 'Australia Has Brought Out Things About Myself That I Thought Wouldn't Exist', *Inside Story*, 4 January 2016, http://insidestory.org.au/australia-has-brought-out-things-about-myself-that-i-thought-wouldnt-exist (accessed 21 January 2016)
21 Richard Sennett, 'Capitalism and the City: Globalization, Flexibility and Indifference', in *Cities of Europe: Changing Contexts, Local Arrangements and the Challenge to Urban Cohesion*, edited by Yuri Kazepov, Blackwell, Oxford, 2005
22 Selvaraj Velayutham, 'Precarious Experiences of Indians in Australia on 457 Temporary Work Visas', *Economic and Labour Relations Review* 24, no. 3 (2013), pp. 346–347
23 Malcolm Fraser, Prime Minister of Australia, 'Multiculturalism: Australia's Unique Achievement', Inaugural Address, Institute of Multicultural Affairs, Melbourne,

30 November 1981
24 Michael Walzer, *Spheres of Justice: A Defense of Pluralism and Equality*, Basic Books, New York, 1983, p. 52
25 Walzer (1983), p. 60
26 Walzer (1983), p. 61
27 Walzer (1983), p. 63
28 Walzer (1983), p. 40
29 Zolberg (2012), p. 1212
30 Joseph Carens, 'Reconsidering Open Borders', *International Migration Review* 33, no. 4 (1999), pp. 1082–1097
31 Walzer (1983), p. 60
32 Joseph Carens, 'An Overview of the Ethics of Immigration', *Critical Review of International Social and Political Philosophy* 17, no. 5 (2014):538-559
33 Dauvergne and Marsden (2014), p. 225
34 Ruhs (2013), p. 197
35 Ruhs (2013), p. 197
36 Ruhs (2013), p. 176
37 Barbara Deegan, 'Visa Subclass 457 Integrity Review Final Report', Department of Immigration and Citizenship, October 2008, p. 10
38 Government of Canada, Immigration and Citizenship, Four-year maximum—work in Canada, http://www.cic.gc.ca/english/work/apply-who-eligible/four-year-maximum.asp (accessed 28 April 2016)
39 Stephanie Silverman, 'At Any Cost: The Injustice of the "4 and 4" Rule in Canada', *Open Democracy*, 29 May 2015, https://www.opendemocracy.net/beyondslavery/stephanie-j-silverman/at-any-cost-injustice-of-%E2%80%9C4-and-4-rule%E2%80%9D-in-canada (accessed 28 April 2016)
40 Canadian Labour Congress, Temporary foreign workers: the revolving door, 23 March 2015, http://canadianlabour.ca/news/news-archive/temporary-foreign-workers-revolving-door (accessed 28 April 2016)
41 Ruhs (2013), p. 177
42 Carens (2010), p. 21
43 Joseph Carens, 'Live-in Domestics, Seasonal Workers, and Others Hard to Locate on the Map of Democracy', *Journal of Political Philosophy* 16, no. 4 (2008), p. 422
44 Carens (2008), p. 435
45 Department of Human Services, Newly arrived resident's waiting period, http://www.humanservices.gov.au/customer/enablers/newly-arrived-residents-waiting-

period (accessed 18 April 2016)
46 *Australian Citizenship Act 2007* pt 2 div 1 s 22
47 Department of Immigration and Border Protection (DIBP), Partner visa (subclasses 820 and 801), https://www.border.gov.au/Trav/Visa-1/801- (accessed 15 January 2016)
48 'If you arrived in Australia on a New Zealand passport and have lived here for at least ten continuous years since 26 February 2001, you may be able to access a once-only payment of Newstart Allowance, Sickness Allowance or Youth Allowance. If you are eligible, payment can be made for a maximum continuous period of up to six months.' Department of Human Services, Australian Government, New Zealand citizens claiming payments in Australia, http://www.humanservices.gov.au/customer/enablers/nz-citizens-claiming-payments-in-australia (accessed 21 November 2014)
49 *Higher Education Legislation Amendment (Miscellaneous Measures) Act 2015,* Schedule 1
50 *Australian Citizenship Act 2007* pt 2 div 1 s 12(b)
51 Carens (2008), p. 419 (The directive in question is European Council Directive 2003/109/EC)
52 Shanthi Robertson, *Transnational Student-Migrants and the State: The Education-Migration Nexus*, Palgrave Macmillan, Melbourne, 2013, p. 38. This means, for example, that a combination of four years of study and three years of work would render temporary migrant eligible.
53 Citizenship and Immigration Canada, Become a permanent resident—live-in caregivers, 19/10/2012, http://www.cic.gc.ca/english/work/caregiver/permanent_resident.asp#require (accessed 16 May 2014)

Conclusion

1 Herman Melville, *Redburn: His First Voyage*, Project Gutenberg ebook edition, 2014 (first published 1849), p. 425
2 Joanna Howe and Alexander Reilly, submission to the Senate Education and Employment References Committee Inquiry into the Impact of Australia's Temporary Work Visa Program on the Australian Labour Market and on Temporary Work Visa Holders, May 2015
3 Department of Immigration and Border Protection, Government response to the Independent Review into the integrity of the subclass 457 programme (recommendation 6.1), https://www.border.gov.au/about/reports-publications/

reviews-inquiries/independent-review-of-the-457-programme/response-to-integrity (accessed 29 April 2016)

4   The lower figure was suggested by an independent review into integrity in the Subclass 457 program—John Azarias et al., 'Robust New Foundations: A Streamlined, Transparent and Responsive System for the 457 Programme', report of an independent review into integrity in the Subclass 457 programme, September 2014 (recommendation 6.1). The higher figure was recommendation 15 of the Senate Education and Employment References Committee report, 'A National Disgrace: The Exploitation of Temporary Work Visa Holders', March 2016.

5   Migration Council Australia, 'More than Temporary: Australia's 457 Visa Program', May 2013, p. 30

6   See David Sparkes, 'Labour-Hire Company Faces Court Over Allegations of Exploiting Pacific Island Workers in 416 Visa Program', ABC Rural, 14 January 2016, http://www.abc.net.au/news/2016-01-13/labor-hire-company-faces-allegations-of-416-visa-breaches/7086100 (accessed 5 February 2016) and Norman Hermant, 'Fijian Seasonal Workers Told to Return to Work for Contractor Accused of Exploitation or Go Home', ABC News Online, 27 March 2016, http://www.abc.net.au/news/2016-03-27/seasonal-workers-to-return-contractor-accused-of-exploitation/7270902 (accessed 4 April 2016)

7   See Peter Mares and Nic Maclellan, 'Neighbours, Making Bilateral Worker Schemes a Win-Win', in Manjula Luthria et al. 'At Home and Away: Expanding Job Opportunities for Pacific islanders Through Labour Mobility', World Bank, Washington, pp. 101–42

8   Peter Mares, 'Workers for All Seasons', *Diplomat*, June–July 2006, pp. 41–3

9   See Jess Doyle and Stephen Howes, 'Australia's Seasonal Worker Program: Demand-Side Constraints and Suggested Reforms', discussion paper, World Bank and Australian National University, January 2015

10 Ben Schneiders and Royce Millar, '"Black Jobs": Rampant Exploitation of Foreign Workers in Australia Revealed', *Sydney Morning Herald*, 1 October 2015

11 Malcolm Fraser, Prime Minister of Australia, 'Multiculturalism: Australia's Unique Achievement', Inaugural Address, Institute of Multicultural Affairs, Melbourne, 30 November 1981

12 Joseph Carens, 'Live-in Domestics, Seasonal Workers, and Others Hard to Locate on the Map of Democracy', *Journal of Political Philosophy* 16, no. 4 (2008), p. 420

Index

Abbott government 52, 92, 187, 188, 194, 200, 205–6
Abbott, Tony 73, 154, 162, 171
aged-care sector
   culturally specific care 207–11, 213–15
   labour agreements 209–11, 212–14
Agribusiness Pty Ltd 242
Alien Son (Waten) 270–73
AMIEU (Australasian Meat Industry Employees Union) 241–42
anti-discrimination law 245
Aristotle 26
Asian migrants 36
assimilation of migrants 14–15
asylum-seeker policy 16
asylum seekers
   assessment of claims 34, 51–52, 187–88, 198
   bridging visas 5, 51, 56, 57, 185, 188, 196–97
   denied resettlement in Australia 186, 187
   enforced separation of families 183, 187, 188–89, 190, 191
   legal services for 180–82, 195, 201–2
   mandatory detention 165
   'no-advantage principle' 186–87, 190
   number of arrivals by boat 192–93
   offshore detention and processing 186
   punitive treatment 192–94
   refugee determination procedure 34, 51–52, 199–202
   resettlement in Australia 186
   resettlement in PNG 186, 203–5
   temporary protection visas 188, 191–99, 194–96
   treatment of those arrived by boat 199
   work rights 189–90, 201
   see also refugees
Asylum Seeker's Assistance Scheme 202
Australasian Meat Industry Employees Union (AMIEU) 241–42
Australia Day 1–2
Australia Post 247–48, 252
Australia Solo Andata (Australia One Way) 31
Australia–China free-trade agreement 263–64
Australia–New Zealand Closer Economic Relations Trade Agreement 132
Australia–New Zealand relationship 154–58, 176–77
Australia–South Korea free-trade agreement 263
Australian citizenship
   benefits of 21
   ceremonies 2, 10
   eligibility for 4–5, 15–16, 17
   nature of 2–4, 9
   pledge 2, 10
   take-up by New Zealanders 134–35
   take-up rates 135
Australian Government Disaster Recovery scheme 75, 76
Australian Industry Group 229
Australian Labor Party 263–64
Australian resident, legal definitions 75–77, 136, 137
Australians, definition 2–3, 5–6, 9–10
AWX Group 242

'back door' migration 157–58, 162–63, 165–69, 178–79
backpackers 32, 48, 50, 234–37, 255
Baiada Group 238–40, 242, 243
Bartlett, Andrew 169
bilateral trade agreements 263
Birch, Bill 164
Birrell, Bob 158, 163, 221, 253
Bishop, Julie 206

'black labour' 245
blackbirding 20
Bondi bludgers 133, 155, 157, 160–61
Border Protection Force 38
Bowen, Chris 9, 21, 92, 190
bridging visas
  for asylum seekers 5, 51, 56, 188, 201
  Bridging Visa B 104
  Bridging Visa E 188, 189
  conditions imposed under 104–5, 118–19, 196–97
  eligibility for 102
  for international student graduates 56
  numbers issued 57
  for permanent residency applicants 97
British subjects 4, 15
Business Council of Australia 229
business organisations, demands for foreign labour 264–68

Calwell, Arthur 13, 15, 131
Canada 34, 47, 123, 265, 279, 287, 291
cancellation of visas 145–49
Carens, Joseph 24–25, 28, 81, 273, 284, 287, 289, 290, 291, 304
Cash, Michaelia 209, 210
Centrelink Special Benefit 189
chicken-processing industry 238–43
childhood immunisation program 77–80, 301
children
  eligibility for permanent residency 295
  enforced separation from parents 85–94, 183, 187, 188
  permanent residency for foreign parents 301
children's rights 92, 319–20
China
  free-trade agreement with Australia 263–64
  secondary students in Australia 121–22
  and work and holiday scheme 267
Chinese-Papua New Guineans 114–15, 121
Christchurch earthquake 75, 154

Christmas Island detention centre 146, 185
circular migration 129
citizenship, democracy and migration 9–10, 18, 24, 281–86
Clark government (NZ) 160–61
Clark, Helen 160
cleaning services industry 249–50
Clibborn, Stephen 232, 246, 252
Cocks, Kevin 237
Comcare scheme 71
communitarianism 282–83
community detention 185
construction industry 229
Convention relating to the Status of Refugees 200
Convention on the Rights of the Child 92, 140
Cook Islanders 166
Costello, Peter 21
criminal deportation 145–47, 148–49
Crock, Mary 193
Cronulla riots 16
cyclical migration 282

Dauvergne, Catherine 276, 285
de facto labour migrants 232
De Fusco, Ilaria 96–97, 99, 100, 101, 103–5, 106, 107, 108–9, 305
Deegan, Barbara 230, 231, 287, 288
demand-driven migration 112, 214–15
democracy *see* liberal democracy
Department of Employment 52
Department of Immigration and Border Protection 38–39, 97, 274
deportation 145–49
detention 145–46
dictation test 8, 17, 173
Die Zeit (newspaper) 262, 263
discrimination 16, 17, 19
displaced persons (DPs), postwar resettlement 12–13
disposable labour 226, 287
domestic violence 83–85, 139, 142–43, 301

'Don's backpackers' 236–37
Downer, Alexander 156
Drummond, David 171
Dutton, Peter 2, 9, 92, 147, 205

East Lorengau refugee transit centre 203
East Timor 265, 286
education export industry 18, 43–44, 121–22, 121–25, 266
education system, internationalisation of 18, 43–44
88 Days (documentary) 31
886 visas 106
emergency assistance 74–76
emigration, core narratives of 7–8
employee entitlements 73–74
employee recruitment 216–18
Employer Nomination Scheme 99, 119, 217–18, 334
employer sponsorship 66, 67, 68, 71, 116, 119, 222–24, 260, 297
employers, role in migrant selection 215–16
English-language classes 82
ethic of reciprocity and obligation 27–28
ethical sourcing auditing 244
European migration 8, 12–16
European Union 262–63, 291
Evans, Chris 112–13, 192
exemption certificates 16–17
expatriates 259
exploitation of migrant workers 221–23, 228–32

Fair Entitlements Guarantee Act 2012 74
Fair Work Ombudsman
  complaints from 457-visa holders 229
  complaints from working holidaymakers 234, 235–36, 238
  greater resources for 302
  investigation of Baiada Group 238–40, 242
  families, enforced separation 183, 187, 188–89, 203, 205–6, 206

Family and Community Services Legislation Amendment (New Zealand citizens) Act 2001 75
family reunion 35–36, 118
family violence 83–85, 139
fast-track refugee processing 199–202
Faulkner, David 137
FEG (Fair Entitlements Guarantee) 74
Ferguson, Martin 162
571 visas 122
flexible workplaces and indifference 279–80
Forbes, Jim 131, 158
Ford, Carina 88, 93–94, 148–49
foreign-language job ads 245
Four Corners (ABC TV) 237, 238, 242, 243, 246, 251
416 visas *see* Seasonal Worker Programme
417 visas *see* working-holidaymaker scheme
444 visas *see* New Zealanders resident in Australia
457 visas *see* temporary skilled-worker scheme
461 visas 152
462 visas *see* work and holiday scheme
485 visas *see* post-study work visa; temporary graduate visa
Fragomen 264
Fraser, Malcolm 9, 15, 18, 34–35, 281, 302–3
Fraser, Michael 246–47
Fraser, Peter 131
Frisch, Max 276
Fronditha Care labour agreement 207–11, 212–14, 227

Galbally Report 34
Gaster, Adam 106, 108, 305
GEERS (General Employee Entitlements and Redundancy Scheme) 73
General Skilled Migration (GSM) stream 175
Germany, migrant workers 262–63
Gibbons, Wayne 165

Gillard, Julia 154, 162, 171, 186–87
Goff, Phil 159, 160, 161, 170, 176
Gold Coast, percentage of New Zealanders 141, 324
Grassby, Al 34
Greece 268
Greek migrants, aged-care facilities 207–11
Gregory, Bob 216
Grigoletti, Michele (Mike) 31, 32
guest workers 20–21, 25
Gulf States 261–62, 281, 286

Haapu, Ngati Kanohi Te Eke (Ko) 147
Hamer, Paul 130, 131, 151–52, 158–59
Hand, Gerry 164–65
Harris, Tony 163
Hawke, Bob 41
Hawke government 35, 43
Hawke–Keating governments 35
Hazara people 184, 188–89, 197–98
Health Insurance Act 137
healthcare system, access to 53–54
Healy, Ernest 221, 253
Hewitt, Claire 65–71, 72, 73
Hewitt, Terry 65, 66–67, 69, 71
high-school education 121–22
Higher Education Loan Program (HELP) 136, 137
Hirst, John 15
Hockings, Peter 237, 243
Holding, Clyde 155, 176
Holt, Harold 17
homelessness 141
Hong Kong 240
hospitality industry 219–22, 232, 250, 265
Houston, Angus 186
Houston expert panel 186, 189
Howard government 35, 41, 43–44, 73, 98, 136, 192–94, 206
Howard, John 6, 20, 159
Howe, Brian 156
Howe, Joanna 264, 298
Huang, Sherry 50
humanitarian intake 35, 36, 201

illegal immigrants 52
Immigration Museum, Melbourne 7–8
immunisation programs 77–80
indefinite temporariness 113, 124–26, 289
Indochinese refugees 18, 34
Inghams Enterprises 238
international education industry 18, 43–44, 121–25, 256, 266–67
international education services 256
International English Language Testing System (IELTS) 110, 213, 265
International Refugee Organisation 13
international students
  aspirations for permanent residency 60
  breaching of visa rules 251
  housing issues 251–52
  improved services for 300–301
  labour market participation and exploitation 245–51, 257
  switching visa categories to stay 61
  work restrictions 300
Iran 184
Iranian asylum seekers 325
Islamic State 184
Israel 268
Italian migrants 30–33

JDA Wokman 204
Jewish immigrants 270–73
job advertisements 245
Johnston, Chris 72–73
Journeaux, Matt 241, 243
juvenile justice system 145

Keating, Paul 41
kefala sponsorship system 261–62
Kennedy, Tim 302
Key, John 135, 145, 154, 160, 171, 172, 175–76
Kinnaird, Bob 263
Kirk, Norman 131
Kukutai, Tahu 150–51, 173
Kumar, Rakesh 248
Kunze, Anne 262
Kuresa, Julius 143–44, 152, 169, 179

Index   353

labour agreements
  in aged care 209–11, 212–14
  and labour-market testing 216–17
  and possibility of permanent
    residency 223–24
  training and skills shortages 218–22
  and transferral of risk from employers
    to temporary migrants 227
labour force
  impact of immigration 253–56
  proportion of temporary migrants 4,
    23, 58–94
labour law 302
labour market, competition for
  jobs 252–53
labour shortages 254–55
labour-hire firms 239–44, 267, 302
labour-market restructuring 279
labour-market testing 217, 264, 297–98
LaCrosse residential tower,
  Melbourne 251–52
Lashkar-e-Jhangvi 188
legal services, for asylum seekers 201
Lekakis, George 208–9, 210, 213–14,
  224–25, 228
levy on employers of 457-visa holders
  298
liberal communitarianism 281–83
liberal democracy
  challenges of temporary
    migration 280–89
  fundamental principles 22, 24–25,
    127
  migration and citizenship 9–10, 18, 24,
    281–86
  and rights of temporary
    migrants 285–86
life insurance 76–77
live-in caregivers 265, 291
Lockyer Valley 237
Logan City, percentage of New
  Zealanders 324
Logan, Sandi 101
Lovisi, Antonio 103–4
'lump of labour fallacy' 253

Lygon St, Carlton 31

McMahon government 131
Malcolm, Aussie 166–67
mandatory detention of asylum
  seekers 165
Manne, David 181, 199
Manus Island detention centre 186,
  203–4, 205, 305
Māori land wars 129
Māori people 130–31, 149–52, 173–74,
  178–79
Mardirossian, Armineh 244
Marsden, Sarah 276, 285
Martinez, Julio 102–3, 106, 107, 108
mass migration 35, 38
medical-treatment visas 117
Medicare, access to 53, 78, 103, 137
Melville, Herman 293
Menzies, Robert 17
metics 26, 27, 28, 95, 303
migrant labour programs 54
migrant workers
  in Europe 262–63
  in Gulf States 261–62
  in Singapore 261
migration, narratives of 121
Migration Act 1958 17, 74, 91
Migration Council Australia 83, 217–18,
  222, 298
migration law, family violence
  exception 84–85
Migration Occupations in Demand List
  (MODL) 44
migration policy 7–8, 18–19, 176–77, 274,
  275–76
migration program
  annual cap on intake 22, 23, 303
  changing patterns 7–8, 18
  conceived through lens of the
    past 33–34, 38
  contingent and contractual nature 8–9
  as economic lever 35
  humanitarian component 34–35, 201
  intake during Whitlam goverment 34

mass migration in postwar period 14, 35, 38
shift from supply-driven to demand-driven system 112, 214–15
shift to temporary migration 36–40, 112, 268–69
size 296–97
staggered processes 19
two-step program 7, 21–23, 37
Migration Review Tribunal 89
ministerial discretion 88, 91–92, 147
mobile global citizens 274–75
Morrison, Scott 145, 146, 273–74, 275–76
Muir, Ricky 200
Muldoon, Robert 160
multiculturalism 8, 9, 21, 29, 34, 281, 294, 303

nannies 265
National Disability Insurance Scheme 137
natural disaster emergency assistance 74–76
Nauru detention centre 186
Nerang Neighbourhood Centre 141–43
net overseas migration, calculation 313n54
Neumann, Klaus 13
'New Australians' 15, 16, 21
New Zealand
amnesty for overstayers 167
Christchurch earthquake 75, 154
cultural diversity 161–62
entitlements of Australians 132, 161
ethnic composition of population 162
exodus to Australia as political issue 160
net migration 162
New Zealand Citizen Family Relationship (Temporary) visa 152
New Zealand citizenship 133
New Zealanders resident in Australia
compensation for workplace injury 72
contradictory status 134
detention and deportation 145–49

domestic violence 139, 142–43
emergency assistance 74–76
employment statistics 157
homelessness 141, 143–45
issuing of visas 132
Māoris 149–52
Medicare; access 53, 78, 137
number 51, 58, 128–30, 135
permanent residency 5, 22, 134, 135, 170–76
rights and entitlements 133, 136–38, 158–59, 170
social vulnerability 138–49, 169, 178–79
status 18, 50–51
superannuation and life insurance 76–77
support in times of crisis 138–41, 169
tax revenue from 157, 159
'temporary' status 133–34
'third country' migrants 162–63, 178–79
and Trans-Tasman Travel Arrangement 57, 130, 131–32, 136, 161, 164, 176–77
uptake of Australian citizenship 134–36, 151
welfare access 37, 51, 75, 133, 136, 138, 156, 157, 158, 160–61, 163, 169–70, 177–78
'no-advantage principle' 186–87, 190
non-European migrants, discrimination against 16–17, 19
Northern Territory Health Department 66, 67, 68–71
Northern Territory WorkSafe 69
Numerical Multifactor Assessment System 35
nursing, linguistically appropriate care 208–9

Oakleigh 207
Oasis Backpacker Hostel, Mildura 235
O'Connor, Brendan 42
O'Grady, John 14, 16

Old, Gae 139
176 visas 106
186 visas *see* Employer Nomination Scheme
O'Neill, Peter 186, 205
Opperman, Hubert 17
'other family' visa class 118, 321
overstayers 52–53, 167
Oz Trade 248

Pacific Islanders 16, 52, 130, 131, 143, 158, 159, 161, 163, 166–68, 169, 173, 178–79, 265
Pacific Labourers Act 1901 130
Palmer, Clive 198, 200
Papua New Guinea
  East Lorengau refugee transit centre 203
  High Court ruling on detention of asylum seekers 205
  Manus Island detention centre 186, 203–4, 205, 305
  National Refugee Resettlement Policy 186, 204
  resettlement of asylum seekers 186, 203–5
  working-holiday scheme 268
'parent non-contributory' visa class 321
parental sacrifices 120–21
partner visas, and family violence 84–85
Pauline Hanson's One Nation Party 191–92
Pawar, Shefali 173
pay-as-you-go migration 214, 256
Pei, Belinda 113–21, 123, 124, 305
people smuggling 186–87, 191
permanent residency
  age limits 175
  backlog of applications 97–98, 105–6, 109, 111
  cost of applying 96–97, 100, 107, 175
  delays in granting 96–97
  eligibility criteria 68, 97
  excluded groups 4–5
  health restrictions 174
  offshore applications 102–3
  points test 34–35, 110, 112, 215

priority group five 99–109
priority processing 97, 98–99
skilled migration applications 97, 98–113, 260
SkillSelect application processing system 109–13
unconditional pathway after set time period 289–92, 294–97, 303–4
permanent settler migration 19
permanent settler model 19–20
Perth 12
Pezzullo, Michael 33, 38–39, 274, 278
Pianelli, Silvia 31
piece work 233–34, 242
Pitt, Keith 243
Pivato, Camilla 278
points test 34–35, 110, 112, 215
population of Australia
  citizens 3
  non-citizens 3–4
  temporary migrants 4
  total 3
post-study work visas 22, 45, 61, 122–23, 267
postwar resettlement of displaced persons 12–13
power 183
priority processing 97
private health insurance 54, 77
Productivity Commission 171, 216, 221, 254, 265
prostitution 139, 144–45
public-interest powers of minister 92–93
Pyne, Christopher 266

Qatar, migrant workers 261
Queensland floods, 2010–11 74–76
queue jumping 97, 118

Rabaul 114, 115
Rapson, Virginia 158, 163
Ray, Robert 156–57
Red Cross 186
Redburn: His First Voyage (Melville) 293–94

Redfern Legal Centre 250, 301
refugee determination procedure 34, 51–52, 199–201
Refugee and Immigration Legal Service (Refugee Legal) 180–82, 195
Refugee Review Tribunal 89
refugees
  barriers to permanent residency 198–99
  Convention relating to the Status of Refugees 200
  definition in Australian migration law 200
  definition in international law 200
  from postwar Europe 12–13
  granting of permanent residency 295–96
  impact of temporary protection visas 5, 52, 194–96
  introduction of temporary visas 192–94
  pathways to permanent residency 198–99
  resettlement of Indochinese 18
  safe haven enterprise visas (SHEV) 198–201
  Syrian crisis 205–6
regional resettlement arrangement 186
Regional Sponsored Migration Scheme 68–71, 99, 334
Reilly, Alex 245–46, 298
'remaining relative' visas 118
repeat migration 129
Restaurant and Catering Australia 265
retail sector 230, 232
Richards, Eric 12, 17
rights of temporary migrants 285–86
Roach, Neville 40–42
Roach Report 41–42
Robertson, George 239, 245
Robertson, Shanthi 50, 64
Romanian migrants in Germany 262–63
rootedness, sense of 271–72
Rose, Vicky 141–43, 152–53, 169, 174–75, 177, 179

Rudd government 45, 97, 98, 109, 123, 186
Rudd, Kevin 186, 187
Ruddock, Philip 162–63, 167, 194
Ruhs, Martin 277, 285–87, 289, 290

safe haven enterprise visas (SHEV) 198–201
Safety, Rehabilitation and Compensation Amendment (Improving Comcare Scheme) Bill 2015 71
Safety, Rehabilitation and Compensation Legislation Amendment Bill 2014 71
Saldana, Marta 102–3, 106, 107, 108
Samoans 166, 167–68
Saudia Arabia 261, 286
Saul, Ben 193
school fees 80–82, 301
Seasonal Worker Programme 52, 265–66, 286, 288, 299–300
seasonal workforce 255
second-class residents 289
Sennett, Richard 279–80
settlement services 82–83, 298–99
settler loss, rates of 13, 19–20
settler-society model 20–21, 23, 28, 38, 302
7-Eleven 246–47, 251, 252
7.30 (ABC TV) 248
Sharma, Mukesh 248
shearers from New Zealand 155, 164–65
Sherman, Richard 138–39
Sherrell, Henry 253, 268
SHEV (safe haven enterprise visas) 198–201
Shop, Distributive and Allied Employees' Association 247
Sidoti, Chris 195, 206
Singapore 261, 286
Singh, Baljit 'Bobby' 248
Sinha, Pallavi 84
Skandalaki, Evgenia 211–13, 277
skilled migrants
  barriers to achieving permanent residency 97–113

in postwar period 35
Skilled Occupation List (SOL) 99, 116, 122
skilled temporary workers
  aspirations for permanent residency 60, 224, 230–31
  barriers to mobility in labour market 223–24, 228
  as 'disposable labour' 226, 287
  employer sponsorship 66, 67, 68, 71, 116, 119, 222–24, 226, 228, 230–31, 260
  exploitation of 221–23, 228–32, 257
  number 42, 55, 57
  as 'shock absorbers' 227
  sponsorship for permanent residency 210, 230–31, 334
  workplace accidents and injuries 69–73
  workplace behaviour 225–27
skills shortages
  determining existence of 227, 264, 298
  training and temporary labour 218–22
SkillSelect 110–13
slave labour 243
Sloane, Judith 253
Slovak Republic 267
Slovenia 267
Social Security Act 76
South Korea 240
Spheres of Justice (Walzer) 26, 281–82
sponsorship by employers 66, 67, 68, 71, 116
sponsorship by family member 106–7
Stevenson-Perks, Quentin 121
Stimson, Sean 88, 250, 251, 301
strawberry picking 233–34
superannuation 76–77
supply-driven migration 112, 214
Swan Services Cleaning Group 74
Syria
  civil war 184–85
  refugee crisis 205–6

Tait, Brian 86
Tait, Judy 86
Tait, Michael 86
Taiwan 240
Tampa affair 193
Taskforce Cadena 238
Tavan, Gwenda 13
Taylor Park, Torquay 1–2
temporary graduate visa
  eligibility requirements 45–46
  introduction 43–45
  nexus with residency 45, 98, 109, 111
  number of visa holders 45, 55, 57
  post-study work stream 61
  revamping of 22, 45, 61, 122–23
  source countries of visa holders 45
  tensions arising from 46–47
  see also international students
temporary labour migration 54, 209–11
temporary migrant labour, increasing business demands for 264–68
temporary migrants
  access to permanent residency 21–23, 210, 260
  administrative and legal status 4–6, 54, 68–73
  aspirations for permanent residency 60–61
  categories 26–27
  differing entitlements 53–54, 301–2
  distinguished from tourists 54
  as human beings rather than units of production 276, 278
  inadequate terminology to describe 25–26
  and indefinite temporariness 113, 124–26, 289
  as *metics* 26, 27, 28, 95
  number 4, 5, 6, 23, 29, 55, 56, 57, 62
  proportion of labour force 23, 58–94
  rights 285
  switching of visas to extend stay in Australia 126–27
  time spent in Australia 61–64
temporary migration
  annual cap on 303–4
  in Australia compared to other countries 260–64

benefits of 276–78
challenges for democracy 280–89
forms 40–53
as global phenomenon 260
need for coherent approach 94–95
open-ended nature 22–23, 59
relationship with permanent residency 27–28
scale 55–64
shift to 36–40
temporary protection visas
  abandonment by Labor governments 192
  and deterrence of asylum seekers 191
  impact on refugees and Australian community 194–96
  introduction 37, 52, 192
  and policy as punishment 191
  purpose and scope 5, 52
  under Howard government 192–94
Temporary Skilled Migration Income Threshold (TSMIT) 172
temporary skilled-worker scheme 5
  background 40–41
  classification of visa holders 42–43
  countries of origin of visa holders 43
  employment conditions 70, 229, 231–32, 260–61
  English-language requirements 265
  introduction 6, 37, 41–42
  and labour agreements 209
  onshore applications 60–61, 314
  original purpose 42
  proposed reforms 297–99
  see also skilled temporary workers
Teua, Francesca 86–87, 89–92
Tham, Joo-Cheong 228
They're a Weird Mob (O'Grady) 14–15, 16
third country movement 162–63, 178–79
Thodi, Mohamed Rashid Ullat 251
time limits on temporary migration 287–88
Tongans 167
tourism industry 255, 256
trachoma 66

trade unions, opposition to labour agreements 209
training, skills shortages and temporary workers 218–22
trans-Tasman migration, history of 129–31
Trans-Tasman Travel Arrangement 57, 130, 131–32, 136, 161, 164, 176–77
Turnbull government 187, 194, 291
Turnbull, Malcolm 135, 154, 171–72

Underhill, Elsa 234–35
United States 260, 267
'unlawful non-citizens' 53
utilitarianism 285

Valiani, Salimah 231, 279
Vanstone, Amanda 198
Velayutham, Selvaraj 221, 232, 280
Victorian Health Department 78, 79
Vietnam 268
'visa dependency' 84
visa subclass 176 106
visa subclass 186 *see* Employer Nomination Scheme
visa subclass 416 *see* Seasonal Worker Programme
visa subclass 417 *see* working-holidaymaker scheme
visa subclass 444 *see* New Zealanders resident in Australia
visa subclass 457 *see* temporary skilled-worker scheme
visa subclass 461 152
visa subclass 462 *see* work and holiday scheme
visa subclass 571 122
visa subclass 886 106
vocational education loans program (VET FEE-HELP) 137
vocational training courses 44, 98
voting rights 4, 9

Walsh, Peter 156

Walzer, Michael 26, 281–82, 283, 284, 287, 289
Waten, Judah 270–73
Watson, Chris 129
Weil, Simone 271
Wells, Bruce 87, 89, 90, 92–93
White Australia policy 8, 13, 16–17, 18, 21, 34, 40–41, 63, 130
White New Zealand policy 130
Whitlam, Gough 17, 34, 131
Williams, Grant 100–101, 105
Williams, Priscilla 163–64
Withers, Glenn 123
wool industry 155
Wooldridge, Michael 191–92
Woolworths 244, 252
work and holiday scheme 48–49, 50, 267–68
workers compensation 69–73
Workers Rehabilitation and Compensation Act (NT) 69, 70
working-holidaymaker scheme 18
  aims and scope 47–48, 49–50
  benefits of scheme 255–56
  as de facto temporary labour scheme 257
  eligibility 50
  foreign recruitment agencies 50
  introduction 47
  number of visas issued 47, 49, 55, 57, 252–53
  proposed reforms 299–300
  reciprocal arrangements with other countries 240, 256
  second 12-month visas 37, 48, 233–34, 237
  tensions arising from 47
working holidaymakers
  exploitation 234–43, 257
  false job vacancy information 235–36
  from Taiwan, Hong Kong and South Korea 240
  impact on employment 255
  inquiries into mistreatment 238
  Italian visa holders 31–32
  qualifying for second 12-month visa 233–34, 237
  vulnerability in labour market 234

youth labour market 253, 254

Zolberg, Aristide 275, 276, 283